Tao Te Ching
Word for Word

道 德 经

Dào dé Jīng

Translation and commentary by Carl Abbott

Santa Cruz, Calironia, 2012

Realizing I don't' know is better;[1]
Not knowing this knowing is dis-ease.
Man alone faults this dis-ease; this so as not to be ill.
The sacred person is not ill, taking his dis-ease as illness.
Man alone has this dis-ease; this is because to him there is no illness.
[2]

Preface

My brother's death in the early 1960's spurred in me the deepest quandary of my life. I was 22, he was 18, and it was the first time I had really been brought face-to-face with death personally. The question, "What is life and death truly?" haunted me for months on end. I couldn't let go; I had to know. One day it dawned on me while riding home from work on the bus: "Life and death are essentially one and the same—two sides of the same coin." That gut realization closely parallels what I regard as the essence of the Taoist point of view. As chapter 2 puts it, *Hence existence and nothing give birth to each other.* Likewise for me, life and death produce each other.

My brother's death was a gift of circumstance for which I am forever grateful. This book is a memorial to him and his profound influence on my life.

Copyright © 2012, Santa Cruz, CA. USA

---

1   This is from chapter 71, perhaps one of the most useful and practical chapters in the book. Going forward each moment *Realizing I don't' know is better,* really is better. Many other chapters speak to this in various ways; this is just the most direct, hit-the-nail-on-the-head one for me. Translating it literally as I do makes some of the lines more impenetrable than most translators would like. The advantage of having it opaque is that understanding happens at a more intuitive level. As chapter 43 puts it, *Not of words teaching, without action advantage.*

2   Excerpts from my translations in the Introduction and Commentary are in *italic*. Excerpts from D.C. Lau's translation are in SMALL CAPS.

Front Cover

The front cover was taken by our mother near our home in
Tucson, Arizona. I've forgotten so much over the years—it
seems like lifetimes ago—yet I do remember this day
walking out on the grassy hill with my little brother.

A Brief Bio

I came across the Tao Te Ching (D.C Lau's translation) in Vietnam
in 1964. Several years later I began learning Chinese. I remained
in Asia for over a decade, working, traveling, and also studying
Tai Chi (Cheng style), yoga (from B.K.S. Iyengar), 'blowing Zen'
Shakuhachi (from Yamaguchi Goro), and karate (at JKA Tokyo).

I settled down in California in 1980, incorporated the
Center for Taoist Thought and Fellowship (now CenterTao),
married, and raised two sons. I began putting this book
together over twenty years ago. While it is now fit to print,
I intend to keep tending it; it is the garden of my mind.

My final take? Perhaps the advantage of all this is a greater
ability to peek under the hood and see reality, or something as
close to it as humanly possible. Knowledge is power, right? So
why isn't the whole world rushing to get on board the Taoist
approach to knowing? Simple: that power does not beef up
the belief that one can control life. If anything, it is just the
opposite, as this excerpt from chapter 2 (page 12) suggests:

> *Hence existence and nothing give birth to each other,*
> *Difficult and easy become one another...*
> *Considering this,*
>   *the wise person manages without doing anything.*

Carl Abbott, 11/28/2012 (This is still a work-in-progress. I was
holding off reprinting it until this current review was finished
in a few years. That doesn't make sense though; after all, this
will be a work-in-progess until to ashes and dust I return.)

Table of Contents

Preface iii

A Brief Bio iv

Introduction. vi

Translation Notes xii

Chapter / Page

Comment / Page

Chapter	Page		Chapter	Page		No.	Page		No.	Page
Chapter 1	1		Chapter 41	.54		1.	109		41.	157
Chapter 2	2		Chapter 42	.56		2.	110		42.	158
Chapter 3	4		Chapter 43	.57		3.	111		43.	159
Chapter 4	5		Chapter 44	.58		4.	112		44.	161
Chapter 5	6		Chapter 45	.59		5.	112		45.	162
Chapter 6	7		Chapter 46	.60		6.	113		46.	164
Chapter 7	7		Chapter 47	.61		7.	113		47.	165
Chapter 8	8		Chapter 48	.62		8.	114		48.	166
Chapter 9	9		Chapter 49	.63		9.	115		49.	167
Chapter 10	.10		Chapter 50	.64		10.	116		50.	169
Chapter 11	.11		Chapter 51	.66		11.	117		51.	171
Chapter 12	.12		Chapter 52	.67		12.	117		52.	172
Chapter 13	.13		Chapter 53	.69		13.	119		53.	173
Chapter 14	.15		Chapter 54	.70		14.	120		54.	175
Chapter 15	.17		Chapter 55	.72		15.	121		55.	177
Chapter 16	.19		Chapter 56	.73		16.	122		56.	179
Chapter 17	.20		Chapter 57	.75		17.	124		57.	180
Chapter 18	.21		Chapter 58	.76		18.	125		58.	182
Chapter 19	.22		Chapter 59	.78		19.	126		59.	183
Chapter 20	.23		Chapter 60	.79		20.	127		60.	184
Chapter 21	.25		Chapter 61	.80		21.	128		61.	186
Chapter 22	.26		Chapter 62	.82		22.	129		62.	188
Chapter 23	.28		Chapter 63	.83		23.	130		63.	190
Chapter 24	.29		Chapter 64	.85		24.	131		64.	192
Chapter 25	.30		Chapter 65	.87		25.	133		65.	194
Chapter 26	.32		Chapter 66	.89		26.	135		66.	196
Chapter 27	.33		Chapter 67	.91		27.	135		67.	197
Chapter 28	.35		Chapter 68	.93		28.	137		68.	199
Chapter 29	.36		Chapter 69	.94		29.	138		69.	201
Chapter 30	.38		Chapter 70	.95		30.	139		70.	203
Chapter 31	.40		Chapter 71	.96		31.	141		71.	205
Chapter 32	.42		Chapter 72	.96		32.	143		72.	206
Chapter 33	.43		Chapter 73	.97		33.	144		73.	207
Chapter 34	.44		Chapter 74	.99		34.	146		74.	209
Chapter 35	.45		Chapter 75	100		35.	148		75.	210
Chapter 36	.46		Chapter 76	101		36.	149		76.	212
Chapter 37	.47		Chapter 77	102		37.	150		77.	214
Chapter 38	.48		Chapter 78	104		38.	152		78.	216
Chapter 39	.51		Chapter 79	105		39.	153		79.	217
Chapter 40	.53		Chapter 80	106		40.	155		80.	218
			Chapter 81	107					81.	219

Introduction

I first came across the Tao Te Ching (D.C. Lau's translation) in 1964 while hitchhiking around Vietnam. A few years later, I began learning to read and write Chinese. Over the years, I translated parts of chapters that puzzled me. This revealed a subtle problem I found in all translations: The process of translating the Chinese phrasing into another language loses some of the straightforward meaning. (Even more problematic, a number of 'translations' are actually interpretations of true translations.)

Of the genuine translations, D.C. Lau's is one of the most faithful to the original. Therefore, I will use a line from his chapter 73 to illustrate one aspect of a problem I see, and my attempt to reduce it.

His translation of 73 says, HEAVEN HATES WHAT IT HATES, WHO KNOWS THE REASON WHY?[1] Now, this doesn't sound so far off base until you compare it with the issue I raise in my comment for the final chapter (81): "So now, ask yourself: is there **good** or **bad** in nature? Does nature **play favorites**; does nature **love** some things more than other things?... "

The Chinese is 天之所恶孰知其故 (tiān zhī suo è/wù shú zhī qí gù), which literally translates as: **sky** (heaven; day; season; nature) **of place** (indicate passive construction, agent of action) **loathe** (dislike; hate fierce; ferocious) **who know** (realize; inform; knowledge) **his** (her; its; that; such) **reason** (cause; on purpose; hence).

The main character in question, 恶 has two spoken variants. One is "è", which means evil; vice; wickedness; fierce; ferocious. The other is "wù", which means loathe; dislike; hate. In my view, the variant that most closely pertains to **sky** (heaven; day; season; nature) is "è", when translated as "fierce, ferocious".

Using "è", I translate the phrase this way, *Nature's ruthlessness, who knows its cause.* With any luck, this is more in line with the impartiality and overall balance expressed throughout

---

1 Excerpts from my translations in the Introduction and Commentary are in italic. Excerpts from D.C. Lau's translation are in SMALL CAPS.

the Tao Te Ching. To be fair, people experiencing misfortune commonly feel life is unjust and even hates them. However, conveying that view of personal bias rather than an impartial one shortchanges the spirit of the Tao Te Ching, in my view.

About ten years ago, I decided to do what I could to remedy some of the translation problems I have encountered over the decades. I do feel, with humble confidence, that this may be one of the more faithful translations available. Reliability, even at the expense of readability, has been my goal—a fool's errand for anyone wishing to publish their work commercially. I suppose I had no choice really, for as chapter 81 says, *True speech isn't beautiful, Beautiful speech isn't true.* Of course that probably means my translation is also one of the least readable ever written. Oh well, that is balanced... what more could I want?

Using This Translation... and Doing It Yourself
Anyone wishing to plumb deeper meaning from their reading of the Tao Te Ching may find my translation helpful when used alongside their favorite, more readable version. If that fails, you can always ponder the included literal Chinese to English translation. In any case, figuring out your own phrasing from the literal occasionally can help shake loose your preconceptions and open the mind some.

Also, go to Wengu (http://wengu.tartarie.com/wg/wengu.php) and Zhongwen (http://www.zhongwen.com/dao.htm). These sites provide a simple way to check out the Tao Te Ching in the original Chinese with character-by-character translations. Just checking out a few original characters can help UNTANGLE A KNOT or two. Wengu also has a choice of comparative translations, including D.C. Lau's.

Why bother, you say? Mixing things up helps you see the Tao Te Ching more as a mirror of your mind than as *the* authoritative source of objective wisdom. Ha! The Tao Te Ching doesn't even consider itself as *the* source... as the disclaimer at the beginning of chapter 1 puts it,

The way possible to think, runs counter to the constant way.
The name possible to express runs counter to the constant name.

Personally, I think of the Tao Te Ching as pointing to *the without shape form, the without substance shape.* All I see when I look deeply enough in that direction is my 'self'. Viewed this way, each of us is the definitive, authoritative source for what we see. As for this so-called 'self', Buddha's Second Noble Truth points out that: "The illusion of self originates and manifests itself in a cleaving to things."

Other Translation Issues

Translators understandably like to use BEAUTIFUL AND PERSUASIVE WORDS to make their translations readable (and thus, publishable). In addition, translators among the intelligentsia who have pinned their life's work on words may succumb to another difficulty: Might this not impede their ability to plumb the depths of the Taoist point of view? I'd say so, considering the importance Taoists place on the *Not of words teaching,* on the view that *Knower not speak; speaker not know,* and on the resulting Taoist reservations about knowledge and the intelligentsia.

Finally, some translators skew their Taoist view to echo the Western humanist paradigm in which they were conditioned. Of course, that would not be a problem for readers also steeped in the humanist paradigm; indeed, nothing else would be palatable. Simply put, we are naturally drawn to that which says what we want to hear.

Can You Trust My Translation?

I've already mentioned one important factor; I don't need to make it beautiful. Readability and understandability always take a back seat to reliability, for me. Here are a few other factors that may support the reliability of my work.

First, I'm not academic or brilliant; I just barely put up with language—especially in matters of Taoist thought. Second, I was never well integrated into Western humanist culture, even before

I left the country[1] – so cultural conditioning was minimal. Living abroad for 15 years, mostly in Asia, allowed me to become even more culturally impartial. Finally, I'm not a biased 'true believer'.

Indeed, considering the Tao Te Ching's low regard for words and names, being a 'true believer' of a Taoist point of view is oxymoronic. Again, as chapter 71 puts it, *Realizing I don't' know is better; Not knowing this knowing is disease..* Considering this, along with chapter 1's disclaimer, how can one ever be a 'true believer' and a 'true' Taoist?

Sometimes the less one knows, the more one knows
Think of this idea as a parallel to 'out of the mouths of babes'. Being deeply steeped in Chinese history, language and culture may not offer the best vantage point when it comes to sensing the nitty-gritty of the Tao Te Ching. It, after all, points to a view utterly 'outside the box'. So, do dig into the nitty-gritty within, without concern for your lack of knowledge. After all…

> *Without going out the door we can know all under heaven.*
> *Without looking out the window we can see Nature's way.*
> *He goes out farther, he realizes less,*
> *Accordingly, the wise person goes nowhere yet knows.*
> *Sees nothing yet understands.*
> *Refrains from acting yet accomplishes.*

You can only understand that which you already know
This is the best tip I can offer; it may also be the most difficult to understand and apply for obvious reasons. The short story, "Duke Huan and the Wheelwright" from Chuang Tzu speaks to this view. Chapter 70 may also allude to this when it says, *Our words are very easy to know, very easy to do. Under heaven none can know, none can do.* I've also posted extensively on CenterTao.org about this from different angles over the years.

---

1   Some years ago I began to truly realize that my 'cultural independent' streak is mainly due to genetics. I also began to realize what a profoundly social species we humans are. A majority are joiners to one degree or another, who identify with groups: political, religious, sports, hobby, professions, etc. A minority, like me and perhaps you, are outliers. For them, the Tao Te Ching can be a real 'soul match'.

Nowhere is this more applicable than in attempting to understand or translate the Tao Te Ching. As I see it, we can only understand that which we have come to know intuitively. The fact that CIRCUMSTANCES BRING US TO MATURITY[1] accounts for why one's intuitive wisdom and understanding deepen over time. The idea that reading the Tao Te Ching will teach you the Taoist point of view is fundamentally flawed. It is like a Rorschach test that only you can take and evaluate; no one 'outside' can. That is what makes the Tao Te Ching all the more valuable.

Overall I'd say the Tao Te Ching, like all scriptures, can put into words that which you know intuitively (feel) yet can't quite find the words to express—It is the 'spokesman' for your soul.

Rising beyond oneself
Considering all I've said above, it should come as no surprise that I don't regard this translation as done. It will always be a work in progress, especially considering my meager writing skills. Anyway, this is just how nature works. Indeed, when the proof copy of this *Word for Word* translation arrived, our family used it right away, and right away, there were 'problems'.

Good problems, it turns out; for now I have an idea of what to do next. My plan is to post a chapter from this *Word for Word* translation on CenterTao.org regularly. Anyone could then contribute corrections, questions, comments, or even other ways to word the chapter. I would be so grateful, and with your help, we could make a truly improved edition possible.

So what 'problem' did the family encounter? We began using *Word for Word* on chapter 51, and immediately everyone had a problem with *power accomplishes*. They all preferred D.C. Lau's CIRCUMSTANCES BRING THEM TO MATURITY. I too am very fond of Lau's phrase, by the way. Even so, it may be redundant in that THINGS GIVE SHAPE implies somewhat the same thing. The other meanings for **power** are influence; momentum; circumstances, so I see where Lau got the CIRCUMSTANCES, but what about BRING THEM TO MATURITY? The other meaning

---

1   Again, excerpts from my translations in the Introduction and Commentary are in italic. Excerpts from D.C. Lau's translation are in SMALL CAPS.

for **accomplish** are <u>become</u>; result. Okay, I agree how that could mean MATURITY, i.e., one <u>becomes</u> mature.

Even so, I feel *power accomplishes* is more profound, provided you appreciate the difference between force and power. In physics, that parallels the difference between voltage and wattage. (Voltage is the electromotive force, the potential; wattage is the actual work accomplished by electrons driven by the electromotive force. W = V × I, where W = watts, V = volts, I = current (amperes). Another way to say this might be, "Put your money where your mouth is". 'Mouth' expresses a potential. 'Money' expresses something relatively more tangible. Finally, to bring it all home, consider chapter 52's, *observe yielding is called powerful.*

Not surprisingly, chapter 52 provided another stumbling block. (I imagine each chapter to offer at least one.) Here it was *squeeze exchange* vs. Lau's BLOCK THE OPENINGS. Lau's is much easier to grasp; it is normal English after all. The character here, however, is not referring to 'openings', but rather to **exchange** (convert; add water, etc) and is usually used in a financial context. A parallel to 'squeeze' is the yogic idea of bandha (bondage, fetter, restrain). 'Reining in' also comes to mind; reining in the urge to fully participate in the exchange to which we happen to be driven towards each moment.

On the other hand, chapter 52 provided a seemingly straightforward win for Lau's choice of words. Here the stumbling block is *not nearly almost* vs. Lau's NOT MEET WITH DANGER. Lau's comes closer to the literal, **no** (*not*) **danger** (*nearly almost*).

So, why did I opt for *not nearly almost*? I felt it offered a subtle, *indistinct and suddenly* side to danger. Pondering all three words (*danger, nearly, almost*) helps me to *rise beyond* my self. Whenever I succeed, I can see *beyond* my mind; it is a peaceful place!

In summary: I don't regard my choice of words as 'the best', let alone the 'truth'. Therefore, I suggest you simply use them as a launch pad, along with the other word-for-word meanings given, and see where it takes you.

I would truly appreciate hearing any corrections, thoughts, or suggestions you have. You can post these on the **Forum** at CenterTao.org or e-mail me at carl@centertao.org The translations, dangling on poetic license as they do, may be satisfactory most of the time. The commentaries, on the other hand, can always benefit from more critical review; after all, I flunked English in school. Ironically, a weakness I've been striving to make up for ever since.

Note: There is a line-for-line consistency between the poetic version and the numbered, literal word for word translation of the Chinese characters below it. This should help make comparisons between them easier. In addition, don't take punctuation too seriously. In times past, this was less important. Even now, I appreciate the fact that there is no use of capitalization in Chinese, and little emphasis on gender precision.

I am grateful to my wife Leslie who has helped my over the years with this project, and to Lynn Cornish for her keen editor's eye. Not only did they do what they could with my English, they have been my muse over the years asking the best of questions!

Translation Notes

Abbreviations I use

<grm> = grammar (e.g., <grm> is (yes <frml> this; that)
<frml> = formal
<conj> = conjuction
<v>   = verb
<p>   = preposition
<adj>   = adjective

Notable 'Outlier' words

yǐ （以）use; take; according to; because of; in order to; so as to; <formal> at (a certain time); on (a fixed date); <conj.> and; as well as *yĭ...wéi...* (以... 为...) take... as; regard.. as.

yĭwéi (以为) think, believe; consider that.

xī (兮) exclamatory or interrogatory
particle at end of questions. !

zāi (哉) is exclamatory or interrogatory
particle at end of questions. !

hū (乎) is a particle <part> sentence-final interrogative
particle; Oh! Ah, expressing doubt or wonder. Used
in the middle of a sentence, it is a classical particle
similar to yú (於)... in (at; from; because; than)

zhī (之) <pronoun> used only as object; <particle> used
to connect the modifier and the word modified; without
actual reference. For me, this translates best as **of** which
my dictionary says is a preposition introducing a noun or
phrase that provides more information about a preceding
word or phrase. Here are some examples of common
usage with the literal word for word in parentheses.

爱国之心 patriotic feeling (love country of heart)
父母之爱 parental love (father mother of love)
自知之明   self-awareness (self know of understand)
世界之大，无奇不有。 There is nothing too strange in this
vast world. (world boundary of big, without strange no have

qí (其) This is a possessive particle; literary
equivalent of 的 or pronoun: him; her; it

zì + rán (自 + 然) self; oneself; one's own; certainly; of course;
from; since + right; correct; so; like that; <formal> <conj.>
but; nevertheless; however. These together are zìrán, which
translates as: natural world; nature; naturally; in the ordinary
course of events; of course; naturally. For me, this gives a
deeper meaning to the word and the workings of "nature".

zhě（者）This is kind of like '... **ness'** (see chapter 40). It is used after an adjective or verb as a substitute for a person or a thing.

不欲□□如玉 Boxes are missing characters. I substitute them with an educated guess.

Translation madness
When my translation gets to feeling nuts, try to remember that there may be 'method to my madness'. Chapter 81 points to it. The less "beautiful" the words are, the more "truth". Not that I am saying something with more truth! The point is, you'll be more intuitive about the point being made when it is being made less clear cut – up to a point. I hope I don't cross that 'point' too often.

It helps to see this in terms of a mirror; what you see is a reflection of your mind- nothing more… ever! True, what the words you see on the page are a result of the workings of my mind, but how you interpret them, understand them (either attracted to or repelled by) mirror your reality. Seeing this can be very helpful for getting a handle on life. Instinct appears to cause us (and animals all) to see the external world as though it really exists in the way we sense it (or frankly exists at all). So powerful is this illusion that few people, and I am guessing no other animals, are able to see past this biological hoodwink. The cognitive ability to do this may be the most significant difference between us and other animals. I suppose it is what makes us 'spiritual', or rather drives us to be 'spiritual'. In other words, the ability to see through the illusion also divides us from the unity that nature's masterful hoodwink offers.

This makes for great irony: the ability to see through the hoodwink separates us from the 'whole', which leaves us in a state of stress and contention. We are engaging in a war between what we imagine should be, and what 'is'. The only way to soften the blow is to look deeper, past our emotion, and recognize that our instinctive emotion is driving what we see in the first place. I guess this is a catch-22, blind-spot, and Peter Principle all rolled into one.

CHAPTER 1

The way possible to think, runs counter to the constant way.
The name possible to express runs counter to the constant name.
Without description, the universe began.
Of the describable universe, the origin.
Hence, normally without desire so as to observe its wonder.
Normally having desire so as to observe its boundary.
These two are the same coming out, yet differ in name.
The same, meaning dark and mysterious.
Dark and dark again, the multitude, of wondrous entrance.

1. **WAY** (road, principle; speak; think, suppose) **APPROVE** (can; may; fit; suit)
   WAY (road, principle; speak; think, suppose), **WRONG** (run counter to)
   ORDINARY (normal; constant; invariable; usually) **WAY** (road, principle;
   speak; think, suppose). 道可道，非常道。 *(dào kě dào fēi cháng dào)*

2. **NAME** (express; describe) **APPROVE** (can; may; fit; suit) **NAME**
   (express; describe), **WRONG** (run counter to) **ORDINARY** (normal;
   constant; invariable; usually) **NAME** (express; describe). 名
   可名，非常名。 *(míng kě míng fēi cháng míng)*

3. **NOTHING** (nil; without) **NAME** (express; describe) **HEAVEN AND EARTH** (world;
   universe) **OF** **BEGINNING** (start). 无名天地之始。 *(wú míng tiān dì zhī shǐ)*

4. **HAVE** (there is; exist) **NAME** (express; describe) **ALL THINGS ON EARTH** **OF**
   MOTHER (origin; parent). 有名万物之母。 *(yǒu míng wàn wù zhī mǔ)*

5. **INCIDENT** (hence; cause) **ORDINARY** (normal; constant; invariable;
   usually) **NOTHING** (nil; without) **DESIRE** **USE** (<v> take <p> according
   to; because of <adj> so as to <conj> and) **OBSERVE** **ITS** **WONDERFUL**
   (excellent). 故常无欲以观其妙。 *(gù cháng wú yù yǐ guān qí miào)*

6. **ORDINARY** (normal; constant; invariable; usually) **HAVE** (there
   is; exist) **DESIRE** **USE** (<v> take <p> according to; because of
   <adj> so as to <conj> and) **OBSERVE** **ITS** **BOUNDARY** (by mere
   luck) 常有欲以观其徼。 *(cháng yǒu yù yǐ guān qí jiǎo)*

7. **THIS** **TWO** (both; either) (者) **SAME** (together) **COME** **OUT** (exceed; go beyond;
   happen) <conj.> **AND** (yet, but) **DIFFERENT** (strange; separate) **NAME** (express;
   describe), 此两者同出而异名， *(cǐ liǎng zhě tóng chū ér yì míng)*

8. **SAME** (together) **SAY** (call; meaning; sense) **OF** **BLACK** (dark;
   mysterious; profound). 同谓之玄。 *(tóng wèi zhī xuán)*

1

9.	**BLACK** (dark; mysterious; profound) **OF** **ALSO** (again) **BLACK** (dark; mysterious; profound), **MANY** (numerous; crowd) **WONDERFUL** (excellent; fine; ingenious; clever; subtle) **OF** **DOOR** (gate; valve; switch). 玄之又玄，众妙之门。 *(xuán zhī yòu xuán, zhòng miào zhī mén)*

CHAPTER 2

All under heaven realizing beauty as beauty, wickedness already.
All realizing goodness as goodness, no goodness already.
Hence existence and nothing give birth to one another,,
Difficult and easy become one another,
Long and short form one another,
High and low incline to one another,,
Sound and tone blend with one another,
Front and back follow one another,.
Considering this,
      the wise person manages without doing anything,
Carries out the indescribable teaching.
Don't all things on earth work and not shirk.
Give birth to and yet not have,
Do and yet not depend on,
Achieves success and yet not dwell.
The simple man alone does not dwell,
Because of this he never leaves.

1.	**SKY** (heaven; weather; nature) **UNDER ALL** (each and every) **KNOW** (realize; be aware of) **BEAUTIFUL** (pretty; good) **OF** **DO** (act; act as; serve as; be; mean) **BEAUTIFUL** (pretty; good), **THIS** **WICKEDNESS** (fierce; ferocious) **STOP** (cease; end; already; thereafter; afterwards; too); 天下皆知美之为美，斯恶已； *(tiān xià jiē zhī měi zhī wéi měi sī ě yǐ)*

2.	**ALL** (each and every) **KNOW** (realize; be aware of) **GOOD** (perfect; kind) **OF** **DO** (act; act as; serve as; be; mean) **GOOD** (perfect; kind), **THIS** **NO** (not) **GOOD** (perfect; kind) **STOP** (cease; end; already; thereafter; afterwards; too). 皆知善之为善， 斯不善已。 *(jiē zhī shàn zhī wéi shàn sī bù shàn yǐ)*

3.	**REASON** (cause; hence) **HAVE** (there is; exist) **NOTHING** (nil; without) **EACH OTHER** (one another; mutually) **GIVE BIRTH TO** (bear; grow; existence; life), 故有无相生， *(gù yǒu wú xiāng shēng)*

4.	**DIFFICULT** (hard) **EASY** (amiable) **EACH OTHER** (one another; mutually) **ACCOMPLISH** (become; result), diction， 难易相成， *(nán yì xiāng chéng)*

2

5. **LONG** (of long duration; steadily; strong point) **SHORT** (brief; weak point; fault) **EACH OTHER** (one another; mutually) **FORM** (shape; appear; contrast), 长短相形， *(cháng duǎn xiāng xíng)*

6. **TALL** (high; above the average) **BELOW** (under; low; inferior) **EACH OTHER** (one another; mutually) **INCLINE** (lean; bend) , 高下相倾， *(gāo xià xiāng qīng)*

7. **SOUND** (news; tidings) **SOUND** (voice; tone; reputation) **EACH OTHER** (one another; mutually) **GENTLE** (harmonious... mix; blend), 音声相和， *(yīn shēng xiāng hé)*

8. **FRONT** (before; former; first) **BACK** (after; later; offspring) **EACH OTHER** (one another; mutually) **TO FOLLOW** (to allow). 前后相随。 *(qián hòu xiāng suí)*

9. <grm> **IS** (yes <frml> this; that) **USE** (<v> take <p> according to; because of <adj> so as to <conj> and) **SAGE** (holy; sacred) **HUMAN** (man; people) **MANAGE NOTHING** (nil; without; no matter whether, what, etc) **DO** (act; act as; serve as; become; be; mean) **OF MATTER** (affair; thing), 是以圣人处无为之事， *(shì yǐ shèng rén chǔ wú wéi zhī shì)*

10. **GO** (do; carry out) **NO** (not) **SPEECH** (word; say; talk; speak) **OF TEACH** (instruct.). 行不言之教。 *(xíng bù yán zhī jiāo)*

11. **ALL THINGS ON EARTH DO** (make; work) **HEREIN** (usu. negative questioning) how; why) <conj.> **AND** (yet, but) **NO** (not) **DICTION** (poetry; take leave; decline; dismiss; discharge; shirk). 万物作焉而不辞。 *(wàn wù zuò yān ér bù cí)*

12. **GIVE BIRTH TO** (bear; grow; existence; life) <conj.> **AND** (yet, but) **NO** (not) **HAVE** (there is; exist) 生而不有， *(shēng ér bù yǒu)*

13. **DO** (act; act as; serve as; become; be; mean) <conj.> **AND** (yet, but) **NO** (not) **RELY ON** (depend on), 为而不恃， *(wéi ér bù shì)*

14. **MERIT** (achievement; result; skill; work) **ACCOMPLISH** (succeed; capable) <conj.> **AND** (yet, but) **NOT RESIDE** (dwell; live; store up). (i.e. not claim credit for oneself.). 功成而弗居。 *(gōng chéng ér fú jū)*

15. **MAN** (a person engaged in manual labor) **ONLY** (alone) **NOT RESIDE** (dwell; live; store up), 夫唯弗居， *(fū wéi fú jū)*

16. <grm> **IS** (yes <frml> this; that) **USE** (<v> take <p> according to; because of <adj> so as to <conj> and) **NO** (not) **GO** (leave; remove; get ride of). 是以不去。 *(shì yǐ bù qù)*

CHAPTER 3

Not to value worthy people, enables people to avoid contending.
Not to value rare goods, enables people to avoid stealing.
Not to catch sight of what suits desire,
    enables people's heart to avoid confusion.
This is because of how the wise person governs;
Empties their hearts, fills their bellies,
Weakens their aspirations, strengthens their bones,
Always enables the people to be unlearned and without desire,
And enables resourceful men to never dare to act also.
Doing without doing, following without exception rules.

1. **NO** (not) **STILL** (yet; value) **VIRTUOUS** (able worthy person), **SEND** (tell to do; use; cause; enable) **PEOPLE** **NO** (not) **CONTEND** (vie; strive; argue). 不尚贤，使民不争。*(bù shàng xián, shǐ mín bù zhēng)*

2. **NO** (not) **EXPENSIVE** (valuable) **RARE** (hard to come by) **OF** **GOODS** (commodity), **SEND** (tell to do; use; cause; enable) **PEOPLE** **NO** (not) **DO** (act; become; be) **STEEL** (rob; thief). 不贵难得之货，使民不为盗。*(bù guì nán dé zhī huò, shǐ mín bù wéi dào)*

3. **NO** (not) **SEE** (catch sight of) **APPROVE** (can; may; need doing; fit; suit) **DESIRE** (longing; wish; want), **SEND** (tell to do; use; cause; enable) **PEOPLE** **THE HEART** (mind; feeling; intention; center; core) **NO** (not) **IN DISORDER** (in confusion). 不见可欲，使民心不乱。*(bù jiàn kě yù, shǐ mín xīn bù luàn)*

4. <grm> **IS** (yes <frml> this; that) **USE** (<v> take <p> according to; because of <adj> so as to <conj> and) **SAGE** (holy; sacred) **HUMAN** (man; people) **OF** **RULE** (govern; manage; order), 是以圣人之治，*(shì yǐ shèng rén zhī zhì)*

5. **VOID** (emptiness; empty) **HIS** (her; its; their) **THE HEART** (mind; feeling; intention; center; core), **SOLID** (true; honest; reality; fruit; seed) **HIS** (her; its; their) **BELLY** (abdomen; stomach), 虚其心，实其腹，*(xū qí xīn, shí qí fù)*

6. **WEAK** (lose (through death) **HIS** (her; its; their) **WILL** (aspiration; ideal), **STRONG** (better) **HIS** (her; its; their) **BONE**; 弱其志，强其骨；*(ruò qí zhì, jiàng qí gǔ)*

7. **ORDINARY** (common; normal; constant; often) **SEND** (tell to do; use; cause; enable) **PEOPLE** **NIL** (without) **KNOW** (be aware of; inform), **NIL** (without) **DESIRE** (longing; wish; want), 常使民无知、无欲，*(cháng shǐ mín wú zhī, wú yù)*

8. **SEND** (tell to do; use; cause; enable) **MAN** (a person engaged in manual labor) **WISDOM** (resourcefulness) (者) **NO** (not) **DARE** **DO** (act; act as; serve as) **ALSO** (too; either). 使夫智者不敢为也。*(shǐ fū zhì zhě bù gǎn wéi yě)*

9. **DO** (act; act as; serve as) **NIL** (without) **DO** (act; act as; serve as), **STANDARD** (norm; rule > imitate; follow) **INVARIABLY** (all without exception) **RULE** (govern; administer; manage; order; peace).
为无为，则无不治。*(wéi wú wéi, zé wú bù zhì)*

CHAPTER 4

The way flushes and employs the virtue of 'less'.
Deep like the ancestor of every-thing.
Subdue its sharpness, separate its confusion,
Soften its brightness, be the same as its dust.
Deep and clear, it appears to exist.
I don't know of whose child it is,
It resembles the ancestor of the Supreme Being.

1. **ROAD** (way, doctrine; speak) **RINSE** (flush) <conj.> **AND** (yet, but) **USE** (employ; hence) **OF** **PERHAPS** (probably; or) **NO** (not) **BE FULL** (have a surplus). 道冲而用之或不盈。*(dào chōng ér yòng zhī huò bù yíng)*

2. **DEEP** (deep pool) **!** **SIMILAR** (like) **TEN THOUSAND** **THING** (matter) **OF** **ANCESTOR** (clan; purpose). 渊兮似万物之宗。*(yuān xī sì wàn wù zhī zōng)*

3. **DEFEAT** (subdue; lower) **HIS** (her; its; their; that; such) **SHARP** (keen; acute; vigor) **SEPARATE** (divide; untie) **HIS** (her; its; their) **CONFUSED** (tangled; disorderly), 挫其锐解其纷，*(cuò qí ruì jiě qí fēn)*

4. **GENTLE** (peace, and, blend, mix) **HIS** (her; its; their; that; such) **LIGHT** (ray; brightness... naked; alone), **SAME** (alike; similar; be the same as; together; in common) **HIS** (her; its; their; that; such) **DUST** (dirt; this world), 和其光，同其尘，*(hé qí guāng, tóng qí chén)*

5. **PROFOUND** (deep; crystal clear) **!** **SIMILAR** (like; seem; appear) **PERHAPS** (probably; or) **EXIST** (live; store; keep). 湛兮似或存。*(zhàn xī sì huò cún)*

6. **I** (we) **NO** (not) **KNOW** (realize; be aware of; tell) **WHO** (someone; anyone) **OF** **SON** (child; person; seed), 吾不知谁之子，*(wú bù zhī shéi zhī zǐ)*

7. **APPEARANCE** (shape; image; resemble) **THE SUPREME BEING** (emperor) **OF** **EARLIER** (before; first; ancestor). 象帝之先。*(xiàng dì zhī xiān)*

CHAPTER 5

The universe is not benevolent,
    and all things serve as grass dogs ('sacrificial lambs').
The wise person is not benevolent,
    and the people serve as grass dogs.
Is not the space between heaven and earth like a bag?
Empty yet doesn't submit,
    moves yet recovers from all its coming and going.
More speech counts as exceptionally limited;
    not in accord with keeping to the middle.

1.   **HEAVEN AND EARTH** (world; universe) **NO** (not) **BENEVOLENT** (humanity; sensitive), **TAKE... AS** (regard.. as) **ALL THINGS ON EARTH** **DO** (act as) **HAY** (fodder) **DOG** (damned). 天地不仁，以万物为刍狗。 *(tiān dì bù rén yǐ wàn wù wéi chú gǒu)*

2.   **SAGE** (holy; sacred) **HUMAN** (man; people) **NO** (not) **BENEVOLENT** (humanity; sensitive), **TAKE... AS** (regard.. as) **COMMON PEOPLE** **DO** (act as) **HAY** (fodder) **DOG** (damned). 圣人不仁，以百姓为刍狗。 *(shèng rén bù rén, yǐ bǎi xìng wéi chú gǒu)*

3.   **HEAVEN AND EARTH** (world; universe) **OF** **BETWEEN** (among; space in between), **ITS** (it; that; such) **JUST AS** (like) **A BAG** (a pocket) **KEY** 乎 (<part> expresses doubt or wonder)? 天地之间，其犹橐钥乎？ *(tiān dì zhī jiān, qí yóu tuó yào hū)*

4.   **VOID** (emptiness) <conj.> **AND** (yet, but) **NO** (not) **BEND** (bow; subdue; submit; in the wrong), **MOVE** (stir; act) <conj.> **AND** (yet, but) **HEAL** (recover; become) **GO OR COME** **OUT** (exceed; go beyond; produce). 虚而不屈，动而愈出。 *(xū ér bù qū, dòng ér yù chū)*

5.   **MANY** (much; more) **SPEECH** (word; say; talk) **COUNT** (be reckoned as exceptionally) **POOR** (poverty-stricken; limit; end), **NO** (not) **IN COMPLIANCE WITH** (according to; like; as) **GUARD** (defend; keep watch; observe) **CENTER** (middle; halfway between two extremes). 多言数穷，不如守中。 *(duō yán shù qióng, bù rú shǒu zhōng)*

CHAPTER 6

The valley's spirit never dies; this is called the profound female.
Of the profound female entrance;
   this is called the origin of the universe.
Continuous, like it exists; in usefulness, not diligent.

1. **VALLEY** (gorge; cereal; grain) **GOD** (supernatural; spirit) **NO** (not) **TO THE DEATH** (extremely; implacable) <grm> **IS** (yes <frml> this; that) **SAY** (meaning) **BLACK** (dark; profound) **FEMALE** (of some birds and animals). 谷神不死是谓玄牝。 *(gǔ shén bù sǐ shì wèi xuán pìn)*

2. **BLACK** (dark; profound) **FEMALE** (of some birds and animals) **OF ENTRANCE** (door) <grm> **IS** (yes <frml> this; that) **SAY** (meaning) **HEAVEN AND EARTH** (world; universe) **ROOT** (foot; base; cause; origin). 玄牝之门是谓天地根。 *(xuán pìn zhī mén shì wèi tiān dì gēn)*

3. **CONTINUOUS** (unbroken) **LIKE** (seem; as if) **EXIST** (live; store), **USE** (employ; apply; expenses; need <frml> hence) **OF** **NO** (not) **DILIGENT** (industrious). 绵绵若存，用之不勤。 *(mián mián ruò cún, yòng zhī bù qín)*

CHAPTER 7

Nature everlasting.
Heaven and earth can long endure,
Because they do not give themselves life,
Hence they can long continue to exist.
The wise person places his life last yet life comes first,
Is outside his life, yet lives life.
Non conforming so as to void personal evil!
Hence he is able to succeed personally.

1. **HEAVEN** (nature; God) **LONG** **THE EARTH** **FOR A LONG TIME.** (i.e., enduring as the universe; everlasting and unchanging) 天长地久。 *(tiān cháng dì jiǔ)*

2. **HEAVEN AND EARTH** (world; universe) **SO** (therefore; as a result) **ABILITY** (energy; can) **LONG** **JUST** (for the time being) **FOR A LONG TIME** (者), 天地所以能长且久者，*(tiān dì suǒ yǐ néng cháng qiě jiǔ zhě)*

3. **USE** (<v> take <p> according to; because of <adj> so as to <conj> and) **HIS** (her; its; their; that; such) **NO** (not) **SELF** (oneself) **GIVE BIRTH TO** (bear; grow; existence; life), 以其不自生，*(yǐ qí bù zì shēng)*

4. **INCIDENT** (happening; reason; cause; hence) **ABILITY** (energy; can) **LONG** (of long duration) **PERDURE** (to continue to exist). 故能长生。 *(gù néng cháng shēng)*

5. <grm> **IS** (yes <frml> this; that) **USE** (<v> take <p> according to; because of <adj> so as to <conj> and) **SAGE** (holy; sacred) **HUMAN** (man; people) **BACK** (behind; rear; after) **HIS/HER/ITS** **BODY** (life; oneself) <conj.> **AND** (yet, but) **BODY** (life; oneself) **EARLIER** (before; first), 是以圣人后其身而身先， *(shì yǐ shèng rén hòu qí shēn ér shēn xiān)*

6. **OUTER** (outward; other) **HIS** (her; its; that; such) **BODY** (life; oneself) <conj.> **AND** (yet, but) **BODY** (life; oneself) **EXIST** (live; survive; keep). 外其身而身存。 *(wài qí shēn ér shēn cún)*

7. **WRONG** (not conform to; run counter to; not) **USE** (<v> take <p> according to; because of <adj> so as to <conj> and) **HIS** (her; its; that; such) **NOTHING** (without) **PERSONAL** (secret; illicit) **EVIL** (heretical; irregular)! 非以其无私邪！ *(fēi yǐ qí wú sī xié)*

8. **INCIDENT** (happening; reason; cause; hence) **ABILITY** (energy; can) **ACCOMPLISH** (succeed; become; turn into; result) **HIS** (her; its; that; such) **PERSONAL** (secret; illicit). 故能成其私。 *(gù néng chéng qí sī)*

CHAPTER 8

Highest good is like water.
Water benefits all things and does not contend,
Dwells in places the multitude loathe.
Therefore, it is somewhat like the way.
In being, satisfactory is location.
In intention, satisfactory is depth and benevolence.
In speech, satisfactory is truth.
In honesty, satisfactory is order.
In work, satisfactory is ability.
In action, satisfactory is time.
He alone does not contend,
Hence there is no blame..

1. **UPPER** (up; higher; better; first) **GOOD** (satisfactory; succeed) **LIKE** (seem; as if) **WATER** (river; lakes, seas). 上善若水。 *(shàng shàn ruò shuǐ)*

2. **WATER** (river; lakes, seas) **GOOD** (satisfactory; succeed) **SHARP** (advantage) **ALL THINGS ON EARTH** <conj.> **AND** (yet, but) **NO** (not) **CONTEND** (argue), 水善利万物而不争， *(shuǐ shàn lì wàn wù ér bù zhēng)*

3. **GET ALONG** (manage <frml> dwell; live) **MANY   HUMAN** (man; people) **OF PLACE   LOATHE** (dislike; hate), 处众人之所恶， *(chǔ zhòng rén zhī suǒ ě)*

4. **CAUSE** (hence; therefore) **SEVERAL** (some) **IN** (at, to, from, by, than, out of) **ROAD** (way, principle, talk, think). 故几于道。 *(gù jī yú dào)*

5. **RESIDE** (dwell; live) **GOOD** (satisfactory; succeed) **THE EARTH** (land; ground; place; locality), 居善地， *(jū shàn dì)*

6. **HEART** (mind; feeling; intention; core) **GOOD** (satisfactory; succeed) **DEEP   AND   BENEVOLENCE** (kindheartedness), 心善渊与善仁， *(xīn shàn yuān yú shàn rén)*

7. **SPEECH** (word; say; talk; speak) **GOOD** (satisfactory; succeed) **TRUE** (trust; faith; believe), 言善信， *(yán shàn xìn)*

8. **STRAIGHT** (upright; honest) **GOOD** (satisfactory; succeed) **RULE** (govern; manage; order; peace; control), 正善治， *(zhēng shàn zhì)*

9. **MATTER** (affair; business; trouble; work; responsibility) **GOOD** (satisfactory; succeed) **ABILITY** (capability; skill), 事善能， *(shì shàn néng)*

10. **MOVE** (stir; act; change; arouse) **GOOD** (satisfactory; succeed) **TIME** (hour; current; present). 动善时。 *(dòng shàn shí)*

11. **HUSBAND** (man <old> a person engaged in manual labor) **ONLY** (alone) **NO** (not) **CONTEND** (vie; strive; argue; dispute), 夫唯不争， *(fū wéi bù zhēng)*

12. **CAUSE** (hence; therefore) **NOTHING** (nil; not have; without) **OUTSTANDING** (particularly; especially; blame). 故无尤。 *(gù wú yóu)*

CHAPTER 9

Grasping and yet full of, not in harmony with oneself;
Surmising and yet of keen spirit, cannot long protect;
Treasures fill a room which no one is able to keep;
Wealth and pride, one's gift to one's blame.
Meritorious deeds that satisfy oneself recede,
This is the way of nature.

1. **HOLD** (grasp; support; maintain; manage) <conj.> **AND** (yet, but) **BE FULL** (be filled with; have a surplus of) **OF   NO** (not) **IN HARMONY WITH** (in compliance with; like; as; if) **HIS** (her; its; that; such) **ONESELF** (personal); 持而盈之不如其己； *(chí ér yíng zhī bù rú qí jǐ)*

2. **ESTIMATE** (surmise; conjecture) <conj.> **AND** (yet, but) **SHARP** (keen; acute; vigor; fighting spirit) **OF** **NO** (not) **CAN** (need doing, able> but; yet) **LONG** (steadily, older; chief; grow) **PROTECT** (keep; preserve; ensure); 揣而锐之不可长保；*(chuǎi ér ruì zhī bù kě cháng bǎo)*

3. **GOLD AND JADE** (treasures) **FULL** (reach the limit) **ROOM** **NO ONE** (nothing) **OF** **ABILITY** (skill) **GUARD** (defend; keep watch); 金玉满堂莫之能守；*(jīn yù mǎn táng mò zhī néng shǒu)*

4. **RICH** (wealthy) **EXPENSIVE** (valuable) <conj.> **AND** (yet, but) **PROUD** (arrogant; conceited), **SELF** (one's own; certainly) **OFFER AS A GIFT** (make a present of something) **HIS** (its; he, it, that; such) **FAULT** (blame; punish). 富贵而骄，自遗其咎。*(fù guì ér jiāo, zì yí qí jiù)*

5. **MERITORIOUS SERVICE** (merit; work) **SATISFY** (fulfil) **BODY** (oneself) **MOVE BACK** (withdraw; quit; recede; ebb; return), 功遂身退，*(gōng suì shēn tuì)*

6. **SKY** (heaven; day; nature) **OF** **ROAD** (way, path; principle; speak; think). 天之道。*(tiān zhī dào)*

CHAPTER 10

Loaded down with life, can you leave with nothing?
Focused in breath, can you compare with a baby?
Washing away the mystery, can you see life as flawless?
Loving the nation, can you govern the people without acting?
When Heavens gate opens wide, can your action be female?
When understanding reaches its full extent, can you know
nothing?
Give birth and raise, give birth and not have;
Act and not depend on;
Be in charge and not rule;
This is called profound moral character.

1. **CARRY** (be loaded with) **SEEK** (operate) **SOUL** (vigor; spirit) **HOLD OR CARRY IN THE ARMS** (embrace; hug), **CAN** (ability) **NOTHING** (nil; without) **LEAVE** (off, from; without) 乎 (<part> expresses doubt or wonder). 载营魄抱一，能无离乎？*(zǎi yíng pò bào yī, néng wú lí hū)*

2. **SPECIAL** (for a particular purpose, expert) **GAS** (air; breath; spirit; get angry) **SEND** (incur; result in) **SOFT** (yielding), **CAN** (ability) **IN COMPLIANCE WITH** (can compare with; like; as; as if) **BABY** 乎 (<part> expresses doubt or wonder)? 专气致柔，能如婴儿乎？*(zhuān qì zhì róu, néng rú yīng ér hū)*

10

3. **WASH AWAY** (eliminate) **BLACK** (dark; profound; abstruse) **LOOK AT** (see; view; read), **CAN** (ability) **NOTHING** (nil; without) **FLAW** (defect; blemish) 乎 (<part> expresses doubt or wonder)? 涤除玄览，能无疵乎？ *(dí chú xuán lǎn, néng wú cī hū)*

4. **LOVE** (like; cherish; take good care of) **COUNTRY** (state; nation) **RULE** (govern; manage; peace) **THE PEOPLE** (civilian), **CAN** (ability) **NOTHING** (nil; without) **DO** (act; act as; serve as; become; be; mean) 乎 (<part> expresses doubt or wonder)? 爱国治民，能无为乎？ *(ài guó zhì mín, néng wú wéi hū)*

5. **SKY** (heaven; weather; nature) **ENTRANCE** (door; gate; valve) **OPEN** (come loose; start; begin) **ENTIRE** (whole; shut; close), **CAN** (ability) **DO** (act; act as; serve as; become; be; mean) **FEMALE** 乎 (<part> expresses doubt or wonder)? 天门开阖，能为雌乎？ *(tiān mén kāi gé, néng wéi cí hū)*

6. **CLEAR** (obvious; understand; know) **FOUR EXTEND** (reach; attain; amount to; understand thoroughly), **CAN** (ability) **NOTHING** (nil; without) **KNOW** (realize; be aware of; tell; knowledge) 乎 (<part> expresses doubt or wonder). 明白四达，能无知乎。 *(míng bai sì dá, néng wú zhī hū)*

7. **GIVE BIRTH TO** (grow; life) **OF**, **RAISE DOMESTIC ANIMALS** **OF**, **GIVE BIRTH TO** (grow; life) <conj.> **AND** (yet, but) **NO** (not) **HAVE** (there is; exist); 生之，畜之，生而不有； *(shēng zhī, chù zhī, shēng ér bù yǒu)*

8. **DO** (act; act as; serve as; become; be; mean) <conj.> **AND** (yet, but) **NO** (not) **RELY ON** (depend on); 为而不恃； *(wéi ér bù shì)*

9. **OLDER** (elder; senior; eldest; oldest; chief) <conj.> **AND** (yet, but) **NO** (not) **SLAUGHTER** (butcher; govern; rule), 长而不宰， *(cháng ér bù zǎi,)*

10. <grm> **IS** (yes <frml> this; that) **SAY** (call; name; meaning; sense) **BLACK** (dark; profound; abstruse) **VIRTUE** (moral character; heart; kindness). 是谓玄德。 *(shì wèi xuán dé.)*

CHAPTER 11

Thirty widths share one hub,
 out of its nothingness, exists the useful vehicle.
Mix water with clay soil, think utensil,
 out of its nothingness exists the useful utensil.
Cut out a door and window, think room,
 out of its nothingness exists the useful room.
Hence, of having what is thought favorable,
 of the nothing think as the useful.

1. **THREE** (more than two; several; many) **TEN** (topmost) **WIDTH OF CLOTH** (size, extent) **SHARE** (together; all) **ONE HUB**, **EQUAL** (out; should; regard as) **HIS** (its; their; that; such) **NOTHING** (nil; without; not), **HAVE** (there is; exist) **VEHICLE** (machine) **OF USE** (apply). 三十幅共一毂，当其无，有车之用。 *(sān shí fú gòng yī gū, dāng qí wú, yǒu chē zhī yòng.)*

2. **MIX WATER WITH CLAY SOIL** **THINK** (believe; consider that) **IMPLEMENT** (utensil), **EQUAL** (out; should; regard as) **HIS** (its; their; that; such) **NOTHING** (nil; without; not), **HAVE** (there is; exist) **IMPLEMENT** (utensil) **OF USE** (apply). 埏埴以为器，当其无，有器之用。 *(shān zhí yǐ wéi qì, dāng qí wú, yǒu qì zhī yòng.)*

3. **CHISEL** (cut a hole) **DOOR** (household; family) **WINDOW** **THINK** (believe; consider that) **ROOM**, **EQUAL** (out; should; regard as) **HIS** (its; their; that; such) **NOTHING** (nil; without; not), **HAVE** (there is; exist) **ROOM** **OF USE** (apply). 凿户牖以为室，当其无，有室之用。 *(záo hù yǒu yǐ wéi shì, dāng qí wú, yǒu shì zhī yòng.)*

4. **INCIDENT** (happening; reason; hence) **HAVE** (there is; exist) **OF** **THINK** (believe; consider that) **SHARP** (favorable; advantage), **NOTHING** (nil; without; not) **OF** **THINK** (believe; consider that) **USE** (apply). 故有之以为利，无之以为用。 *(gù yǒu zhī yǐ wéi lì, wú zhī yǐ wéi yòng.)*

CHAPTER 12

The five colors make people's eyes blind,
The five sounds make people's ears deaf,
The five taste make people's mouths brittle,
Rushed hunting make people's hearts go crazy.
Goods hard to come by make people behave harmfully.
Because of this, the wise person acts for the belly, not the eye,
Hence, he leaves that and takes this.

1. **FIVE** **COLOR** (look; expression) **COMMAND** (order; make; cause) **HUMAN** (man; people) **EYE** (item; look) **BLIND**, 五色令人目盲， *(wǔ sè lìng rén mù máng,)*

2. **FIVE** **SOUND** (news; tidings; tone) **COMMAND** (order; make; cause) **HUMAN** (man; people) **EAR** (on both sides) **DEAF**, 五音令人耳聋， *(wǔ yīn lìng rén ěr lóng,)*

3. **FIVE** **TASTE** (flavor; smell) **COMMAND** (order; make; cause) **HUMAN** (man; people) **MOUTH** (opening; entrance) **BRIGHT** (clear; brittle; frank), 五味令人口爽， *(wǔ wèi lìng rén kǒu shuǎng,)*

4. **GALLOP** **TO HUNT** (cultivate land) **HUNT** **COMMAND** (order; make; cause) **HUMAN** (man; people) **HEART** (mind; feeling; intention; core) **ISSUE** (deliver) **GO CRAZY**, 驰骋畋猎令人心发狂， *(chí chěng tián liè lìng rén xīn fā kuáng,)*

5. **HARD TO COME BY** (rare) **OF GOODS** (commodity; money) **COMMAND** (order; make; cause) **HUMAN** (man; people) **GO** (prevail;; circulate; do) **HINDER** (harm). 难得之货令人行妨。 *(nán dé zhī huò lìng rén xíng fāng.)*

6. <grm> **IS** (yes <frml> this; that) **USE** (<v> take <p> according to; because of <adj> so as to <conj> and) **SAGE** (holy; sacred) **HUMAN** (man; people), **DO** (act; serve as; become; be) **BELLY** (abdomen; stomach) **NO** (not) **DO** (act; serve as; become; be) **EYE** (item; look), 是以圣人，为腹不为目， *(shì yǐ shèng rén, wéi fù bù wéi mù,)*

7. **INCIDENT** (happening; reason; hence) **GO** (leave; remove) **THAT** (those; the other; another) **TAKE** (get; seek; adopt) **THIS**. 故去彼取此。 *(gù qù bǐ qǔ cǐ.)*

CHAPTER 13

Bestowing favor and disgrace likewise startle;
Treasure and trouble likewise seem personal.
Why say bestowing favor and disgrace likewise startle?
Bestowing favor supports the low.
Gain seems to startle,
Loss seems to startle,
This says bestowing favor and disgrace likewise startle.
Why say treasure and trouble likewise seem personal?
I have great trouble means I have a body,
Come the day I have no body, what trouble have I?
Hence, regarding the body as treasure supports all under heaven,
Likewise trustworthy for all under heaven.
Taking care in use of the body supports all under heaven,
Likewise worthy of serving as support for all under heaven.

1. **DOTE ON** (bestow favor) **DISGRACE** (dishonor; insult) **LIKE** (seem; if, you) **START** (be frightened; surprise), 宠辱若惊， *(chǒng rǔ ruò jīng.)*

2. **EXPENSIVE** (valuable; precious) **BIG** (greatly; fully) **TROUBLE** (disaster; worry) **LIKE** (seem; if, you) **BODY** (life; personally). 贵大患若身。 *(guì dà huàn ruò shēn.)*

3. **CARRY** (what, how, why, which) **SAY** (call; name; meaning) **DOTE ON** (bestow favor) **DISGRACE** (dishonor; insult) **LIKE** (seem; if, you) **START** (be frightened; surprise)? 何谓宠辱若惊？ *(hé wèi chǒng rǔ ruò jīng?)*

4. **DOTE** on (bestow favor) **DO** (act; serve as; be, mean; support) **BELOW** (down; lower; inferior; next). 宠为下。 *(chǒng wéi xià.)*

13

5. **GET** (obtain, gain) **OF** **LIKE** (seem; if, you) **START** (be frightened; surprise), 得之若惊 *(dé zhī ruò jīng)*

6. **LOSE** (miss; let slip; fail; mistake) **OF** **LIKE** (seem; if, you) **START** (be frightened; surprise), 失之若惊 *(shī zhī ruò jīng)*

7. <grm> **IS** (yes <frml> this; that) **SAY** (call; name; meaning) **DOTE ON** (bestow favor) **DISGRACE** (dishonor; insult) **LIKE** (seem; if, you) **START** (be frightened; surprise). 是谓宠辱若惊。 *(shì wèi chŏng rŭ ruò jīng.)*

8. **CARRY** (what, how, why, which) **SAY** (call; name; meaning) **EXPENSIVE** (valuable; precious) **BIG** (greatly; fully) **TROUBLE** (disaster; worry) **LIKE** (seem; if, you) **BODY** (life; personally)? 何谓贵大患若身？ *(hé wèi guì dà huàn ruò shēn?)*

9. **I** (we) **SO** (therefore; as a result) **HAVE** (there is; exist) **BIG** (greatly; fully) **TROUBLE** (disaster; anxiety; worry) (者), **DO** (act; serve as; be, mean; support) **I** (we) **HAVE** (there is; exist) **BODY** (life; personally), 吾所以有大患者，为吾有身， *(wú suŏ yĭ yŏu dà huàn zhĕ, wéi wú yŏu shēn,)*

10. **REACH** (come up to; in time for; and) **I** (we) **NOTHING** (nil; not have; there is not; without) **BODY** (life; personally), **I** (we)) **HAVE** (there is; exist) **CARRY** (what, how, why, which) **TROUBLE** (disaster; anxiety; worry)? 及吾无身，吾有何患？ *(jí wú wú shēn, wú yŏu hé huàn?)*

11. **INCIDENT** (reason; hence) **EXPENSIVE** (valuable; precious) **TAKE AS** (regard... as..) **BODY** (life; personally) **DO** (act; serve as; be, mean; support) **LAND UNDER HEAVEN** (the world), 故贵以身为天下， *(gù guì yĭ shēn wéi tiān xià,)*

12. **LIKE** (seem; if, you) **APPROVE** (can; may; be worth (doing); fit; suit <adv.> but; yet) **SEND** (post; mail; entrust; depend on) **LAND UNDER HEAVEN** (the world). 若可寄天下。 *(ruò kě jì tiān xià.)*

13. **LOVE** (like; treasure; take care of) **TAKE AS** (regard... as..) **BODY** (life; personally) **DO** (act; serve as; be, mean; support) **LAND UNDER HEAVEN** (the world), 爱以身为天下， *(ài yĭ shēn wéi tiān xià,)*

14. **LIKE** (seem; if, you) **APPROVE** (can; may; be worth (doing); fit; suit <adv.> yet) **HOLD IN THE PALM** (serving as a support; entrust) **LAND UNDER HEAVEN** (the world). 若可托天下。 *(ruò kě tuō tiān xià.)*

CHAPTER 14

Of watched for, yet not seen is called smooth.
Of listened to, yet not heard is called rarefied.
Of handled yet not held is called minute.
These three are unfathomable, so they blend and serve as One.
Its upper part is not taken in, its lowest part is not hidden,
Unending, it cannot be named, and returns again to nothing.
This is called the of without shape form,
     the of without substance shape,
This is called the suddenly trance-like.
Moving toward it, you will not see its head,
Following behind, you will not see its back.
Hold of the ancient way in order to manage today.
The ability to know the ancient beginning,
     this is called the way's discipline.

1. **LOOK AT** (regard; inspect; watch) **OF** **NO** (not) **SEE** (not meet) **NAME**
    (fame; reputation; well-known) **SAY** (call; name) **SMOOTH** (safe;
    exterminate). 视之不见名曰夷。 *(shì zhī bù jiàn míng yuē yí.)*

2. **LISTEN** (hear; obey / allow) **OF** **NO** (not) **HEAR** (news; story; smell) **NAME**
    (fame; reputation; well-known) **SAY** (call; name) **HOPE** (rare; scarce;
    uncommon). 听之不闻名曰希。 *(tīng zhī bù wén míng yuē xī.)*

3. **ROLL ROUND WITH HAND** **OF** **NO** (not) **GET** (obtain, gain) **NAME**
    (fame; reputation; well-known) **SAY** (call; name) **MINUTE** (tiny).
    抟之不得名曰微。 *(tuán zhī bù dé míng yuē wēi.)*

4. **THIS** **THREE** (者) **CANNOT** (must not) **SEND** (extend; deliver; result in) **CLOSELY**
    QUESTION (interrogate), **REASON** (cause; hence) **MIX** (confuse; pass for)
    <conj.> **AND** (yet, but) **DO** (act; serve as; become; be; mean) **ONE**. 此三者
    不可致诘，故混而为一。 *(cǐ sān zhě bù kě zhì jié, gù hún ér wéi yī.)*

5. **HIS** (its; they; that; such) **UPPER** (up; upward; higher; superior) **NO** (not)
    RECEIVE (accept; put away; take in; collect; control), **HIS** (its; they; that;
    such) **BELOW** (down; under; underneath; lower; inferior) **NO** (not) **HAVE**
    HAZY NOTIONS ABOUT (be ignorant of; hide; conceal), (**NEGLECT**), 其上不
    □（收），其下不昧（忽），*(qí shàng bù, shōu, qí xià bù mèi, (hū))*

6. **ROPE** (restrict; unending) **CANNOT** (must not) **NAME** (fame; reputation; well-known), **DUPLICATE** (turn over; answer; again) **GO BACK TO** (return) **IN** (at, to, from, by, than, out of) **NOTHING** (nil; not have, without) **THING** (matter; the outside world). 绳绳不可名，复归于无物。 *(shéng shéng bù kě míng, fù guī yú wú wù.)*

7. <grm> **IS** (yes <frml> this; that) **SAY** (call; name; meaning; sense) **NOTHING** (nil; not have) **FORM** (shape; state; condition) **OF FORM** (shape; state; condition), **NOTHING** (nil; not have, without) **THING** (matter; the outside world) **OF ELEPHANT** (appearance; shape; image; be like; resemble), 是谓无状之状，无物之象， *(shì wèi wú zhuàng zhī zhuàng, wú wù zhī xiàng,)*

8. <grm> **IS** (yes <frml> this; that) **SAY** (call; name; meaning; sense) **SUDDENLY** (seem; as if) **DIM** (in a trance; seemingly). 是谓惚恍。 *(shì wèi hū huǎng.)*

9. **GREET** (welcome; receive; move towards) **OF NO** (not) **SEE** (not meet) **HIS** (its; they; that; such) **HEAD** (first; leader; chief), 首之不见其首， *(shǒu zhī bù jiàn qí shǒu,)*

10. **TO FOLLOW** (to comply with / to allow) **OF NO** (not) **SEE** (not meet) **HIS** (its; they; that; such) **BACK** (behind; rear; after; afterwards). 随之不见其后。 *(suí zhī bù jiàn qí hòu.)*

11. **HOLD** (grasp; manage) **ANCIENT** (age-old) **OF ROAD** (way, speak; think) **OF USE** (<v> take <p> according to; because of <adj> so as to <conj> and) **DRIVE A CARRIAGE** (resist, keep out) **PRESENT-DAY** (now) **OF HAVE** (there is; exist). 执古之道以御今之有。 *(zhí gǔ zhī dào yǐ yù jīn zhī yǒu.)*

12. **ABILITY** (skill <physics> energy; can) **KNOW** (realize; notify; knowledge) **ANCIENT** (age-old) **BEGINNING** (start), <grm> **IS** (yes <frml> this; that) **SAY** (call; name; meaning; sense) **ROAD** (way, speak; think) **DISCIPLINE** (put down in writing; record). 能知古始，是谓道纪。 *(néng zhī gǔ shǐ, shì wèi dào jì.)*

CHAPTER 15

Of old, the adept student was minutely subtle,
 open and deep beyond knowledge.
He alone cannot be known, hence his strength lies in allowing.
He prepares as if fording a river in winter;
 as if like in fear of neighbors;
Solemn that seems to allow; vanishing like ice that melts away;
Honest that is like simple; broad that is like a valley;
Blending that is like muddy water; tranquil that is like the sea.
Circular[1] as if without end.
Who can be muddy as well as still to gently clarify.
Who can be calm as well as aroused to gently live.
Keeping to this way, he desires not to be full.
Therefore,
 only he who is not full can shelter and yet newly become.

1. **ANCIENT** **OF** **GOOD** (be good at) **DO** (act; serve as; be; mean) **BACHELOR** (scholar) (者), **MINUTE** (tiny) **WONDERFUL** (subtle) **BLACK** (dark; profound) **OPEN** (through; connect; whole), **DEEP** (difficult; profound) **CANNOT** (should not; must not) **KNOW** (knowledge). 古之善为士者，微妙玄通，深不可识。*(gǔ zhī shàn wéi shì zhě, wēi miào xuán tōng, shēn bù kě shí.)*

2. **HUSBAND** (man) **ONLY** (alone) **CANNOT** (should not; must not) **KNOW** (knowledge), **REASON** (cause; hence) **STUBBORN** (unyielding) **DO** (act; serve as; be; mean) **OF** **HOLD** (permit; allow). 夫唯不可识，故强为之容。*(fū wéi bù kě shí, gù jiàng wéi zhī róng.)*

3. **TO COMFORT** (to ease) **!** **LIKE** (seem; as if) **WINTER** **WADE** (ford; experience) **RIVER**; **JUST AS** (like; still) **!** **LIKE** (seem; as if) **FEAR** (respect) **FOUR** **NEIGHBOR**; 豫兮若冬涉川；犹兮若畏四邻；*(yù xī ruò dōng shè chuān; yóu xī ruò wèi sì lín;)*

4. **MAJESTIC** (solemn; dignified) **!** **HIS** (its; that; such) **LIKE** (seem; as if) **HOLD** (permit; allow); **MELT** (vanish) **!** **LIKE** (seem; as if) **ICE** (put on the ice; feel cold) **OF** **SUPPORT** (bring; handle) **EXPLAIN** (dispel; let go); 俨兮其若容；涣兮若冰之将释；*(yǎn xī qí ruò róng; huàn xī ruò bīng zhī jiāng shì;)*

---

1 This character is missing from the original so I had to use my poetic license: 圆 yuan = round; circular; spherical

5. **HONEST** (sincere) **!** **HIS** (its; that; such) **LIKE** (seem; as if) **SIMPLE** (plain); **VAST** (spacious; free from petty ideas) **!** **HIS** (its; that; such) **LIKE** (seem; as if) **VALLEY;** 敦兮其若朴；旷兮其若谷； *(dūn xī qí ruò pò; kuàng xī qí ruò gǔ;)*

6. **MIX** (confuse; pass for) **!** **HIS** (its; that; such) **LIKE** (seem; as if) **TURBID** (muddy; deep and thick); **TRANQUIL** (placid, quiet) **!** **HIS** (its; that; such) **LIKE** (seem; as if) **SEA** (extra large); 混兮其若 浊；澹兮其若海； *(hún xī qí ruò zhuó; dàn xī qí ruò hǎi;)*

7. **ROUND** (circular; spherical)* **!** **LIKE** (seem; as if) **NOTHING** (nil; without) **STOP** (to; till; only). □兮若无止。 *([] xī ruò wú zhǐ.)*

8. **WHO** (which; what) **ABILITY** (capability; skill; able) **TURBID** (muddy; deep and thick) **USE** (<v> take <p> according to; because of <adj> so as to <conj> and) **STILL** (quiet; calm) **OF** **SLOWLY** (gently) **UNMIXED** (clear; distinct; settle). 孰能浊以静之徐清。 *(shú néng zhuó yǐ jìng zhī xú qīng.)*

9. **WHO** (which; what) **ABILITY** (capability; skill; able) **PEACEFUL** (quiet; tranquil; calm) **USE** (<v> take <p> according to; because of <adj> so as to <conj> and) **MOVE** (stir; change; arouse) **OF** **SLOWLY** (gently) **GIVE BIRTH TO** (bear; grow; life). 孰能安以动之徐生。 *(shú néng ān yǐ dòng zhī xú shēng.)*

10. **PROTECT** (maintain; preserve) **THIS** **ROAD** (way, speak; think) (者) **NO** (not) **DESIRE** (longing; about to) **BE FULL OF** (have a surplus of). 保此道者不欲盈。 *(bǎo cǐ dào zhě bù yù yíng.)*

11. **HUSBAND** (man) **ONLY** (alone) **NO** (not) **BE FULL OF** (have a surplus of) **REASON** (cause; hence) **ABILITY** (capability; skill; able) **COVER** (shelter; hide) <conj.> **AND** (yet, but) **NEW** (fresh) **ACCOMPLISH** (become; fully grown). 夫 唯不盈故能蔽而新成。 *(fū wéi bù yíng gù néng bì ér xīn chéng.)*

CHAPTER 16

Devote effort to emptiness, sincerely watch stillness.
Everything 'out there' rises up together, and I watch again.
Everything 'out there', one and all, return again to their root cause.
Returning to the root cause is called stillness,
     this means answering to one's destiny;
Answering to one's destiny is called the constant,
     knowing the constant is called honest.
Not knowing the constant, rash actions lead to ominous results.
Knowing the constant allows, allowing therefore impartial,
Impartial therefore whole, whole therefore natural,
Natural therefore the way.
The way therefore long enduring, nearly rising beyond oneself.

1. **SEND** (extend; devote effort to) **VOID** (emptiness) **THE UTMOST
    POINT** (extreme; pole) **DEFEND** (keep watch) **STILL** (quiet) **SINCERE**
    (earnest). 致虚极守静笃。 *(zhì xū jí shǒu jìng dǔ.)*

2. **TEN THOUSAND** (myriad) **THING** (matter; the outside world) **AND**
    (furthermore, simultaneously) **DO** (make; rise; get up; write), **I** (we)
    USE (<v> take <p> according to; because of <adj> so as to <conj>
    and) **LOOK AT** (watch; observe) **DUPLICATE** (answer; recover; again).
    万物并作，吾以观复。 *(wàn wù bìng zuò, wú yǐ guān fù.)*

3. **HUSBAND** (man) **THING** (matter; the outside world) **ALL** (every)
    EACH (every; various) **DUPLICATE** (answer; recover; again) **RETURN**
    (converge) **HIS** (its; their; that; such) **ROOT** (base; cause; origin). 夫
    物芸芸各复归其根。 *(fū wù yún yún gè fù guī qí gēn.)*

4. **RETURN** (converge) **ROOT** (base; cause; origin) **SAY** (call; name) **STILL**
    (quiet; calm), <grm> **IS** (yes <frml> this; that) **SAY** (call; name; meaning;
    sense) **DUPLICATE** (answer; recover; again) **LIFE** (lot; destiny; order).
    归根曰静，是谓复命； *(guī gēn yuē jìng, shì wèi fù mìng;)*

5. **DUPLICATE** (answer; recover; again) **LIFE** (lot; destiny; order) **SAY** (call; name)
    ORDINARY (normal; constant), **KNOW** (realize; be aware of; tell) **ORDINARY**
    (normal; constant) **SAY** (call; name) **BRIGHT** (light; distinct; open; honest).
    复命曰常，知常曰明。 *(fù mìng yuē cháng, zhī cháng yuē míng.)*

6. **NO** (not) **KNOW** (realize; be aware of; tell) **ORDINARY** (normal;
    constant), **ABSURD** (preposterous; presumptuous; rash) **DO**
    (make; rise; get up; write) **OMINOUS** (crop failure; terrible). 不
    知常，妄作凶。 *(bù zhī cháng, wàng zuò xiōng.)*

7. **KNOW** (realize; be aware of; tell) **ORDINARY** (normal; constant) **ALLOW** (contain; hold), **ALLOW** (contain; hold) **BE** (so; therefore; only then; you) **COMMON** (public; impartial; just), 知常容，容乃公，*(zhī cháng róng, róng nǎi gōng,)*

8. **COMMON** (public; impartial; just) **BE** (so; therefore; only then; you) **COMPLETE** (whole; entire; full), **COMPLETE** (whole; entire; full) **BE** (so; therefore; only then; you) **SKY** (heaven; nature), 公乃全，全乃天，*(gōng nǎi quán, quán nǎi tiān,)*

9. **SKY** (heaven; nature) **BE** (so; therefore; only then; you) **ROAD** (way, principle; speak; think). 天乃道，*(tiān nǎi dào,)*

10. **ROAD** (way, principle; speak; think) **BE** (so; therefore; only then; you) **FOR A LONG TIME** (long), **SINK** (rise beyond; disappear; hide; die) **BODY** (life; oneself; personally) **NO** (not) **DANGER** (nearly almost). 道乃久，没身不殆。*(dào nǎi jiǔ, méi shēn bù dài.)*

CHAPTER 17

The greatest heights exist below what we realize,
Next comes what we praise.
Next comes what we fear.
Next comes what we bully.
When trust is lacking, there is no trust.
Long drawn out speech is noble,
Meritorious accomplishment is fulfilling,
The people all say, "I am natural".

1. **HIGHEST** (greatest; excessively; too) **UPPER** (higher; superior; better), **BELOW** (under; lower; inferior) **KNOW** (realize; notify) **HAVE** (exist) **OF**. 太上，下知有之。*(tài shàng, xià zhī yǒu zhī.)*

2. **HIS** (her; its; their; that; such) **ORDER** (sequence; next) **PARENT** (relative; intimate) <conj.> **AND** (yet, but) **REPUTATION** (fame; praise) **OF**. 其次亲而誉之。*(qí cì qīn ér yù zhī.)*

3. **HIS** (her; its; their; that; such) **ORDER** (sequence; next) **FEAR** (respect) **OF**. 其次畏之。*(qí cì wèi zhī.)*

4. **HIS** (her; its; their; that; such) **ORDER** (sequence; next) **INSULT** (bully) **OF**. 其次侮之。*(qí cì wǔ zhī.)*

5. **TRUE** (confidence; trust; faith; believe in) **NOT** **FOOT** (enough; ample) **HERE** (herein; how; why), **HAVE** (exist) **NO** (not) **TRUE** (confidence; trust; faith; believe in) **HERE** (herein; how; why). 信不足焉，有不信焉。*(xìn bù zú yān, yǒu bù xìn yān.)*

6. **LONG-DRAWN-OUT** (leisurely) **!** **HIS** (her; its; their; that; such) **EXPENSIVE** (precious; noble) **SPEECH** (word; say; speak), 悠兮其贵言，*(yōu xī qí guì yán.)*

7. **MERIT** (achievement; skill; work) **ACCOMPLISH** (succeed; become) **THING** (business; trouble) **SATISFY** (fulfil), 功成事遂，*(gōng chéng shì suì,)*

8. **THE COMMON PEOPLE ALL** (each and every) **SAY** (call; name; meaning; sense) **I AT EASE** (natural; free from affectation). 百姓皆谓我自然。*(bǎi xìng jiē wèi wǒ zì rán.)*

CHAPTER 18

When the great way is given up, there is benevolence and justice;
When intelligence increases, there is great falseness;
When intimacy lacks harmony, there is mourning kindness;
When the county is confused and chaotic, there are loyal officials.

1. **BIG** (great; loud) **ROAD** (way, path; principle) **GIVE UP** (abolish; waste; useless) **HAVE** (exist) **BENEVOLENCE** (kindheartedness) **JUSTICE** (relationship); 大道废有仁义；*(dà dào fèi yǒu rén yì;)*

2. **INTELLIGENT WISDOM** (resourcefulness) **GO OR COME OUT** (exceed; go beyond) **HAVE** (exist) **BIG** (great; loud) **FALSE** (fake); 慧智出有大伪；*(huì zhì chū yǒu dà wěi;)*

3. **SIX** **PARENT** (relative; intimate) **NO** (not) **GENTLE** (harmony, and, blend) **HAVE** (exist) **FILIAL PIETY** (mourning) **KIND** (loving; b/ mother); 六亲不和有孝慈；*(liù qīn bù hé yǒu xiào cí;)*

4. **COUNTRY** (state; nation) **DARK** (dim; confused; muddled) **IN DISORDE**r (in confusion; chaos) **HAVE** (exist) **OFFICIAL LOYAL TO HIS SOVEREIGN**. 国家昏乱有忠臣。*(guó jiā hūn luàn yǒu zhōng chén.)*

CHAPTER 19

Cut off the sage, discard wisdom,
And the people benefit a hundred fold;
Cut off benevolence, discard justice,
And the people resume devout kindness;
Cut off cleverness, discard advantage,
And robbers will not exist;
These three, considering culture, are not enough.
For this reason, make something to belong to,
See simply, embrace the plain, and have few personal desires.

1. **CUT OFF** (sever; exhausted) **SAGE** (holy; sacred) **THROW AWAY** (discard)
   WISDOM (resourcefulness), 绝圣弃智， *(jué shèng qì zhì,)*

2. **THE PEOPLE** **SHARP** (favorable; advantage; benefit) **HUNDRED**
   (numerous) **TIMES** (-fold); 民利百倍； *(mín lì bǎi bèi;)*

3. **CUT OFF** (sever; exhausted) **BENEVOLENCE** (kindheartedness; humanity) **THROW
   AWAY** (discard) **JUSTICE** (relationship; meaning), 绝仁弃义， *(jué rén qì yì,)*

4. **THE PEOPLE** **DUPLICATE** (turn round; recover; resume) **FILIAL PIETY**
   (mourning) **KIND** (loving; mother); 民复孝慈； *(mín fù xiào cí;)*

5. **CUT OFF** (sever; exhausted) **SKILLFUL** (clever; deceitful) **THROW AWAY** (discard)
   SHARP (favorable; advantage; benefit), 绝巧弃利， *(jué qiǎo qì lì,)*

6. **ROBBERS** (bandits) **NOTHING** **HAVE** (there is; exist);
   盗贼无有； *(dào zéi wú yǒu;)*

7. **THIS** **THREE** (several) (者), **THINK** (believe; consider) **LANGUAGE**
   (culture; civil) **NO** (not) **FOOT** (enough; ample). 此三者，
   以为文不足。 *(cǐ sān zhě, yǐ wéi wén bù zú.)*

8. **INCIDENT** (cause; hence) **COMMAND** (decree; make; cause) **HAVE** (there is;
   exist) **WHAT ONE BELONGS TO**, 故令有所属， *(gù lìng yǒu suǒ shǔ,)*

9. **SEE** (catch sight of) **SIMPLE** (quiet; vegetable) **EMBRACE** (hug) **SIMPLE**
   (plain) **FEW** (little; lose) **PERSONAL** (secret) **FEW** (scant; tasteless) **DESIRE**
   (wish; want). 见素抱朴少私寡欲。 *(jiàn sù bào pò shǎo sī guǎ yù.)*

CHAPTER 20

Cut off learning and be without worry,
Of participation and pandering, both differ by how much?
Of good and evil, both differ how then?
Of man's actual fear, one cannot, not fear.
Neglect such that has no end!
Crowd of people bustle about
Like enjoying excessive sacrifice,
Like ascending a springtime terrace,
I alone am anchored without anticipation,
Like an infant, not a child;
Breathing in and out with a place to return to.
Crowd of people all have more than enough,
I alone seem left behind.
I am foolish of human mind also.
Innocent, conventional people are clear.
I alone am drowsy;
Normal people discern difference,
I alone am subdued.
Crowd of people all have appointments to keep,
I alone am stupid and out of the way.
I alone am different from people,
And value feeding the mother.

1. **CUT OFF** (sever; exhausted) **STUDY** (imitate; learning) **NOTHING** (nil; not have) **WORRY** (sorrow; anxiety; concern), 绝学无忧， *(jué xué wú yōu,)*

2. **YES OF GIVE** (participate in) **PLAY UP TO** (pander to), **MUTUALLY** (each other) **GO** (leave; remove) **HOW MUCH**? 唯之与 阿，相去几何？ *(wéi zhī yú ā, xiāng qù jǐ hé?)*

3. **GOOD** (perfect; be adept in) **OF GIVE** (participate in) **EVIL** (vice; wickedness), **MUTUALLY** (each other) **GO** (leave; remove) **LIKE** (seem, as if) **HOW MUCH**? 善之与恶，相去若何？ *(shàn zhī yú ě, xiāng qù ruò hé?)*

4. **HUMAN** (man; people) **OF ACTUALLY** (place) **FEAR** (respect), **CANNOT** (should not) **NO** (not) **FEAR** (respect). 人之所 畏，不可不畏。 *(rén zhī suǒ wèi, bù kě bù wèi.)*

5. **WASTE** (famine; neglect) **!** **HIS** (its; their, that; such) **HAVE** **NOT** (not) **ENTREAT** (center; b/end; finish) final particle at end of questions) **!** 荒兮其未央哉！ *(huāng xī qí wèi yāng zāi!)*

6. **MANY** (crowd) **HUMAN** (man; people) **BRIGHT** (sunny; prosperous; bustling) 众人熙熙 *(zhòng rén xī xī)*

7. **IN COMPLIANCE WITH** (according to; as; if > go to) **ENJOY** **HIGHEST** (greatest; excessively) **SACRIFICE** (prison; jail; firm) 如享太牢 *(rú xiǎng tài láo)*

8. **IN COMPLIANCE WITH** (according to; as; if > go to) **SPRING** (love; lust; life) **ASCEND** (mount; publish) **PLATFORM** (terrace; support). 如春登台。 *(rú chūn dēng tái.)*

9. **I** (we; self) **ONLY** (single; alone) **BE AT ANCHOR** (moor; berth) **!** **HIS** (its; their, that; such) **HAVE NOT** (did not; not) **SIGN** (omen; portent, foretell), 我独泊兮其未兆， *(wǒ dú bó xī qí wèi zhào,)*

10. **IN COMPLIANCE WITH** (according to; as; if > go to) **BABY INFANT** **OF** **HAVE NOT** (did not; not) **CHILD**； 如婴儿之未孩； *(rú yīng ér zhī wèi hái;)*

11. **BREATHE OUT** (scold)" **!** **LIKE** (seem; as if; if) **NOTHING** (nil; not have) **PLACE** **GO BACK TO** (return; give back to; turn over to). □□兮若无所归。 *([] [] xī ruò wú suǒ guī.)*

12. **MANY** (crowd) **HUMAN** (man; people) **ALL** (each and every) **HAVE** (there is; exist) **SURPLUS** (more than; over; beyond), 众人皆有余， *(zhòng rén jiē yǒu yú,)*

13. <conj.> **AND** (yet, but) **I** (we; self) **ONLY** (single; alone) **LIKE** (seem; as if; if) **OFFER AS A GIFT** (lose; leave behind; keep back; not give). 而我独若遗。 *(ér wǒ dú ruò yí.)*

14. **I** (we; self) **FOOLISH** (stupid; fool) **HUMAN** (man; people) **OF** **HEART** (mind; feeling; core) **ALSO** (too; as well; either) **!** (exclaimation particle at end of questions) 我愚人之心也哉！ *(wǒ yú rén zhī xīn yě zāi!)*

15. **CONFUSED** (innocent) **!** **CUSTOM** (popular; common) **HUMAN** (man; people) **CLEAR** (obvious). 沌沌兮俗人昭昭。 *(dùn dùn xī sú rén zhāo zhāo.)*

16. **I** (we; self) **ONLY** (single; alone) **DROWSY** (sleepy); 我独昏昏； *(wǒ dú hūn hūn;)*

17. **CUSTOM** (common) **HUMAN** (man; people) **EXAMINE** (look into; scrutinize), 俗人察察， *(sú rén chá chá,)*

18. **I** (we; self) **ONLY** (single; alone) **BORED** (depressed) **STUFFY** (close; muffled, subdued). 我独闷闷。 *(wǒ dú mēn mēn.)*

19. **MANY** (crowd) **HUMAN** (man; people) **ALL** (each and every) **HAVE** (there is; exist) **USE** (<v> take <p> according to; because of <adj> so as to <conj> and) . 众人皆有以， *(zhòng rén jiē yǒu yǐ,)*

20. <conj.> **AND** (yet, but) **I** (we; self) **ONLY** (single; alone) **STUPID** (stubborn; mischievous) **JUST** (for the time being; even; both...and....) **LOW** (vulgar < despise < an out-of-the-way place). 而我独顽且鄙。 *(ér wǒ dú wán qiě bǐ.)*

21. **I** (we; self) **ONLY** (single; alone) **DIFFERENT** (strange; surprise; other) **IN** (at, to, from, by, than, out of) **HUMAN** (man; people), 我独异于人， *(wǒ dú yì yú rén,)*

22. <conj.> **AND** (yet, but) **EXPENSIVE** (costly; dear; highly valued) **BRING FOOD TO** (feed) **MOTHER**. 而贵食母。 *(ér guì shí mǔ.)*

CHAPTER 21

The opening of moral character allows only the way through.
Of the way serving the outside world,
    only suddenly, only indistinct.
Indistinct and suddenly, among which exist a shape.
Suddenly and indistinct, among which exists the outside world.
Deep and dark in which exists essence.
Its essence is more than real.
In which exists trust.
From ancient times up to the present,
Its reputation never left
    because of the experience of the multitude.
Why do I know the multitude are of just this condition?
Because of this.

1. **HOLE** (opening) **VIRTUE** (character; heart) **OF** **HOLD** (allow, permit) **ONLY** (alone) **ROAD** (way, principle, speak; think) <grm> **IS** (yes <frml> this; that) **FROM** (through > ever; follow). 孔德之容惟道是从。 *(kǒng dé zhī róng wéi dào shì cōng.)*

2. **ROAD** (way, principle, speak; think) **OF** **DO** (serve as; be; for) **THING** (matter; the outside world) **ONLY** (but; thinking) **SUDDENLY** (seemingly) **ONLY** (but; thinking) **INDISTINCT**. 道之为物惟恍惟惚。 *(dào zhī wéi wù wéi huǎng wéi hū.)*

3. **INDISTINCT** **!** **SUDDENLY** (seemingly) **!** **HIS** (its; their, that; such) **AMONG** (in which) **HAVE** (there is; exist) **ELEPHANT** (appearance; shape; image). 惚兮恍兮其中有象。 *(hū xī huǎng xī qí zhōng yǒu xiàng.)*

4. **SUDDENLY** (seemingly) **!** **INDISTINCT** **!** **HIS** (its; their, that; such) **AMONG** (in which) **HAVE** (there is; exist) **THING** (matter; the outside world). 恍兮惚兮其中有物。 *(huǎng xī hū xī qí zhōng yǒu wù.)*

5. **DEEP** (quiet and elegant) **!** **DARK** (obscure; deep; profound; stupid) **!** **HIS** (its; their, that; such) **AMONG** (in which) **HAVE** (there is; exist) **REFINED** (choice; essence). 窈兮冥兮其中有精。 *(yǎo xī míng xī qí zhōng yǒu jīng.)*

6. **HIS** (her; its; their; that; such) **REFINED** (choice; essence) **VERY** (extremely; more than) **TRUE** (real; unmistakably). 其精甚真。 *(qí jīng shén zhēn.)*

7. **HIS** (its; their, that; such) **AMONG** (in which) **HAVE** (there is; exist) **TRUE** (trust; have faith in; believe in). 其中有信。 *(qí zhōng yǒu xìn.)*

8. **SELF** (certainly; from; since) **ANCIENT** (age-old) **REACH** (come up to; and) **MODERN** (present-day; now), 自古及今， *(zì gǔ jí jīn,)*

9. **HIS** (its; their, that; such) **NAME** (fame; reputation) **NO** (not) **GO** (leave; remove) **USE** (<v> take <p> according to; because of <adj> so as to <conj> and) **READ** (inspect; experience) **MANY** (crowd; multitude) **JUST** (only). 其名不去以阅众甫。 *(qí míng bù qù yǐ yuè zhòng fǔ.)*

10. **I** (we) **WHO** (why) **KNOW** (realize; tell) **MANY** (crowd; multitude) **JUST** (only) **OF** **FORM** (shape; condition; account) **?** 吾何以知众甫之状哉？ *(wú hé yǐ zhī zhòng fǔ zhī zhuàng zāi?)*

11. **USE** (<v> take <p> according to; because of <adj> so as to <conj> and) **THIS**. 以此。 *(yǐ cǐ.)*

CHAPTER 22

Bent follows whole, crooked follows straight,
Hollow follows filled, worn-out follows new.
Little follows satisfaction, much follows bewilderment.
The wise person uses this to hold the One,
    and models all under heaven.
He does not see his self for he is honest;
    he does not exist for he is clear;
He does not attack himself for he has merit;
    he is not self important for he endures;
He alone does not contend,
    for nothing under heaven is able to contend with him.
This is the ancient point of view: bent follows whole.
How can it be that emptiness speaks! Complete sincerity returns.

1. **BENT** (crooked, wrong) **STANDARD** (norm; rule > imitate; follow) **COMPLETE** (whole; make perfect), **CROOKED** (twist; treat unjustly) **STANDARD** (norm; rule > imitate; follow) **STRAIGHT** (upright; frank), 曲则全，枉则直， *(qū zé quán, wǎng zé zhí,)*

2. **HOLLOW** (low-lying) **STANDARD** (norm; rule > imitate; follow) **BE** full of (have a surplus of), **SHABBY** (worn-out; ragged) **STANDARD** (norm; rule > imitate; follow) **NEW** (fresh). 洼则盈，敝则新 *(wā zé yíng, bì zé xīn)*

3. **FEW** (little; lack) **STANDARD** (norm; rule > imitate; follow) **GET** (obtain, satisfied, complacent), **MUCH** (many; more) **STANDARD** (norm; rule > imitate; follow) **BE PUZZLED** (be bewildered; delude). 少则得，多则惑。 *(shǎo zé dé, duō zé huò.)*

4. <grm> **IS** (yes <frml> this; that) **USE** (<v> take <p> according to; because of <adj> so as to <conj> and) **SAGE** (holy; sacred) **HUMAN** (man; people) **HOLD IN THE ARMS** (hug; cherish) **ONE** (single; alone; whole; all) **DO** (act; serve as; become; be; mean) **LAND UNDER HEAVEN** **TYPE** (style; form> mood; mode). 是以圣人抱一，为天下式。 *(shì yǐ shèng rén bào yī, wéi tiān xià shì.)*

5. **NO** (not) **SELF** (oneself; certainly) **SEE** (catch sight of_ appear) **HAPPENING** (reason; cause; hence) **BRIGHT** (clear, distinct, honest); **NO** (not) **NATURALLY** (of course) **HAPPENING** (reason; cause; hence) **CLEAR** (evident; conspicuous). 不自见故明；不自是故彰； *(bù zì jiàn gù míng; bù zì shì gù zhāng;)*

6. **NO** (not) **SELF** (oneself; certainly) **FELL** (cut down; attack) **HAPPENING** (reason; cause; hence) **HAVE** (there is; exist) **MERIT** (exploit; achievement; result; work); **NO** (not) **SELF** (oneself; certainly) **PITY** (self-important; conceited; reserved) **HAPPENING** (reason; cause; hence) **LONG** (of long duration; regularly; forte). 不自伐故有功；不自矜故长； *(bù zì fá gù yǒu gōng; bù zì jīn gù cháng;)*

7. **HUSBAND** (man) **ONLY** (alone) **NO** (not) **CONTEND** (vie; strive; argue; dispute), **HAPPENING** (reason; cause; hence) **LAND UNDER HEAVEN** **NO ONE** (nothing) **CAN** (be able to) **TAKE PART IN** (participate in) **OF** **CONTEND** (vie; strive; argue). 夫唯不争，故天下莫能与之争。 *(fū wéi bù zhēng, gù tiān xià mò néng yú zhī zhēng.)*

8. **ANCIENT** (age-old) **OF** **WHAT IS CALLED** (so-called): [**BENT** (crooked, wrong) **STANDARD** (norm; rule > imitate; follow) **COMPLETE** (whole; make perfect) (者)] 古之所谓：「曲则全者」 *(gǔ zhī suǒ wèi: [qū zé quán zhě])*

9. **HOW CAN IT BE THAT** **VOID** (emptiness) **SPEECH** (word) **!** **SINCERE** (honest;> really) **COMPLETE** (whole; make perfect)' <conj.> **AND** (yet, but) **GO** back to (return; converge; come together) **OF**. 岂虚言哉！诚全而归之。 *(qǐ xū yán zāi! chéng quán ér guī zhī.)*

CHAPTER 23

Infrequent speech is natural.
Fluttering breezes change direction,
    sudden showers can't last the day.
What does this? Heaven and earth.
Even heaven and earth unable to long continue,
And so what about people?
Hence, following the way is the same as the way.
Following virtue is the same as virtue,
Following loss is the same as loss.
Together in the way, the way happily satisfies;
Together in virtue, virtue happily satisfies;
Together in loss, loss happily satisfies;
When trust is not sufficient herein, there exists no trust herein.

1. **HOPE** (rare; scarce; uncommon) **SPEECH** (word; say; talk) **AT EASE** (natural; free from affectation). 希言自然。 *(xī yán zì rán.)*

2. **HENCE FLUTTER WIND NO** (not) **END** (death; after all) **FACING** (towards), **SUDDEN** (abrupt) **RAIN NO** (not) **END** (death; after all) **SUN** (day; time). 故飘风不终朝，骤雨不终日。 *(gù piāo fēng bù zhōng cháo, zhòu yǔ bù zhōng rì.)*

3. **WHO** (which; what) **DO** (act; act as; serve as; become; be; mean) **THIS** (者)? **HEAVEN AND EARTH** (world; universe; field of activity). 孰为此者？天地。 *(shú wèi cǐ zhě? tiān dì.)*

4. **HEAVEN AND EARTH** (world; universe; field of activity) **STILL** (yet; set great store by) **NO** (not) **CAN** (be able to) **FOR A LONG TIME** (long), 天地尚不能久， *(tiān dì shàng bù néng jiǔ,)*

5. <conj.> **AND** (yet, but) **CONDITION** (situation; compare;> moreover; besides) **IN** (at, to, from, by, than, out of) **HUMAN** (man; people) 乎 (<part> expresses doubt or wonder)? 而况于人乎？ *(ér kuàng yú rén hū?)*

6. **HENCE BE ENGAGED IN** (deal with) **IN** (at, to, from, than) **ROAD** (way, principle; speak; think) (者), **SAME** (similar; together) **IN** (at, to, from, than) **ROAD** (way, principle; speak; think). 故从事于道者，同于道。 *(gù cóng shì yú dào zhě, tóng yú dào.)*

7. **VIRTUE** (moral character; heart) (者) **SAME** (similar; together) **IN** (at, to, from, than) **VIRTUE** (moral character; heart). 德者同于德。 *(dé zhě tóng yú dé.)*

8. **LOSE** (miss; fail; mistake) (者) **SAME** (similar; together) **IN** (at, to, from, than) **LOSE** (miss; fail; mistake). 失者同于失。 *(shī zhě tóng yú shī.)*

9. **SAME** (similar; together) **IN** (at, to, from, than) **ROAD** (way, principle; speak; think) (者) **ROAD** (way, principle; speak; think) **ALSO** **HAPPY** (cheerful; enjoy) **GET** (result in; satisfied_need; must) **OF**; 同于道者道亦乐得之； *(tóng yú dào zhě dào yì lè dé zhī;)*

10. **SAME** (similar; together) **IN** (at, to, from, than) **VIRTUE** (moral character; heart) (者) **VIRTUE** (moral character; heart) **ALSO** **HAPPY** (cheerful; enjoy) **GET** (result in; satisfied_need; must) **OF**; 同于德者德亦乐得之； *(tóng yú dé zhě dé yì lè dé zhī;)*

11. **SAME** (similar; together) **IN** (at, to, from, than) **LOSE** (miss; fail; mistake) (者) **LOSE** (miss; fail; mistake) **IN** (at, to, from, than) **HAPPY** (cheerful; enjoy) **GET** (result in; satisfied_need; must) **OF**. 同于失者失于乐得之。 *(tóng yú shī zhě shī yú lè dé zhī.)*

12. **TRUE** (trust; believe) **NO** (not) **FOOT** (sufficient; as much as) **HERE** (herein; how; why) **HAVE** (there is; exist) **NO** (not) **TRUE** (trust; believe) **HERE** (herein; how; why). 信不足焉有不信焉。 *(xìn bù zú yān yǒu bù xìn yān.)*

CHAPTER 24

What we look forward to, does not exist;
What we chase after, will not prevail.
Seeing your self, is not honest;
Of course, this is not evident.
Attacking your self is without merit;
Self pity does not endure.
Such ways are called surplus food and superfluous forms.
Matters of the outside world, perhaps fierce,
Hence one who has the way does not dwell in them.

1. **STAND ON TIPTOE** (look forward to) (者) **NO** (not) **STAND** (found; exist; live); 企者不立； *(qǐ zhě bù lì;)*

2. **STEP** (stride; go beyond) (者) **NO** (not) **GO** (be current; prevail; do; competent). 跨者不行。 *(kuà zhě bù xíng.)*

3. **SELF** (one's own; certainly) **SEE** (catch sight of_ appear; become visible) (者) **NO** (not) **BRIGHT** (clear; honest; know); 自见者不明； *(zì jiàn zhě bù míng;)*

4. **NATURALLY** (of course) (者) **NO** (not) **CLEAR** (evident; conspicuous). 自是者不彰。 *(zì shì zhě bù zhāng.)*

5. **SELF** (one's own; certainly) **FELL** (cut down; strike; attack) (者) **NOTHING** (without; not; regardless of) **MERIT** (achievement); 自伐者无功； *(zì fá zhě wú gōng;)*

6. **SELF** (one's own; certainly) **PITY** (sympathize with; self-important; conceited) (者) **NO** (not) **OF LONG DURATION** (forte). 自矜者不长。 *(zì jīn zhě bù cháng.)*

7. **HIS** (her; its; their, he, she, it, they; that; such) **EXIST** (be living) **ROAD** (way, principle; speak; think) **ALSO** (too; as well; either) **SAY** (call; name); **SURPLUS** (more than; over) **BRING FOOD TO** (feed) **SUPERFLUOUS** (redundant; be cumbersome) **FORM** (entity; look). 其在道也曰：余食赘形。 *(qí zài dào yě yuē: yú shí zhuì xíng.)*

8. **MATTER** (the outside world as distinct from oneself) **PERHAPS** (or> someone) **EVIL** (fierce, dislike; hate) **OF**, 物或恶之， *(wù huò è zhī,)*

9. **HAPPENING** (reason; hence) **HAVE** (there is; exist) **ROAD** (way, principle; speak; think) (者) **NO** (not) **PLACE** (part, be situated in; manage> dwell; live). 故有道者不处。 *(gù yǒu dào zhě bù chǔ.)*

CHAPTER 25

The outside world passes for the beginning of Heaven and Earth.
Still and silent, it alone does not change.
Goes round yet doesn't harm,
It can serve as the mother of all under heaven and earth.
We don't know its name,
Powerful, of words we call it the way,
Striving, of reputation we call it great.
Great we call death, death we call distant, distant we call reversal.
Hence, the way is great, heaven is great,
    earth is great, and people are also great.
In the center there exists four 'greats', and people reside as one.
People follow earth, earth follows heaven, heaven follows the way,
And the way follows that which is natural,
    and free from affectation.

1. **HAVE** (there is; exist) **MATTER** (the outside world) **MIX** (confuse; pass for) **ACCOMPLISH** (become; turn into) **EARLIER** (first) **HEAVEN AND EARTH** (universe) **GIVE BIRTH TO** (existence). 有物混成 先天地生。 *(yǒu wù hún chéng xiān tiān dì shēng.)*

2. **STILL** (silent; solitary) **!** **FEW** (silent; deserted) **!** **ONLY** (single; alone) **STAND** (set up) **NO** (not) **CHANGE** (rectify), 寂兮寥兮独立不改， *(jì xī liáo xī dú lì bù gǎi,)*

3. **MAKE A CIRCUIT** (all) **GO** (be current; prevail; do; competent) <conj.> **AND** (yet, but) **NO** (not) **DANGER** (nearly almost), 周行而不殆， *(zhōu xíng ér bù dài,)*

4. **CAN** (may) **THINK** (believe; consider that) **LAND UNDER HEAVEN** **MOTHER**. 可以为天下母。 *(kě yǐ wéi tiān xià mú.)*

5. **I** (we) **NO** (not) **KNOW** (realize; tell) **SELF** (one's own; certainly) **NAME** (fame; reputation), 吾不知其名， *(wú bù zhī qí míng,)*

6. **STUBBORN** (unyielding> powerful> strive) **WORD** **OF** **SAY** (call) **ROAD** (way, principle; speak; think). 强字之日道。 *(jiàng zì zhī yuē dào.)*

7. **STUBBORN** (unyielding> powerful> strive) **DO** (become; mean, stand for, support) **OF** **NAME** (fame; reputation) **SAY** (call) **BIG** (great; heavy rain, loud etc). 强为之名曰大。 *(jiàng wéi zhī míng yuē dà.)*

8. **BIG** (great; heavy rain, loud etc) **SAY** (call) **PASS** (die), **PASS** (die) **SAY** (call) **FAR** (distant), **FAR** (distant) **SAY** (call) **REVERSE** (turn over; in an opposite direction; revolt). 大曰逝， 逝曰远， 远曰反。 *(dà yuē shì, shì yuē yuǎn, yuǎn yuē fǎn.)*

9. **REASON** (cause; hence) **ROAD** (way, principle; speak; think) **BIG** (great; heavy rain, loud etc), **SKY** (heaven; day; nature) **BIG** (great; heavy rain, loud etc), **EARTH** **BIG** (great; heavy rain, loud etc), **HUMAN** (man; people) **ALSO** **BIG** (great; heavy rain, loud etc). 故道大、 天大、 地大、 人亦大。 *(gù dào dà, tiān dà, dì dà, rén yì dà.)*

10. **FIELD** (region, area) **CENTER** (middle; in; among) **HAVE** (there is; exist) **FOUR** **BIG** (great; heavy rain, loud etc), <conj.> **AND** (yet, but) **HUMAN** (man; people) **RESIDE** (dwell; live) **HIS** (its, he, it, that; such) **ONE** **HERE** (how; why). 域中有四大， 而人居其一焉。 *(yù zhōng yǒu sì dà, ér rén jū qí yī yān.)*

11. **HUMAN** (man; people) **METHOD** (follow; model after) **EARTH**, **EARTH** **METHOD** (follow; model after) **SKY** (heaven; day; nature), **SKY** (heaven; day; nature) **METHOD** (follow; model after) **ROAD** (way, principle; speak; think), 人法地， 地法天， 天法道， *(rén fǎ dì, dì fǎ tiān, tiān fǎ dào,)*

12. **ROAD** (way, principle; speak; think) **METHOD** (follow; model after) **NATURAL** (free from affectation). 道法自然。 *(dào fǎ zì rán.)*

CHAPTER 26

The heavy is the root of the light,
The still is the ruler of the restless.
Because of this, the gentleman throughout the day,
    never abandons seriousness.
Although, he flourishes, watches, enjoys and dwells detached.
How wasteful to be in charge, yet take life lightly.
Light follows the loss of the root.
Restless follows the loss of the gentleman.

1. **HEAVY** (important; repeat) **DO** (act as; be, mean; support) **LIGHT** (softly) **ROOT** (cause; origin), 重为轻根， *(chóng wéi qīng gēn,)*

2. **STILL** (quiet; calm) **DO** (act as; be, mean; support) **RASH** (impetuous; restless) **SOVEREIGN** (gentleman, supreme ruler). 静为躁君。 *(jìng wéi zào jūn.)*

3. <grm> **IS** (yes <frml> this; that) **USE** (<v> take <p> according to; because of <adj> so as to <conj> and) **GENTLEMAN END** (eventually; entire; all) **DAY GO** (be current; prevail; do) **NO** (not) **LEAVE** (off, from) **WEIGHT** (degree of seriousness; propriety). 是以君子终日行不离轻重。 *(shì yǐ jūn zǐ zhōng rì xíng bù lí qīng zhòng.)*

4. **THOUGH** (although; even if) **HAVE** (there is; exist) **GROW LUXURIANTLY** (flourish, honor) **WATCH A SWALLOW** (comfort, enjoy) **MANAGE** (dwell; live) **ALOOF** (detached). 虽有荣观燕处超然。 *(suī yǒu róng guān yān chú chāo rán.)*

5. **HOW** (why, to no avail) **TEN THOUSAND** (myriad) **A WAR CHARIOT OF HOST** (owner) <conj.> **AND** (yet, but) **USE** (<v> take <p> according to; because of <adj> so as to <conj> and) **BODY** (life; personally) **LIGHT** (softly) **LAND UNDER HEAVEN**. 奈何万乘之主而以身轻天下。 *(nài hé wàn chéng zhī zhǔ ér yǐ shēn qīng tiān xià.)*

6. **LIGHT** (softly) **STANDARD** (norm; rule > imitate; follow) **LOSE** (miss; let slip) **ROOT** (cause; origin), 轻则失根， *(qīng zé shī gēn,)*

7. **RASH** (impetuous; restless) **STANDARD** (norm; rule > imitate; follow) **LOSE** (miss; let slip) **GENTLEMAN**. 躁则失君。 *(zào zé shī jūn.)*

CHAPTER 27

Adept at prevailing without the rut of an outward sign.
Adept at speech without the flaw of banishment and blame.
Adept at counting without a plan or paper.
Adept at closing without locking, yet cannot be opened.
Adept at a conclusion without restriction, yet cannot be undone.
Using this, the wise person is:
Always adept at helping people because he abandons no one.
Always adept at helping things because he abandons nothing.
This says he follows the pattern honestly.
Thus, those who are adept are models for those not adept.
Those not adept support those who are adept.
Neither value the model nor love the supporter.
This wisdom, although perplexing,
Is called an essential wonder.

1. **GOOD** (be adept in) **GO** (be current; prevail; do) **NOTHING** (without;
    not) **THE TRACK OF A WHEEL** (rut; > way; idea) **MARK** (trace; an
    outward sign). 善行无辙迹。 *(shàn xíng wú chè jì.)*

2. **GOOD** (be adept in) **SPEECH** (word; say; talk) **NOTHING**
    (without; not) **FLAW** (defect; shortcoming) **BANISH** (censure;
    blame). 善言无瑕谪。 *(shàn yán wú xiá zhé.)*

3. **GOOD** (be adept in) **NUMBER** (count) **NO** (not) **USE** (apply <polite> eat
    <frml> hence) **COUNTER** (prepare; plan) **PLAN** (strategy; bamboo slips
    used for writing on). 善数不用筹策。 *(shàn shǔ bù yòng chóu cè.)*

4. **GOOD** (be adept in) **SHUT** (close; stop up; obstruct) **NOTHING** (without;
    not) **SHUT   DOOR LOCK** <conj.> **AND** (yet, but) **NO** (not) **APPROVE** (can) **OPEN**
    (start). 善闭无关楗而不可开。 *(shàn bì wú guān jiàn ér bù kě kāi.)*

5. **GOOD** (be adept in) **TIE** (settle; conclude; affidavit) **NOTHING** (without;
    not) **ROPE** (restrain) **MAKE AN APPOINTMENT** (arrange; restrain) <conj.>
    AND (yet, but) **NO** (not) **APPROVE** (can) **SEPARATE** (divide; untie). 善
    结无绳约而不可解。 *(shàn jiē wú shéng yāo ér bù kě jiě.)*

6. <grm> **IS** (yes <frml> this; that) **USE** (<v> take <p> according
    to; because of <adj> so as to <conj> and) **SAGE** (holy; sacred)
    HUMAN (man; people). 是以圣人 *(shì yǐ shèng rén)*

7. **ORDINARY** (normal; constant; often) **GOOD** (be adept in) **RESCUE** (save; salvage; help; relieve; succour) **HUMAN** (man; people), **HAPPENING** (reason; cause; hence) **NOTHING** (without; not) **THROW AWAY** (discard; abandon) **HUMAN** (man; people). 常善救人，故无弃人。 *(cháng shàn jiù rén, gù wú qì rén.)*

8. **ORDINARY** (normal; constant; often) **GOOD** (be adept in) **RESCUE** (save; salvage; help; relieve; succour) **MATTER** (the outside world), **HAPPENING** (reason; cause; hence) **NOTHING** (without; not) **THROW AWAY** (discard; abandon) **MATTER** (the outside world). 常善救物，故无弃物。 *(cháng shàn jiù wù, gù wú qì wù.)*

9. \<grm\> **IS** (yes \<frml\> this; that) **SAY** (call; name; meaning; sense) **MAKE A SURPRISE ATTACK ON RAID** (follow the pattern of; carry on as before) **BRIGHT** (clear; honest; know). 是谓袭明。 *(shì wèi xí míng.)*

10. **HAPPENING** (reason; cause; hence) **GOOD** (be adept in) **HUMAN** (man; people) (者) **NO** (not) **GOOD** (be adept in) **HUMAN** (man; people) **OF** **TEACHER** (master; model; example). 故善人者不善人之师。 *(gù shàn rén zhě bù shàn rén zhī shī.)*

11. **NO** (not) **GOOD** (be adept in) **HUMAN** (man; people) (者) **GOOD** (be adept in) **HUMAN** (man; people) **OF** **MONEY** (expenses; subsidize; support; natural ability). 不善人者善人之资。 *(bù shàn rén zhě shàn rén zhī zī.)*

12. **NO** (not) **VALUE** (expensive, precious; noble; > your) **SELF** (one's own; certainly) **TEACHER** (master; model; example), **NO** (not) **LOVE** (like; treasure; take care of) **SELF** (one's own; certainly) **MONEY** (expenses; subsidize; support; natural ability), 不贵其师、不爱其资， *(bù guì qí shī, bù ài qí zī,)*

13. **THOUGH** (although; even if) **WISDOM** (resourcefulness) **BIG** (great) **BE CONFUSED** (be lost; perplex; fascinate; enchant), 虽智大迷， *(suī zhì dà mí,)*

14. \<grm\> **IS** (yes \<frml\> this; that) **SAY** (call; name; meaning; sense) **DEMAND** (force, important; want; ask for) **WONDERFUL** (excellent; fine; ingenious; clever; subtle). 是谓要妙。 *(shì wèi yāo miào.)*

CHAPTER 28

Know its male, abide by its female,
    and be a small stream for all under heaven.
Serving as a small stream for all under heaven,
    constant virtue will never leave you,
And you will again return to infancy.
Know its white, abide by its black,
    and serve as a model for all under heaven.
Being a pattern for all under heaven,
    constant virtue will never be in error,
And you will again return to moderation.
Know its honor, abide by its disgrace,
    and be a valley for all under heaven.
Being a valley for all under heaven,
    constant virtue will be sufficient,
And you will again return to simplicity.
Simplicity loosens the standard,
    and allows a wise person to serve as an elder.
This is how even the greatest control never cuts.

1. **KNOW** **ITS** **MALE** (powerful, imposing), **DEFEND** (observe, abide by, close to) **ITS** **FEMALE**, **SERVE AS** (be, mean) **HEAVEN UNDER** **SMALL STREAM**. 知其雄，守其雌，为天下溪。 *(zhī qí xióng, shǒu qí cí, wéi tiān xià xī.)*

2. **SERVE AS** (be, mean) **HEAVEN UNDER** **SMALL STREAM**, **ALWAYS** **VIRTUE** (integrity) **NO** (not) **LEAVE**, 为天下溪，常德不离， *(wéi tiān xià xī, cháng dé bù lí,)*

3. **DUPLICATE** (again) **RETURN** **IN** (at, to, from, by, than, out of) **BABY**. 复归于婴儿。 *(fù guī yú yīng ér.)*

4. **KNOW** **ITS** **WHITE** (pure, clear), **DEFEND** (observe, abide by, close to) **ITS** **BLACK**, **SERVE AS** (be, mean) **HEAVEN UNDER** **TYPE** (style, pattern) 知其白，守其黑，为天下式。 *(zhī qí bái, shǒu qí hēi, wéi tiān xià shì.)*

5. **SERVE AS** (be, mean) **HEAVEN UNDER** **TYPE** (style, pattern), **ALWAYS** **VIRTUE** (integrity) **NO** (not) **ERROR** (mistake), 为天下式，常德不忒， *(wéi tiān xià shì, cháng dé bù tè,)*

6. **DUPLICATE** (again) **RETURN** **IN** (at, to, from, by, than, out of) **WITHOUT** **EXTREME**. 复归于无极。 *(fù guī yú wú jí.)*

7. **KNOW** **ITS** **FLOURISH** (honor, glory), **DEFEND** (observe, abide by, close to) **ITS** **DISGRACE** (dishonor), **SERVE AS** (be, mean) **HEAVEN UNDER** **VALLEY**. 知其荣，守其辱，为天下谷。 (*zhī qí róng, shǒu qí rǔ, wéi tiān xià gǔ.*)

8. **SERVE AS** (be, mean) **HEAVEN UNDER** **VALLEY**, **ALWAYS** **VIRTUE** (integrity) **BE** (therefore, only then, your) **FOOT** (sufficient;, full), 为天下谷，常德乃足， (*wéi tiān xià gǔ, cháng dé nǎi zú,*)

9. **DUPLICATE** (again) **RETURN** **IN** (at, to, from, by, than, out of) **SIMPLE** (plain). 复归于朴。 (*fù guī yú pò.*)

10. **SIMPLE** (plain) **BREAK-UP** (come loose) **STANDARD** (norm; rule > imitate; follow) **SERVE AS** (be, mean) **IMPLEMENT** (capacity, talent), **SAGE** (holy; sacred) **HUMAN** (man; people) **USE** **OF** **STANDARD** (norm; rule > imitate; follow) **SERVES AS** (be, mean) **PUBLIC ELDER** (senior, chief, head). 朴散则为器，圣人用之则为官长。 (*pò sǎn zé wéi qì, shèng rén yòng zhī zé wéi guān cháng.*)

11. **INCIDENT** (happening, cause, intentionally, therefore) **BIG** **MAKE** (control, regulate, system) **NO** (not) **CUT**. 故大制不割。 (*gù dà zhì bù gē.*)

CHAPTER 29

With desire choosing anything, of doing I see no satisfied end.
All under heaven is divine capacity,
    nothing can be done to it either.
Doing decays, grasping loses.
In the external world of man, someone leads, someone follows.
Someone sighs, someone blows.
Someone strives, someone wins.
Someone subdues, someone ruins.
Because of this, the wise man leaves the extremes,
    the luxurious, and the safe behind.

1. **SUPPORT** (take; will, prod> with, by means of) **DESIRE** (wish; about to) **TAKE** (get; aim at; seek; choose) **LAND UNDER HEAVEN** <conj.> **AND** (yet, but) **DO** (act as; be, mean; support) **OF**, **I** (we) **SEE** (catch sight of) **HIS** (its, he, it, that; such) **NO** (not) **GET** (obtain, <frml> satisfied) **STOP** (cease; end <frml> thereafter). 将欲取天下而为之，吾见其不得已。 (*jiāng yù qǔ tiān xià ér wéi zhī, wú jiàn qí bù dé yǐ.*)

2. **LAND UNDER HEAVEN** **GOD** (deity; magical; spirit; mind) **IMPLEMENT** (utensil; ware; organ; capacity; talent), **NO** (not) **APPROVE** (can <adv.> but; yet) **DO** (act as; be, mean; support) **ALSO** (too; as well; either), 天下神器，不可为也， (*tiān xià shén qì, bù kě wéi yě,*)

3.   **DO** (act as; be, mean; support) (者) **BE DEFEATED** (lose; beat; fail; decay) **OF**,   **HOLD** (grasp; manage; observe; catch) (者) **LOSE** (miss; mishap; defect; mistake) **OF**. 为者败之，执者失之。 *(wéi zhě bài zhī, zhí zhě shī zhī.)*

4.   **HUSBAND** (man) **MATTER** (the outside world) **PERHAPS** (or; either... or...; > someone) **GO** (be current; prevail; do) **PERHAPS** (or; either...or...; > someone) **TO FOLLOW** (to comply with / to allow), 夫物或行或随、 *(fū wù huò xíng huò suí,)*

5.   **PERHAPS** (or; either...or...; > someone) **SIGH**   **PERHAPS** (or; either... or...; > someone) **BLOW** (puff; boast; brag; break off; break up; fall through), 或□或吹、 *(huò [] huò chuī,)*

6.   **PERHAPS** (or; either...or...; > someone) **STRIVE** (strong; powerful; better_unyielding) **PERHAPS** (or; either...or...; > someone) **WIN** (beat; gain (profit), 或强或赢、 *(huò jiàng huò yíng,)*

7.   **PERHAPS** (or; either...or...; > someone) **DEFEAT** (frustrate; subdue; lower) **PERHAPS** (or; either...or...; > someone) **DESTROY** (ruin). 或挫或隳。 *(huò cuò huò huī.)*

8.   <grm> **IS** (yes <frml> this; that) **USE** (<v> take <p> according to; because of <adj> so as to <conj> and) **SAGE** (holy; sacred) **HUMAN** (man; people) **GO** (remove) **VERY** (extremely; more than), **GO** (remove) **LUXURIOUS** (extravagant; excessive; inordinate; extravagant), **GO** (remove) **SAFE** (peaceful; extreme; most). 是以圣人去甚、去奢、去泰。 *(shì yǐ shèng rén qù shén, qù shē, qù tài.)*

CHAPTER 30

In using the way to assist in managing people,
Avoid strong arming anything under heaven.
Such affairs easily rebound.
Where masters live, why do thorn bushes grow?
Where armies have been, years of crop failure follow.
Those most adept have results, yet stop,
    not daring not to seek better.
Have results yet don't pity.
Have results yet don't attack.
Have results yet don't be proud.
Have results yet not complacent afterwards.
Have results yet don't strong arm.
The strong standard always, is not of the dao,
Not of the dao (Tao) ends early.

1. **USE** (<v> take <p> according to; because of <adj> so as to <conj>
   and) **ROAD** (way, principle; speak; think) **ASSIST HUMAN** (man; people)
   HOST (owner) (者), 以道佐人主者， *(yǐ dào zuǒ rén zhǔ zhě,)*

2. **NO** (not) **USE** (<v> take <p> according to; because of <adj> so as to <conj>
   and) **WEAPONS** (army; troops) **STRIVE** (strong; powerful; better,_unyielding)
   LAND UNDER HEAVEN. 不以兵强天下。 *(bù yǐ bīng jiàng tiān xià)*

3. **HIS** (its, he, it, that; such) **MATTER** (affair; thing; business; involvement) **GOOD**
   (be easy) **GO** (give back; return; repay). 其事好还。 *(qí shì hǎo hái.)*

4. **TEACHER** (master; model; example) **OF PLACE DWELL CHASTE**
   TREE (vitex) **THORN BUSHES GIVE BIRTH TO** (existence) **HERE**
   (herein; (usu. negative questioning) how; why). 师之所
   处荆棘生焉。 *(shī zhī suǒ chǔ jīng jí shēng yān.)*

5. **ARMY** (troops) **OF BACK** (after) **CERTAINLY** (must) **HAVE** (there is; exist) **CROP**
   FAILURE (fierce; terrible; murder) **YEAR** (annual; yearly; age; a period in
   history; harvest). 军之后必有凶年。 *(jūn zhī hòu bì yǒu xiōng nián.)*

6. **GOOD** (perfect; kind; be adept in) **HAVE** (there is; exist) **FRUIT** (result;
   really; as expected) <conj.> **AND** (yet, but) **STOP** (cease; end; already;>
   thereafter; afterwards; too), **NO** (not) **BOLD** (daring; be certain; venture)
   USE (<v> take <p> according to; because of <adj> so as to <conj> and)
   TAKE (aim at; seek; choose) **STRIVE** (strong; powerful; better_unyielding).
   善有果而已，不敢以取强。 *(shàn yǒu guǒ ér yǐ, bù gǎn yǐ qǔ jiàng.)*

7. **FRUIT** (result; really; as expected) <conj.> **AND** (yet, but) **DON'T PITY** (sympathize with; self-important; conceited; restrained; reserved). 果而勿矜。 *(guǒ ér wù jīn.)*

8. **FRUIT** (result; really; as expected) <conj.> **AND** (yet, but) **DON'T FELL** (cut down; strike; attack). 果而勿伐。 *(guǒ ér wù fá.)*

9. **FRUIT** (result; really; as expected) <conj.> **AND** (yet, but) **DON'T PROUD** (arrogant; conceited). 果而勿骄。 *(guǒ ér wù jiāo.)*

10. **FRUIT** (result; really; as expected) <conj.> **AND** (yet, but) **NO** (not) **GET** (result in;> satisfied, complacent;> be finished, be ready) **STOP** (cease; end; already; > thereafter; afterwards; too). 果而不得已。 *(guǒ ér bù dé yǐ.)*

11. **FRUIT** (result; really; as expected) <conj.> **AND** (yet, but) **DON'T STRIVE** (strong; powerful; better_unyielding). 果而勿强。 *(guǒ ér wù jiàng.)*

12. **MATTER** (the outside world) **STRONG** (strengthen; make better) **STANDARD** (norm; rule > imitate; follow) **OLD** (aged; of long standing; old;for a long time; always), <grm> **IS** (yes <frml> this; that) **SAY** (call; name; meaning; sense) **NO** (not) **ROAD** (way, principle; speak; think), 物壮则老，是谓不道， *(wù zhuàng zé lǎo, shì wèi bù dào,)*

13. **NO** (not) **ROAD** (way, principle; speak; think) **EARLY MORNING** (long ago; as early as; for a long time; early; in advance) **STOP** (cease; end; already;> thereafter; afterwards; too). 不道早已。 *(bù dào zǎo yǐ.)*

CHAPTER 31

For the good person, weapons are inauspicious tools – even evil.
Hence, one who has the way gets along without them.
A person of noble character dwells normally noble left,
The use of weapons normally noble right.
Weapons are inauspicious tools,
Not the tools of a person of noble character,
Having no alternative but to use them,
Indifferent to fame or gain, to lightly act is best.
Victorious but not beautiful,
That beauty in cheerfully killing people.
Man cheerfully killing people,
    normally never get their way in the world.
Auspicious affairs still left, burial affairs still right.
The partisan general dwells on the left,
    the superior general dwells right.
Speaks at funeral places.
Murder of many, takes sorrowful tears,
    defeat takes management of the mourning rites.

1.   **HUSBAND** (man) **GOOD** (fine; beautiful) **WEAPONS** (army; troops) (者)
NO (not) **AUSPICIOUS** (propitious; lucky) **OF** **UTENSIL** (ware; talent),
MATTER (the outside world) **PERHAPS** (or; either…or…; > someone)
EVIL (vice; wickedness; fierce; ferocious) **OF**, 夫佳兵者不祥之
器，物或恶之，*(fū jiā bīng zhě bù xiáng zhī qì, wù huò ě zhī,)*

2.   **INCIDENT** (cause; intentionally; hence) **HAVE** (exist) **ROAD** (way, principle;
speak; think) (者) **NO** (not) **GET ALONG WITH** (be situated in; deal with
_ place; point; part) 故有道者不处。*(gù yǒu dào zhě bù chǔ.)*

3.   **A MAN OF NOBL**e character (gentleman) **DWELL** (live; stay; store up) **STANDARD**
(norm; rule > imitate; follow) **EXPENSIVE** (precious; noble; > your) **LEFT** (east;
heretical; wrong; different), 君子居则贵左，*(jūn zǐ jū zé guì zuǒ,)*

4.   **USE** (apply <frml> hence) **WEAPONS** (army; troops) **STANDARD** (norm;
rule > imitate; follow) **EXPENSIVE** (precious; noble; > your) **RIGHT**
(west; right thinking). 用兵则贵右。*(yòng bīng zé guì yòu.)*

5.   **WEAPONS** (army; troops) (者) **OMINOUS** (inauspicious) **OF** **UTENSIL**
(ware; talent), 兵者不祥之器，*(bīng zhě bù xiáng zhī qì,)*

6. **WRONG** (not conform to <infrml> must) **A MAN OF NOBLE CHARACTER** (gentleman) **OF** **UTENSIL** (ware; talent), 非君子之器， *(fēi jūn zǐ zhī qì,)*

7. **ACT AGAINST ONE'S WILL** (have no alternative but to; have to) <conj.> **AND** (yet, but) **USE** (apply <frml> hence) **OF**, 不得已而用之， *(bù dé yǐ ér yòng zhī,)*

8. **INDIFFERENT TO FAME OR GAIN** (quiet; tranquil; calm; not care at all) **THIN** (light; tasteless; weak) **DO** (act as; be, mean; support) **UPPER** (higher; superior). 恬淡为上。 *(tián dàn wéi shàng.)*

9. **VICTORY** (success; surpass; be superior to; get the better of; superb) <conj.> **AND** (yet, but) **NO** (not) **BEAUTIFUL** (good), 胜而不美， *(shèng ér bù měi,)*

10. <conj.> **AND** (yet, but) **BEAUTIFUL** (good) **OF** (者), <grm> **IS** (yes <frml> this; that) **HAPPY** (cheerful) **KILL** (murder) **HUMAN** (man; people). 而美之者，是乐杀人。 *(ér měi zhī zhě, shì lè shā rén.)*

11. **HUSBAND** (man) **HAPPY** (cheerful) **KILL** (murder) **HUMAN** (man; people) (者), **STANDARD** (norm; rule > imitate; follow) **NO** (not) **CAN** **GET** **WILL** (aspiration; ideal; mark; sign) **IN** (at, to, from, by, than, out of) **LAND UNDER HEAVEN** **ALREADY** (indeed; really; how). 夫乐杀人者，则不可得志于天下矣。 *(fū lè shā rén zhě, zé bù kě dé zhì yú tiān xià yǐ.)*

12. **LUCKY** (auspicious; propitious) **MATTER** (affair; thing; business; involvement) **STILL** (yet; esteem, set great store by) **LEFt** (east; heretical; wrong; different), **UNLUCKY** **MATTERS** (death, burial) **STILL** (yet; esteem, set great store by) **RIGHT** (west; right thinking). 吉事尚左，凶事尚右。 *(jí shì shàng zuǒ xiōng shì shàng yòu.)*

13. **LEANING** (partial) **SUPPORT** (bring; handle, will> lead, command) **ARMY** (troops) **DWELL** (live; house; store up) **LEFT** (east; heretical; wrong; different), **UPPER** (higher; superior) **SUPPORT** (bring; handle, will> lead, command) **ARMY** (troops) **DWELL** (live; house; store up) **RIGHT** (west; right thinking). 偏将军居左，上将军居右。 *(piān jiàng jūn jū zuǒ, shàng jiàng jūn jū yòu.)*

14. **SPEECH** (word; say; talk) **USE** (<v> take <p> according to; because of <adj> so as to <conj> and) **OBSEQUIES** (funeral) **GET ALONG WITH** (be situated in; deal with _ place; point; part) **OF**. 言以丧礼处之。 *(yán yǐ sāng lǐ chǔ zhī.)*

15. **KILL** (murder) **HUMAN** (man; people) **OF** **MANY** (numerous; crowd; multitude), **USE** (<v> take <p> according to; because of <adj> so as to <conj> and) **GRIEVED** (sorrowful) **WEEP** (sob; tears) **OF**, **DEFEAT** (triumph over; vanquish; overcome) **USE** (<v> take <p> according to; because of <adj> so as to <conj> and) **OBSEQUIES** (funeral) **GET ALONG WITH** (be situated in; deal with _ place; point; part) **OF**. 杀人之众，以悲哀泣之，战胜以丧礼处之。 *(shā rén zhī zhòng, yǐ bēi āi qì zhī, zhàn shèng yǐ sāng lǐ chǔ zhī.)*

CHAPTER 32

The way constant is without name.
Simple though small,
    nothing under heaven can subjugate it either.
Great men, if able to abide by it,
All things would take the role of guest.
Heaven and earth would join and let sweet dew fall,
The people, not ordered and yet self balanced.
Only when restricted, are there names.
Names already exist,
Man handles the realization to stop.
Knowing to stop [he] can be without danger.
Just as the way exists under heaven,
The river of a valley flows to the great river and the sea.

1. **ROAD** (way, principle; speak; think) **ORDINARY** (normal; constant; often) **NOTHING** (without; not) **NAME** (fame; reputation). 道常无名。 *(dào cháng wú míng.)*

2. **SIMPLE** (plain) **THOUGH** (even if) **SMALL** (young) **LAND UNDER HEAVEN** **NO ONE** (nothing; no; don't) **CAN** (be able to) **OFFICIAL** (subject) **ALSO** (either). 朴虽小天下莫能臣也。 *(pò suī xiǎo tiān xià mò néng chén yě.)*

3. **A HIGH OFFICIAL** **KING** (<frml> great) **LIKE** (seem; as if > you) **CAN** (be able to) **GUARD** (observe; abide by) **OF**, 侯王若能守之， *(hóu wáng ruò néng shǒu zhī,)*

4. **TEN THOUSAND** (myriad) **MATTER** (the outside world) **SUPPORT** (take; bring; handle; be going to) **SELF** (oneself; certainly) **GUEST**. 万物将自宾。 *(wàn wù jiāng zì bīn.)*

5. **HEAVEN AND EARTH** (universe) **APPEARANCE** (mutually) **SHUT** (join; combine) **USE** (<v> take <p> according to; because of <adj> so as to <conj> and) **FALL** (drop; lower) **SWEET** (willingly, of one's own accord) **DEW** (manna), 天地相合以降甘露， *(tiān dì xiāng hé yǐ jiàng gān lòu,)*

6. **THE PEOPLE** (civilian) **NO ONE** (nothing; none; no) **OF COMMAND** (decree; make; cause) <conj.> **AND** (yet, but) **SELF** (oneself; certainly) **EQUAL** (even; without exception; all). 民莫之令而自均。 *(mín mò zhī lìng ér zì jūn.)*

7. **BEGINNING** (start; only then) **MAKE** (formulate; restrict; control) **HAVE** (there is; exist) **NAME** (fame; reputation), 始制有名， *(shǐ zhì yǒu míng,)*

8. **NAME** (fame; reputation) **ALSO** (too) **ALREADY** (<conj.> since; both... and...) **HAVE** (there is; exist), 名亦既有 , *(míng yì jì yǒu,)*

9. **HUSBAND** (man) **ALSO** (too) **SUPPORT** (take; bring; take care of; do something; handle) **KNOW** (realize; tell) **STOP** (to; till; only), 夫亦将知止 , *(fū yì jiāng zhī zhǐ,)*

10. **KNOW** (realize; tell) **STOP** (to; till; only) **CAN** (may) **NO** (not) **DANGER** (nearly almost). 知止可以不殆。 *(zhī zhǐ kě yǐ bù dài.)*

11. **EXAMPLE** (analogy) **ROAD** (way, principle; speak; think) **OF** **EXIST** (be living) **LAND** **UNDER** **HEAVEN**, 譬道之在天下 , *(pì dào zhī zài tiān xià.)*

12. **JUST AS** (like; still) **RIVER** (plain) **VALLEY** (gorge; cereal; grain) **OF** **IN** (at, to, from, by, than, out of) **RIVER** **SEA** (big lake). 犹川谷之于江海。 *(yóu chuān gǔ zhī yú jiāng hǎi.)*

CHAPTER 33

Knowledge of people is resourceful,
Knowledge of self is honesty.
Victory over others is power,
Victory over self is striving.
Being content is wealth.
Striving to prevail is will.
Not losing place is endurance.
Dead, but not gone,
This is longevity.

1. **KNOW** (realize; tell) **HUMAN** (man; people) (者) **WISDOM** (resourcefulness; wit), 知人者智 , *(zhī rén zhě zhì,)*

2. **SELF** (oneself; certainly) **KNOW** (realize; tell) (者) **BRIGHT** (clear; honest; know). 自知者明。 *(zì zhī zhě míng.)*

3. **VICTORY** (success; surpass; be superior to) **HUMAN** (man; people) (者) **HAVE** (exist) **POWER** (strength, ability), 胜人者有力 , *(shèng rén zhě yǒu lì,)*

4. **SELF** (oneself; certainly) **VICTORY** (success; surpass; be superior to) (者) **STRIVE** (strong; powerful; better_unyielding). 自胜者强。 *(zì shèng zhě jiàng.)*

5. **BE CONTENT WITH ONE'S LOT** (者) **RICH** (wealthy; abundant). 知足者富。 *(zhī zú zhě fù.)*

6. **STRIVE** (strong; powerful; better_unyielding) **GO** (be current; prevail; do) (者) **HAVE** (exist) **WILL** (aspiration; ideal; keep in mind; records; annals; mark; sign). 强行者有志。 *(qiáng xíng zhě yǒu zhì.)*

7. **NO** (not) **LOSE** (miss; let slip; fail to achieve, mistake) **HIS** (its, he, it, that; such) **PLACE** (者) **FOR A LONG TIME** (long; of a specified duration). 不失其所者久。 *(bù shī qí suǒ zhě jiǔ.)*

8. **DIE** (to the death; extremely; inflexible) <conj.> **AND** (yet, but) **NO** (not) **FLEE** (run away; lose; be gone; die; perish) (者), 死而不亡者， *(sǐ ér bù wáng zhě,)*

9. **LONGEVITY** (life; age; birthday). 寿。 *(shòu.)*

CHAPTER 34

The great way flows, such as it may left and right.
All things on earth depend on it for existence,
    and it never declines,
Meritorious accomplishment yet anonymous.
Clothes and supports all things on earth yet doesn't master.
Always without desire befits the name small.
All things on earth return here, Why?
Not being their master befits the name great.
Because of its ultimate non-self, it becomes great.
Hence it can accomplish its greatness.

1. **BIG** (great) **ROAD** (way, principle; speak; think) **FLOAT** (be suffused with; flood; inundate) **!** , **HIS** (its, he, it, that; such) **APPROVE** (befits, can, but; yet) **THE LEFT** [and] **RIGHT SIDES** (around; about). 大道泛兮，其可左右。 *(dà dào fàn xī, qí kě zuǒ yòu.)*

2. **ALL THINGS ON EARTH** **RELY ON** (depend on) **OF** **USE** (<v> take <p> according to; because of <adj> so as to <conj> and) **GIVE BIRTH TO** (existence) <conj.> **AND** (yet, but) **NO** (not) **DICTION** (take leave; decline; shirk), 万物恃之以生而不辞， *(wàn wù shì zhī yǐ shēng ér bù cí,)*

3. **MERIT** (achievement) **ACCOMPLISH** (succeed; become) <conj.> **AND** (yet, but) **NO** (not) **NAME** (fame; reputation) **HAVE** (exist). 功成而不名有。 *(gōng chéng ér bù míng yǒu.)*

4. **CLOTHING** **SUPPORT** (raise; keep; grow; foster) **ALL THINGS ON EARTH** <conj.> **AND** (yet, but) **NO** (not) **DO** (act as; be, mean; support) **HOST** (owner, master), 衣养万物而不为主， *(yī yǎng wàn wù ér bù wéi zhǔ,)*

5. **ORDINARY** (normal; constant; often) **NOTHING** (without; not) **DESIRE** (longing; wish; want; about to) **APPROVE** (befits, can, but; yet) **NAME** (fame; reputation) **AT** (in, from, to) **SMALL** (little; for a while; young). 常无欲可名於小。 *(cháng wú yù kě míng yú xiǎo.)*

6. **ALL THINGS ON EARTH** **GO BACK TO** (return; give back to; come together) **HERE**
    (herein; (usu. neg question) how; why), 万物归焉， *(wàn wù guī yān,)*

7. <conj.> **AND** (yet, but) **NO** (not) **DO** (act as; be, mean; support)
    HOST (owner), **APPROVE** (befits, can, but; yet) **NAME** (fame;
    reputation) **DO** (act as; be, mean; support) **BIG** (great). 而不
    为主，可名为大。 *(ér bù wéi zhǔ, kě míng wéi dà.)*

8. **USE** (<v> take <p> according to; because of <adj> so as to <conj>
    and) **HIS** (its, he, it, that; such) **END** (death; eventually; after all; whole;
    all) **NO** (not) **SELF** (oneself; certainly) **DO** (act as; be, mean; support)
    BIG (great), 以其终不自为大， *(yǐ qí zhōng bù zì wéi dà,)*

9. **HAPPENING** (reason; cause; on purpose; hence) **CAN** (be able
    to) **ACCOMPLISH** (succeed; become) **HIS** (its, he, it, that; such)
    BIG (great). 故能成其大。 *(gù néng chéng qí dà.)*

CHAPTER 35

Hold the great image and all under heaven come toward you.
Coming toward you but without harm,
   its quiet equanimity greatest.
Happily offering enticement, passing visitors stop.
Of the way passing through the mouth, tasteless its non-flavor.
Of watching, not enough to see.
Of listening to, not enough to hear.
Of using, not enough already.

1. **HOLD** (manage; stick to, carry out; observe) **BIG** (great) **ELEPHANT**
    (appearance; image; resemble) **LAND UNDER HEAVEN** **GO** (in
    the direction of; toward; past; previous <preposition> to;
    toward). 执大象天下往。 *(zhí dà xiàng tiān xià wàng.)*

2. **GO** (in the direction of; toward; past; previous <preposition> to; toward)
    <conj.> **AND** (yet, but) **NO** (not) **EVIL** (harm; calamity; impair; kill), **PEACEFUL**
    (quiet; calm) **FLAT** (even; smooth; equal > tie; equal; impartial) **HIGHEST**
    (greatest; excessively; too). 往而不害安平太。 *(wàng ér bù hài ān píng tài.)*

3. **HAPPY** (cheerful, music) **GIVE** (offer, support > and; together
    with_ take part in) **CAKES** (pastry; bait; > entice), **CROSS** (past;
    through; over; exceed) **VISITOR** (traveler; customer) **STOP** (to;
    till; only). 乐与饵，过客止。 *(lè yú ěr, guò kè zhǐ.)*

4. **ROAD** (way, principle; speak; think) **OF** **SPEAK** (utter; exit) **THIN** (light; tasteless; weak) **IN** (at; from; because; than) **HIS** (its, he, it, that; such) **NOTHING** (without) **TASTE** (flavor; smell; interest). 道之出口淡乎其无味。 *(dào zhī chū kǒu dàn hū qí wú wèi.)*

5. **LOOK AT** (regard; watch) **OF** **NO** (not) **FOOT** (leg; enough; full; as much as) **SHOW** (one can well perceive). 视之不足见。 *(shì zhī bù zú jiàn.)*

6. **LISTEN** (hear; obey / allow) **OF** **NO** (not) **FOOT** (leg; enough; full; as much as) **HEAR** (news; story; reputation; smell). 听之不足闻。 *(tīng zhī bù zú wén.)*

7. **USE** (apply <frml> hence) **OF** **NO** (not) **FOOT** (leg; enough; full; as much as) **ALREADY** (<conj.> since; both... and...). 用之不足既。 *(yòng zhī bù zú jì.)*

CHAPTER 36

In desiring to inhale, one must first open up.
In desiring weakness, one must first strive.
In desiring to let go, one must first begin.
In desiring to get, one must first give.
This saying is little understood.
Weakness is superior to strength.
Fish can't escape from the deep,
A country's weapons can't instruct the people.

1. **SUPPORT** (bring; handle, will> lead, command) **DESIRE** (longing; wish; want; about to) **INHALE THROUGH THE NOSE** **OF** **CERTAINLY** (must) **SOLID** (firm <frml> in the first place) **OPEN** (spread; stretch) **OF**.[1] 将欲歙之，必固张之。 *(jiāng yù shè zhī, bì gù zhāng zhī.)*

2. **SUPPORT** (bring; handle, will> lead, command) **DESIRE** (longing; wish; want; about to) **WEAK** (inferior <frml> a little less) **OF CERTAINLY** (must) **SOLID** (firm <frml> in the first place) **STRIVE** (make an effort; powerful) **OF**. 将欲弱之，必固强之。 *(jiāng yù ruò zhī, bì gù jiàng zhī.)*

3. **SUPPORT** (bring; handle, will> lead, command) **DESIRE** (longing; wish; want; about to) **GIVE UP** (abandon; waste) **OF**, **CERTAINLY** (must) **SOLID** (firm <frml> in the first place) **PROSPER** (begin; encourage > get up) **OF**. 将欲废之，必固兴之。 *(jiāng yù fèi zhī, bì gù xīng zhī.)*

---

1   of [之] connects modifier and word modified.

4. **SUPPORT** (bring; handle, will> lead, command) **DESIRE** (longing; wish; want; about to) **TAKE** (get; seek) **OF**, **CERTAINLY** (must) **SOLID** (firm <frml> in the first place) **GIVE** (participate in) **OF** . 将欲取之，必固与之。 *(jiāng yù qǔ zhī, bì gù yú zhī.)*

5. <grm> **IS** (yes <frml> this; that) **SAY** (call; name; meaning; sense) **MINUTE** (tiny) **BRIGHT** (clear; honest; know). 是谓微明。 *(shì wèi wēi míng.)*

6. **WEAK** (delicate) **VICTORY** (success; surpass; be superior to) **FIRM** (staunch; unyielding). 柔弱胜刚强。 *(róu ruò shèng gāng qiáng)*

7. **FISH** **NO** (not) **CAN** **TAKE OFF** (cast off; escape from > neglect> if) **IN** (at, to, from, by, than, out of) **DEEP POOL** (deep), 鱼不可脱于渊， *(yú bù kě tuō yú yuān,)*

8. **COUNTRY** (state; of our country) **OF** **SHARP** **WEAPON** (good tool) **NO** (not) **CAN** **SHOW** (notify; instruct) **HUMAN** (man; people). 国之利器不可以示人。 *(guó zhī lì qì bù kě yǐ shì rén.)*

CHAPTER 37

The way normally does nothing, yet there is nothing not done.
If kings and noblemen will abide by this,
Everything will self transform.
Transform yet desire rises,
Press it down using nameless simplicity,
Of nameless simplicity, man also supports without desire.
No desire, using stillness, all under heaven supports self calm.

1. **ROAD** (way, principle; speak; think) **ORDINARY** (normal; constant; often) **NOTHING** (without; not) **DO** (act as; be, mean; support), <conj.> **AND** (yet, but) **NOTHING** (without; not) **NO** (not) **DO** (act as; be, mean; support). 道常无为，而无不为。 *(dào cháng wú wéi, ér wú bù wéi.)*

2. **NOBLEMAN** (high official) **KING** (grand; great) **LIKE** (seem; as if > you) **CAN** (be able to) **GUARD** (defend; keep watch; observe; abide by; close to; near) **OF**, 侯王若能守之， *(hóu wáng ruò néng shǒu zhī,)*

3. **ALL THINGS ON EARTH** **SUPPORT** (bring; handle, will> lead, command) **SELF** (oneself; certainly) **SPEND** (expend\\change; transform; dissolve). 万物将自化。 *(wàn wù jiāng zì huā.)*

4. **CHANGE** (turn; transform; convert; influence) <conj.> **AND** (yet, but) **DESIRE** (wish; want; about to) **DO** (make; rise; get up; write; compose; become), 化而欲作， *(huā ér yù zuò,)*

5. **I** (we) **SUPPORT** (bring; handle, will> lead, command) **PRESS DOWN** (keep down; ease; guard) **OF** **USE** (<v> take <p> according to; because of <adj> so as to <conj> and) **NOTHING** (without; not) **NAME** (fame; reputation) **OF** **SIMPLE** (plain). 吾将镇之以无名之朴。 *(wú jiāng zhèn zhī yǐ wú míng zhī pò.)*

6. **NOTHING** (without; not) **NAME** (fame; reputation) **OF** **SIMPLE** (plain), **HUSBAND** (man) **ALSO** (too) **SUPPORT** (bring; handle, will> lead, command) **NOTHING** (without; not) **DESIRE** (wish; want; about to). 无名之朴，夫亦将无欲。 *(wú míng zhī pò, fū yì jiāng wú yù.)*

7. **NO** (not) **DESIRE** (wish; want; about to) **USE** (<v> take <p> according to; because of <adj> so as to <conj> and) **STILL** (quiet; calm), **LAND UNDER HEAVEN** **SUPPORT** (bring; handle, will > lead, command) **SELF** (oneself; certainly) **CALM** (stable; decide, fix > surely). 不欲以静，天下将自定。 *(bù yù yǐ jìng, tiān xià jiāng zì dìng.)*

CHAPTER 38

Superior virtue is not virtuous, and so has virtue.
Inferior virtue never deviates from virtue, and so is without virtue.
Superior virtue: without doing, and without believing.
Inferior virtue: without doing, yet believing.
Superior benevolence: doing, yet without believing.
Superior justice: doing and believing.
Superior ritual: doing and when none respond,
Normally roles up sleeves and throws.
Hence, virtue follows loss of way.
Benevolence follows loss of virtue.
Justice follows loss of benevolence.
Ritual follows loss of justice.
Ways of chaos follow loss of loyalty and thinning faith in ritual.
Foreknowledge of the way, magnificent yet a beginning of folly.
The great man dwells in the thick, not in the thin.
Dwells in the true, not in the magnificent.
Hence, he leaves that and takes this.

1. **UPPER** (higher; superior) **VIRTUE** (moral character; heart) **NO** (not) **VIRTUE** (moral character; heart) <grm> **IS** (yes <frml> this; that) **USE** (<v> take <p> according to; because of <adj> so as to <conj> and) **HAVE** (exist) **VIRTUE** (moral character; heart). 上德不德是以有德。 *(shàng dé bù dé shì yǐ yǒu dé.)*

2. **BELOW** (down; inferior) **VIRTUE** (moral character; heart) **NO** (not) **LOSE** (deviate from the normal) **VIRTUE** (moral character; heart) <grm> **IS** (yes <frml> this; that) **USE** (<v> take <p> according to; because of <adj> so as to <conj> and) **NOTHING** (without) **VIRTUE** (moral character; heart). 下德不失德是以无德。 *(xià dé bù shī dé shì yǐ wú dé.)*

3. **UPPER** (higher; superior) **VIRTUE** (moral character; heart) **NOTHING** (without; not) **DO** (act as; be, mean; support) <conj.> **AND** (yet, but) **NOTHING** (without) **THINK** (believe; consider). 上德无为而无以为。 *(shàng dé wú wéi ér wú yǐ wéi.)*

4. **BELOW** (down; under; inferior; next) **VIRTUE** (moral character; heart) **NOTHING** (without) **DO** (act as; be, mean; support) <conj.> **AND** (yet, but) **HAVE** (exist) **THINK** (believe; consider). 下德无为而有以为。 *(xià dé wú wéi ér yǒu yǐ wéi.)*

5. **UPPER** (higher; superior) **BENEVOLENCE** (kindheartedness; humanity; sensitive) **DO** (act as; be, mean; support) **OF** <conj.> **AND** (yet, but) **NOTHING** (without) **THINK** (believe; consider). 上仁为之而无以为。 *(shàng rén wéi zhī ér wú yǐ wéi.)*

6. **UPPER** (higher; superior) **JUSTICE** (righteous; equitable; relationship; meaning) **DO** (act as; be, mean; support) **OF** <conj.> **AND** (yet, but) **HAVE** (exist) **THINK** (believe; consider). 上义为之而有以为。 *(shàng yì wéi zhī ér yǒu yǐ wéi.)*

7. **UPPER** (higher; superior) **CEREMONY** (rite; courtesy; etiquette) **DO** (act as; be, mean; support) **OF** <conj.> **AND** (yet, but) **NO ONE** (nothing; none; no) **OF** **USE** (<v> take <p> according to; because of <adj> so as to <conj> and) **ANSWER** (respond; agree (to do sth.); should), 上礼为之而莫之以应， *(shàng lǐ wéi zhī ér mò zhī yǐ yīng,)*

8. **STANDARD** (norm; rule > imitate; follow) **PUSH UP ONE'S SLEEVES AND BARE ONE'S ARMS** (in excitement or agitation) <conj.> **AND** (yet, but) **THROW** (toss; cast; throw away; cast aside) **OF**. 则攘臂而扔之。 *(zé rǎng bì ér rēng zhī.)*

9. **HENCE** (therefore; consequently) **LOSE** (let slip; deviate from the normal) **ROAD** (way, principle; speak; think) <conj.> **AND** (yet, but) **AFTER THAT** (then) **VIRTUE**. 故失道而后德。 *(gù shī dào ér hòu dé.)*

10. **LOSE** (deviate from the normal) **VIRTUE** (moral character; heart) <conj.> **AND** (yet, but) **AFTER THAT** (then) **BENEVOLENCE** (kindheartedness; humanity; sensitive). 失德而后仁。 *(shī dé ér hòu rén.)*

11. **LOSE** (deviate from the normal) **BENEVOLENCE** (kindheartedness; humanity; sensitive) <conj.> **AND** (yet, but) **AFTER THAT** (then) **JUSTICE** (righteous; equitable; relationship; meaning). 失仁而后义。 *(shī rén ér hòu yì.)*

12. **LOSE** (deviate from the normal) **JUSTICE** (righteous; equitable; relationship; meaning) <conj.> **AND** (yet, but) **AFTER THAT** (then) **CEREMONY** (rite; courtesy; etiquette). 失义而后礼。 *(shī yì ér hòu lǐ.)*

13. **HUSBAND** (man) **CEREMONY** (rite; courtesy; etiquette) (者) **LOYAL** (honest) **TRUE** (confidence; trust; faith; believe) **OF** **THIN** (weak; infertile; poor) <conj.> **AND** (yet, but) **IN A MESS** (disorder; chaos) **OF** **ROAD** (way, principle; speak; think). 夫礼者忠信之薄而乱之首。 *(fū lǐ zhě zhōng xìn zhī báo ér luàn zhī shǒu.)*

14. **FRONT** (forward; before) **KNOW** (knowledge) (者), **ROAD** (way, principle; speak; think) **OF** **MAGNIFICENT** (prosperous; flourishing; best part) <conj.> **AND** (yet, but) **FOOLISH** (stupid; make a fool of; fool) **OF** **BEGINNING** (start;> only then). 前识者，道之华而愚之始。 *(qián shí zhě, dào zhī huá ér yú zhī shǐ.)*

15. <grm> **IS** (yes <frml> this; that) **USE** (<v> take <p> according to; because of <adj> so as to <conj> and) **TRUE MAN** (real man), **GET ALONG** (manage; > dwell; live) **HIS** (its, he, it, that; such) **THICK** (deep; kind), **NO** (not) **DWELL** (live; store up) **HIS** (its, he, it, that; such) **THIN** (flimsy; weak). 是以大丈夫，处其厚，不居其薄。 *(shì yǐ dà zhàng fu, chǔ qí hòu, bù jū qí báo.)*

16. **GET ALONG** (manage; > dwell; live) **HIS** (its, he, it, that; such) **TRUE** (real; honest; fact), **NO** (not) **DWELL** (live; store up) **HIS** (its, he, it, that; such) **MAGNIFICENT** (prosperous; flourishing; best part). 处其实，不居其华。 *(chǔ qí shí, bù jū qí huá.)*

17. **HENCE** (therefore; consequently) **GO** (remove) **THAT** (those; the other; another) **TAKE** (get; aim at; seek; assume) **THIS**. 故去彼取此。 *(gù qù bǐ qǔ cǐ.)*

CHAPTER 39

All that came before fulfills the One.
Heaven fulfills the One and is clear.
Earth fulfills the One and is tranquil.
Mind fulfills the One and is effective.
Valley fulfills the One and is full.
Existence fulfills the One and grows.
Rulers fulfill the One and support the empire faithfully.
The One causes.
Heaven without clarity brings dreadful splitting.
Earth without tranquility brings dreadful waste.
Mind without effectiveness brings dreadful stoppage.
Valley without fullness brings dreadful exhaustion.
Existence without growth brings dreadful extinction.
Rulers without faithfulness bring dreadful setbacks.
Hence, the precious take the lowly as the origin.
The high take low as the base.
This, and so rulers call themselves solitary, scant, pathetic
Is this not taking the lowly as a foundation of heresy?
No.
Extreme fame is without fame.
Not to desire is comparable to beauty.
Jewelry is comparable to stone.

1. **FORMER TIME** (the past) **OF NEED** (have to_ get, obtain, gain >
    satisfied) **ONE** (者). 昔之得一者。 *(xī zhī dé yī zhě.)*

2. **SKY** (heaven; day; nature; God) **NEED** (have to_ get, obtain, gain > satisfied)
    ONE USE (<v> take <p> according to; because of <adj> so as to <conj> and)
    UNMIXED (clear; thoroughly; settle). 天得一以清。 *(tiān dé yī yǐ qīng.)*

3. **EARTH NEED** (have to_ get, obtain, gain > satisfied) **ONE USE** (take; so as
    to_and; as well as) **PEACEFUL** (tranquil). 地得一以宁。 *(dì dé yī yǐ zhù.)*

4. **GOD** (spirit; mind; smart) **NEED** (have to_ get, obtain, gain > satisfied)
    ONE USE (<v> take <p> according to; because of <adj> so as to <conj>
    and) **QUICK** (clever; effective). 神得一以灵。 *(shén dé yī yǐ líng.)*

5. **VALLEY** (grain) **NEED** (have to_ get, obtain, gain > satisfied) **ONE USE**
    (<v> take <p> according to; because of <adj> so as to <conj> and)
    BE FULL OF (have a surplus of). 谷得一以盈。 *(gǔ dé yī yǐ yíng.)*

6. **ALL THINGS ON EARTH** **NEED** (have to_ get, obtain, gain > satisfied) **ONE** **USE** (<v> take <p> according to; because of <adj> so as to <conj> and) **GIVE BIRTH** (bear; grow; existence; life). 万物得一以生。 *(wàn wù dé yī yǐ shēng.)*

7. **NOBLEMAN** (high official) **KING** (<frml> great) **NEED** (have to_ get, obtain, gain > satisfied) **ONE** **THINK** (believe; consider that) **LAND UNDER HEAVEN** **LOYAL** (faithful; divination). 侯王得一以为天下贞。 *(hóu wáng dé yī yǐ wéi tiān xià zhēn.)*

8. **HIS** (its, he, it, that; such) **SEND** (deliver; devote; result in) **OF**. 其致之。 *(qí zhì zhī.)*

9. **SKY** (heaven; day; nature; God) **NOTHING** (without) **USE** (<v> take <p> according to; because of <adj> so as to <conj> and) **UNMIXED** (clear; thoroughly; settle) **SUPPORT** (bring; handle, will> lead, command) **FEAR** (dread; terrify; intimidate) **SPLIT** (crack). 天无以清将恐裂。 *(tiān wú yǐ qīng jiāng kǒng liè.)*

10. **EARTH** **NOTHING** (without) **USE** (<v> take <p> according to; because of <adj> so as to <conj> and) **PEACEFUL** (tranquil) **SUPPORT** (bring; handle, will> lead, command) **FEAR** (dread; terrify; intimidate) **GIVE UP** (abandon; abolish; waste; useless). 地无以宁将恐废。 *(dì wú yǐ zhù jiāng kǒng fèi.)*

11. **GOD** (spirit; mind; smart) **NOTHING** (without) **USE** (<v> take <p> according to; because of <adj> so as to <conj> and) **QUICK** (clever; effective) **SUPPORT** (bring; handle, will> lead, command) **FEAR** (dread; terrify; intimidate) **HAVE A REST** (stop work,etc.). 神无以灵将恐歇。 *(shén wú yǐ líng jiāng kǒng xiē.)*

12. **VALLEY** (grain) **NOTHING** (without) **USE** (<v> take <p> according to; because of <adj> so as to <conj> and) **BE FULL OF** (have a surplus of) **SUPPORT** (bring; handle, will> lead, command) **EXHAUST** (use up). 谷无以盈将恐竭。 *(gǔ wú yǐ yíng jiāng kǒng jié.)*

13. **ALL THINGS** (10,000 things, all things on earth) **NOTHING** (without) **USE** (<v> take <p> according to; because of <adj> so as to <conj> and) **GIVE BIRTH** (bear; grow; existence; life) **SUPPORT** (bring; handle, will> lead, command) **FEAR** (dread; terrify; intimidate) **EXTINGUISH** (submerge; destroy). 万物无以生将恐灭。 *(wàn wù wú yǐ shēng jiāng kǒng miè.)*

14. **NOBLEMAN** (high official) **KING** (<frml> great) **NOTHING** (without) **USE** (<v> take <p> according to; because of <adj> so as to <conj> and) **LOYAL** (faithful; divination) **SUPPORT** (bring; handle, will> lead, command) **FEAR** (dread; terrify; intimidate) **FALL** (suffer a setback). 侯王无以贞将恐蹶。 *(hóu wáng wú yǐ zhēn jiāng kǒng jué.)*

15. **HENCE** (on purpose; intentionally) **EXPENSIVE** (precious; noble) **TAKE... AS** (regard.. as) **INEXPENSIVE** (cheap; lowly; humble) **THE ROOT** (basis; origin; native), 故贵以贱为本， *(gù guì yǐ jiàn wéi běn,)*

16. **TALL** (high; above the average) **TAKE... AS** (regard.. as) **BELOW** (down; under; underneath; lower; inferior) **BASE** (foundation; basic; key; primary). 高以下为基。 *(gāo yǐ xià wéi jī.)*

17.   <grm> **IS** (yes <frml> this; that) **USE** (<v> take <p> according to; because of <adj> so as to <conj> and) **NOBLEMAN** (high official) **KING** (<frml> great) **SELF** (oneself; certainly) **FIT** (match; suit> call> say) **FATHERLESS** (orphaned; solitary), **FEW** (scant; tasteless; widowed), **NO** (not) **VALLEY** (grain). 是以侯王自称孤、寡、不谷。 *(shì yǐ hóu wáng zì chēng gū, guǎ, bù gǔ.)*

18. **THIS** **WRONG** (not conform to) **TAKE... AS** (regard.. as) **INEXPENSIVE** (cheap; lowly; humble) **ROOT OF A PLANT** (foundation; origin) **EVIL** (heretical; irregular; unhealthy environment)? 此非以贱为本邪？ *(cǐ fēi yǐ jiàn wéi běn xié?)*

19. **WRONG** (not conform to) 乎 (<part> expresses doubt or wonder). 非乎。 *(fēi hū.)*

20. **TO** (until; > extremely; most) **REPUTATION** (fame; praise; eulogize) **NOTHING** (without) **REPUTATION** (fame; praise; eulogize). 至誉无誉。 *(zhì yù wú yù.)*

21. **NO** (not) **DESIRE** (longing; wish; want; about to) ☐ ☐ **IN COMPLIANCE WITH** (according to; like; as; as if > if; > go to) **JADE** (pure, beautiful [of a person]). 不欲☐☐如玉 *(bù yù [] [] rú yù)*

22. **NECK-ORNAMENT** **IN COMPLIANCE WITH** (according to; like; as; as if > if; > go to) **STONE** (rock; stone inscription). 珞珞如石。 *(luò luò rú dàn.)*

CHAPTER 40

In the opposite direction, of the way 'it' moves.
Loss through death, of the way 'it' uses.
All under heaven is born in having
Having is born in nothing.

1. **TURN OVER** (in an opposite direction; in reverse; inside out) (者) **ROAD** (way, principle; speak; think) **OF** **MOVE** (stir; act; change; use; arouse). 反者道之动。 *(fǎn zhě dào zhī dòng.)*

2. **WEAK** (inferior <frml> lose through death) (者) **ROAD** (way, principle; speak; think) **OF** **USE** (employ > eat; drink; > hence). 弱者道之用。 *(ruò zhě dào zhī yòng.)*

3. **UNDER HEAVEN ALL THINGS ON EARTH** **GIVE BIRTH TO** (bear; grow; existence; life) **IN** (at, to, from, by, than, out of) **HAVE** (exist), 天下万物生于有， *(tiān xià wàn wù shēng yú yǒu,)*

4. **HAVE** (exist) **GIVE BIRTH TO** (bear; grow; existence; life) **IN** (at, to, from, by, than, out of) **NOTHING** (without; not). 有生于无。 *(yǒu shēng yú wú.)*

CHAPTER 41

The superior student hearing the way, diligently travels it.
The average student hearing the way,
   seem to live it, seems to lose it.
The inferior student hearing the way, really ridicules it.
Without this ridicule, it could not be the way.
Hence, we advocate saying,
The bright way seems hazy and hidden.
Entering the way seems like moving backwards.
The smooth way seems rough(*).
Superior virtue seems like a valley.
Great purity seems disgraceful.
Vast virtue seems insufficient.
Established virtue seems stolen.
Truthful promises seem capricious
Great honesty is without whispers.
Great capacity is a long time coming.
Great sound is scarce sound.
Great appearance is without form.
The way hides from view without name.
The way alone masters perfect forgiveness and accomplishment.

1. **UPPER** (higher; superior) **BACHELOR** (scholar; person) **HEAR** (news; story; smell) **ROAD** (way, principle; speak; think) **DILIGENT** (frequently) <conj.> **AND** (yet, but) **GO** (be current; prevail; do) **OF**. 上士闻道勤而行之。 *(shàng shì wén dào qín ér xíng zhī.)*

2. **CENTER** (middle; in; among) **BACHELOR** (scholar; person) **HEAR** (news; story; smell) **ROAD** (way, principle; speak; think) **LIKE** (seem; as if; if) **EXIST** (live; store; keep) **LIKE** (seem; as if; if) **FLEE** (lose; die; conquer). 中士闻道若存若亡。 *(zhōng shì wén dào ruò cún ruò wáng.)*

3. **BELOW** (down; lower; inferior; next) **BACHELOR** (scholar; person) **HEAR** (news; story; smell) **ROAD** (way, principle; speak; think) **BIG** (great) **SMILE** (laugh; ridicule) **OF**. 下士闻道大笑之。 *(xià shì wén dào dà xiào zhī.)*

4. **NO** (not) **SMILE** (laugh; ridicule) **NO** (not) **FOOT** (leg; enough; full; as much as) **THINK** (believe; consider)
ROAD (way, principle; speak; think). 不笑不足
以为道。 *(bù xiào bù zú yǐ wéi dào.)*

5. **INCIDENT** (hence; cause) **BUILD** (construct; set up; propose; advocate) **SPEECH** (word; say; talk) **HAVE** (exist) **OF**. 故建言有之。 *(gù jiàn yán yǒu zhī.)*

6. **BRIGHT** (clear; honest; know) **ROAD** (way, principle; speak; think) **LIKE** (seem; as if; if) **HAVE HAZY NOTIONS ABOUT** (be ignorant of; hide). 明道若昧。 *(míng dào ruò mèi.)*

7. **ADVANCE** (enter; receive; eat; take) **ROAD** (way, principle; speak; think) **LIKE** (seem; as if; if) **MOVE BACK** (retreat; cause to move back; remove). 进道若退。 *(jìn dào ruò tuì.)*

8. **SMOOTH** (safe; exterminate) **ROAD** (way, principle; speak; think) **LIKE** (seem; as if; if) **ROUGH**[1]. 夷道若□。 *(yí dào ruò [].)*

9. **UPPER** (higher; superior) **VIRTUE** (moral character; heart) **LIKE** (seem; as if; if) **VALLEY** (grain). 上德若谷。 *(shàng dé ruò gǔ.)*

10. **BIG** (great) **WHITE** (clear; pure) **LIKE** (seem; as if; if) **DISGRACE** (dishonor; bring humiliation to; insult). 大白若辱。 *(dà bái ruò rǔ.)*

11. **WIDE** (vast; expand; spread) **VIRTUE** (moral character; heart) **LIKE** (seem; as if; if) **NO** (not) **FOOT** (leg; enough; full; as much as). 广德若不足。 *(guǎng dé ruò bù zú.)*

12. **BUILD** (construct; set up; establish; advocate) **VIRTUE** (moral character; heart) **LIKE** (seem; as if; if) **STEAL** (pilfer; secretly; on the sly; find (time)). 建德若偷。 *(jiàn dé ruò tōu.)*

13. **NATURE** (character; simple <frml> pledge, promise) **TRUE** (real; genuine) **LIKE** (seem; as if; if) **CHANGE** (of one's attitude or feeling). 质真若渝。 *(zhì zhēn ruò yú.)*

14. **BIG** (great) **SQUARE** (upright; honest; direction; side; method) **NOTHING** (without; not) **CORNER** (nook; outlying place). 大方无隅。 *(dà fāng wú yú.)*

15. **BIG** (great) **UTENSIL** (ware; talent) **EVENING** (far on in time; late) **ACCOMPLISH** (become; result). 大器晚成。 *(dà qì wǎn chéng.)*

16. **BIG** (great) **SOUND** (news; tidings; tone) **HOPE** (rare; scarce; uncommon) **SOUND** (voice; tone). 大音希声。 *(dà yīn xī shēng.)*

17. **BIG** (great) **ELEPHANT** (appearance; shape; image) **NOTHING** (without; not) **FORM** (body; entity; appear). 大象无形。 *(dà xiàng wú xíng.)*

1 The character here is missing from the original. This happens from time to time and is indicated by a big sqare box(□). Like others, 'rough' seemed to fit the 'story line' here.

18. **ROAD** (way, principle; speak; think) **HIDDEN FROM VIEW** (conceal; dormant; lurking) **NOTHING** (without; not) **NAME** (given name; fame). 道隐无名。 *(dào yǐn wú míng.)*

19. **HUSBAND** (man, master) **ONLY** (alone) **ROAD** (way, principle; speak; think) **GOOD** (perfect; kind; be good at) **BORROW OR LEND** (shift responsibility, forgive) **AND** **ACCOMPLISH** (become; result). 夫唯道善贷且成。 *(fū wéi dào shàn dài qiě chéng.)*

CHAPTER 42

The way gave birth to the whole.
The whole gave birth to difference.
Difference gave birth to the many.
The many gave birth to all things.
All things suffer the negative and embrace the positive.
Clashing spirits considered harmonious,
Of people displaced, solitary, scant, not of the valley,
Yet kings and princes consider this a suitable match.
Hence, the outside world perhaps loses as well as benefits,
    and benefits as well as loses.
Of people's religious teaching, I also teach,
The backbone of effort seldom results in one's death.
I will take this teaching of my ancestors just so.

1. **ROAD** (way, principle; speak; think) **GIVE BIRTH TO** (existence) **ONE** (single; same; whole). 道生一。 *(dào shēng yī.)*

2. **ONE** (single; same; whole) **GIVE BIRTH TO** (existence) **TWO** (different). 一生二。 *(yī shēng èr.)*

3. **TWO** (different) **GIVE BIRTH TO** (existence) **THREE** (more than two; several; many). 二生三。 *(èr shēng sān.)*

4. **THREE** (more than two; several; many) **GIVE BIRTH TO** (existence) **ALL THINGS ON EARTH.** 三生万物。 *(sān shēng wàn wù.)*

5. **ALL THINGS ON EARTH** **CARRY ON BACK** (suffer; owe> negative) **YIN** (feminine or negative) <conj.> **AND** (yet, but) **HOLD IN ARMS** **THE SUN** (open; belonging to this world; yang, masculine or positive principle in nature), 万物负阴而抱阳， *(wàn wù fù yīn ér bào yang,)*

6. **VIGOROUSLY** (facing_pour boiling water on; flush> opposition) **GAS** (air; breath; spirit; enrage) **THINK** (believe; consider) **GENTLE** (kind; harmonious; peace> and). 冲气以为和。 *(chōng qì yǐ wéi hé.)*

7. **HUMAN** (man; people) **OF** **PLACE** **LOATHE** (dislike; hate), **ONLY** (alone) **FATHERLESS** (orphaned; solitary; 'I' used by feudal princes) **FEW** (scant; tasteless; widowed) **NO** (not) **VALLEY** (gorge; grain), 人之 所恶，唯孤、寡不谷， *(rén zhī suǒ ě, wéi gū, guǎ bù gǔ,)*

8. <conj.> **AND** (yet, but) **PRINCES AND DUKES** (the nobility) **THINK** (believe; consider) **FIT** (match; suit), 而王公以为称， *(ér wáng gōng yǐ wéi chèn,)*

9. **HAPPENING** (reason; cause; hence; therefore) **THING** (matter; the outside world) **PERHAPS** (or; either...or...; > someone) **DECREASE** (lose; damage; > sarcastic > shabby) **OF** <conj.> **AND** (yet, but) **BENIFIT** (advantage; increase), **PERHAPS** (or; either...or...; > someone) **BENIFIT** (advantage; increase; increasingly) **OF** <conj.> **AND** (yet, but) **DECREASE** (lose; damage; > sarcastic > shabby). 故物 或损之而益，或益之而损。 *(gù wù huò sǔn zhī ér yì, huò yì zhī ér sǔn.)*

10. **HUMAN** (man; people) **OF** **PLACE** **TEACH** (instruct; religion), **I** (we; self) **ALSO** (too) **TEACH** (instruct; religion) **OF**, 人之所 教，我亦教之， *(rén zhī suǒ jiāo, wǒ yì jiāo zhī,)*

11. **STRIVE** (strong; powerful; better_unyielding) **ROOF BEAM** (bridge; ridge)(者), **NO** (not) **NEED** (must,_get, result in;> satisfied> be finished) **HIS** (its, he, it, that; such) **DIE** (extremely; to death; implacable; rigid). 强梁者，不得其死。 *(qiáng liáng zhě, bù dé qí sǐ.)*

12. **I** (we) **SUPPORT** (bring; handle, will> lead, command) **THINK** (believe; consider) **TEACH** (instruct; religion) **FATHER** (elderly man in ancient times) **JUST** (only). 吾将以为教父甫。 *(wú jiāng yǐ wéi jiào fù fǔ.)*

CHAPTER 43

The most flexible of all things under heaven
    surpasses the most resolute.
Without existence entering that without space between,
    I know non action has the advantage.
Not of words teaching, without action advantage.
All under heaven rarely reach this.

1. **LAND UNDER HEAVEN OF TO** (until > extremely; most) **SOFT** (supple; flexible; soften; gentle; yielding; mild), **SPEED** (gallop; spread > turn eagerly towards) **GALLOP** (give free rein to) **LAND UNDER HEAVEN OF TO** (until > extremely; most) **HARD** (firm; strong; firmly; resolutely). 天下之至柔，驰骋天下之至坚。 *(tiān xià zhī zhì róu, chí chěng tiān xià zhī zhì jiān.)*

2. **NOTHING** (without; not) **HAVE** (exist) **ENTER** (join; be admitted into) **NOTHING** (without; not) **SPACE IN BETWEEN** (opening; among; within a definite time or space), **I** (we) <grm> **IS** (yes <frml> this; that) **TAKE... AS** (regard... as) **KNOW** (realize; tell) **NOTHING** (without; regardless) **OF HAVE** (exist) **BENEFIT** (profit; beneficial; increase). 无有入无间，吾是以知无为之有益。 *(wú yǒu rù wú jiàn, wú shì yǐ zhī wú wéi zhī yǒu yì.)*

3. **NO** (not) **SPEECH** (word; say; talk) **OF TEACH** (instruct.), **NOTHING** (without; not) **DO** (act as; be, mean; support) **OF BENEFIT** (profit; advantage; beneficial; increase). 不言之教，无为之益 *(bù yán zhī jiāo, wú wéi zhī yì)*

4. **LAND UNDER HEAVEN HOPE** (rare; scarce; uncommon) **REACH** (come up to; in time for; and) **OF**. 天下希及之。 *(tiān xià xī jí zhī.)*

CHAPTER 44

Name and body, which is intimate.
Body and goods, which is excessive.
Gain and loss, which is defective.
For this reason, the more we love, the greater the cost.
The more we hold on, the deeper the loss.
Knowing contentment, never dishonorable.
Knowing when to stop, never dangerous.
Then you can long endure.

1. **NAME** (fame; reputation) **TAKE PART IN** (give; offer; grant; support > and; together with) **BODY** (life; oneself; personally) **WHO** (which; what) **PARENT** (close; intimate; oneself). 名与身孰亲。 *(míng yú shēn shú qīn.)*

2. **BODY** (life; oneself; personally) **TAKE PART IN** (give; offer; grant; support > and; together with) **GOODS** (commodity; money; idiot) **WHO** (which; what) **MANY** (more; excessive). 身与货孰多。 *(shēn yú huò shú duō.)*

3. **GET** (obtain, gain <frml> satisfied, complacent) **TAKE PART IN** (give; offer; grant; support > and; together with) **FLEE** (lose; be gone; die; subjugate) **WHO** (which; what) **ILL** (sick; fault; defect). 得与亡孰病。 *(dé yú wáng shú bìng.)*

4.   <grm> **IS** (yes <frml> this; that) **INCIDENT** (reason; cause; hence) **VERY** (extremely; more than) **LOVE** (like; treasure) **CERTAINLY** (must) **BIG** (great) **FEE** (dues; expenses; cost; wasteful). 是故甚爱必大费。 *(shì gù shén ài bì dà fèi.)*

5.   **MUCH** (more; too many; excessive) **STORING PLACE** (hide; conceal; store) **CERTAINLY** (must) **THICK** (deep; kind; large; generous; rich or strong in flavor) **FLEE** (lose; be gone; die; subjugate). 多藏必厚亡。 *(duō cáng bì hòu wáng.)*

6.   **BE CONTENT WITH ONE'S LOT** **NO** (not) **DISGRACE** (dishonor; bring humiliation to; insult). 知足不辱。 *(zhī zú bù rǔ.)*

7.   **KNOW** (realize; tell) **STOP** (to; till; only) **NO** (not) **DANGER** (nearly almost). 知止不殆。 *(zhī zhǐ bù dài.)*

8.   **CAN** (may, pretty good) **OLDER** (develop_ long; of long duration; regularly; strong point) **FOR A LONG TIME** (long; of a specified duration). 可以长久。 *(kě yǐ cháng jiǔ.)*

CHAPTER 45

Great accomplishment seems incomplete, its use doesn't harm.
Great fullness seems dynamic[1], its use doesn't end.
Great straightness seems bent.
Great cleverness seems clumsy.
Great debate seems slow in speech.
Still surpasses impetuous,
Cold surpasses heat.
Clear and still keeps all-under-heaven honest.

1.   **BIG** (great) **ACCOMPLISH** (become; result) **LIKE** (seem; as if > if > you) **LACK** (incomplete; be absent; vacancy), **HIS** (its; that; such) **USE** (apply <frml> hence) **NO** (not) **FRAUD** (abuse; disadvantage; harm). 大成若缺，其用不弊。 *(dà chéng ruò quē, qí yòng bù bì.)*

---

1   Translating this line was a little tricky. Dynamic felt like a decent compromise. Interestingly, there is a dual character word, chong cao, (冲操),which is chong (the 'pour boiling water on') combined with cao (grasp; do; behavior), Together they mean keep one's integrity by being contented with simple life. Sure enough, being content with simple life has an eternal – never ending – feel.

    I can be content with simple life when it feels dynamic enough. So I suppose dynamic is not such a bad translation for chong or chong cao. Of course that begs the question; how to make a simple life feel dynamic? Certainly not by *impetuous* behavior, although that is THE BY-PATH PEOPLE OFTEN PREFER. Like Great perfection, contentment is something that is created in the eye of the beholder.

2. **BIG** (great) **BE FULL OF** (have) **LIKE** (seem; as if > if > you) **POURING BOILING WATER ON** (rinse, flush; rush; clash, important place), **HIS** (its; that; such) **USE** (apply <frml> hence) **NO** (not) **POOR** (limit; end; extremely). 大盈若冲，其用不穷。 *(dà yíng ruò chōng, qí yòng bù qióng.)*

3. **BIG** (great) **STRAIGHT** (perpendicular; just; frank; stiff; directly; simply) **LIKE** (seem; as if > if > you) **BEND** (bow; crook; subdue; wrong; injustice). 大直若屈。 *(dà zhí ruò qū.)*

4. **BIG** (great) **CLEVER** (deceitful; artful; opportunely; coincidentally; as it happens) **LIKE** (seem; as if > if > you) **CLUMSY** (awkward; dull > my). 大巧若拙。 *(dà qiǎo ruò zhuó.)*

5. **BIG** (great) **ARGUE** (dispute; debate) **LIKE** (seem; as if > if > you) **SLOW** (of speech). 大辩若讷。 *(dà biàn ruò nè.)*

6. **STILL** (quiet; calm) **VICTORY** (surpass; wonderful; be equal to) **RASH** (impetuous; restless), 静胜躁， *(jìng shèng zào,)*

7. **COLD** (tremble (with fear) **VICTORY** (surpass; wonderful; be equal to) **HEAT** (hot; warm; ardent; craze; fad; envious; popular). 寒胜热。 *(hán shèng rè.)*

8. **QUIET** (peaceful and quiet) **DO** (act as; be, mean; support) **LAND UNDER HEAVEN** **STRAIGHT** (upright; main; honest). 清静为天下正。 *(qīng jìng wéi tiān xià zhēng.)*

CHAPTER 46

All under heaven, having the way,
Retreating horses fertilize the fields.
All under heaven, without the way,
Army horses breed in the suburbs.
Of misfortunes,
    none are greater than not being content with one's lot.
Of faults, none are greater than longing for gain.
Therefore, in being contented with one's lot,
    enough is usually enough indeed.

1. **LAND UNDER HEAVEN** **HAVE** (exist) **ROAD** (way, principle; speak; think), 天下有道， *(tiān xià yǒu dào,)*

2. **STEP BACK** (retreat; decline; > yet; while) **WALK** (go; move; visit) **HORSE** **USE** (<v> take <p> according to; because of <adj> so as to <conj> and) **EXCREMENT** (feces> apply manure). 却走马以粪。 *(què zǒu mǎ yǐ fèn.)*

3. **LAND UNDER HEAVEN** **NOTHING** (without; not) **ROAD** (way, principle; speak; think), 天下无道， *(tiān xià wú dào,)*

4. **ARMY** (military affairs) **HORSE** **GIVE BIRTH TO** (existence) **IN** (at, to, from, by, than, out of) **SUBURBS** (outskirts). 戎马生于郊。 *(róng mǎ shēng yú jiāo.)*

5. **MISFORTUNES** (disaster; ruin) **NO ONE** (nothing; none; no; not; don't) **BIG** (large; great; main) **IN** (at, to, from, by, than, out of) **NO** (not) **BE CONTENT WITH ONE'S LOT**. 祸莫大于不知足。 *(huò mò dà yú bù zhī zú.)*

6. **FAULT** (blame; censure; punish) **NO ONE** (nothing; none; no; not; don't) **BIG** (large; great; main) **IN** (at, to, from, by, than, out of) **DESIRE** (wish; want; about to; on the point of) **GET** (obtain, gain > satisfied_need; must). 咎莫大于欲得。 *(jiù mò dà yú yù dé.)*

7. **HAPPENING** (reason; cause; hence) **BE CONTENT WITH ONE'S LOT OF FOOT** (leg; enough; full; as much as) **OF** **ORDINARY** (normal; constant; often; usually) **FOOT** (leg; enough; full; as much as) **ALREADY** (indeed; really; how). 故知足之足常足矣。 *(gù zhī zú zhī zú cháng zú yǐ.)*

CHAPTER 47

Without going out the door we can know all under heaven.
Without looking out the window we can see Nature's way.
He goes out farther, he realizes less,
Accordingly, the wise person goes nowhere yet knows.
Sees nothing yet understands.
Refrains from acting yet accomplishes.

1. **NO** (not) **GO OR COME OUT** (exceed; put forth) **DOOR** (household; family; (bank) account) **KNOW** (realize; tell; knowledge) **LAND UNDER HEAVEN**. 不出户知天下。 *(bù chū hù zhī tiān xià.)*

2. **NO** (not) **PEEP** (spy) **WINDOW** **SEE** (catch sight of) **SKY** (heaven; weather; nature; God) **ROAD** (way, principle; speak; think). 不窥牖见天道。 *(bù kuī yǒu jiàn tiān dào.)*

3. **HIS** (its, he, it, that; such) **GO OR COME OUT** (exceed; put forth) **FULL** (overflowing; more) **FAR** (distant; remote), **HIS** (its, he, it, that; such) **KNOW** (realize; tell; knowledge) **FULL** (overflowing; more) **FEW** (little; less; be short). 其出弥远，其知弥少。 *(qí chū mí yuǎn, qí zhī mí shǎo.)*

4. <grm> **IS** (yes <frml> this; that) **USE** (<v> take <p> according to; because of <adj> so as to <conj> and) **SAGE** (holy; sacred) **HUMAN** (man; people) **NO** (not) **GO** (be current; prevail; do) <conj.> **AND** (yet, but) **KNOW** (realize; tell; knowledge). 是以圣人不行而知。 *(shì yǐ shèng rén bù xíng ér zhī.)*

5. **NO** (not) **SEE** (appear, become visible) <conj.> **AND** (yet, but) **BRIGHT** (light; clear; open; honest; understand). 不见而明。 *(bù jiàn ér míng.)*

6. **NO** (not) **DO** (act as; be, mean; support) <conj.> **AND** (yet, but) **ACCOMPLISH** (become; result). 不为而成。 *(bù wéi ér chéng.)*

CHAPTER 48

Doing knowledge, day by day increase.
Doing the way, day by day decrease.
Of decreasing and decreasing,
Until without doing.
Without doing, and not supporting.
Take all under heaven ordinary, use without responsibility,
As well as with responsibility,
Not enough use, take all under heaven.

1. **DO** (act as; be_stand for, support) **STUDY** (imitate; knowledge) **SUN** (day; daily) **BENIFIT** (profit; advantage; increase; increasingly). 为学日益。 *(wéi xué rì yì.)*

2. **DO** (act as; be_stand for, support) **ROAD** (way, principle; speak; think) **SUN** (day; daily) **DECREASE** (lose; damage> sarcastic; caustic; cutting> mean; shabby). 为道日损。 *(wéi dào rì sǔn.)*

3. **DECREASE** (lose; damage> sarcastic; caustic; cutting> mean; shabby) **OF** **ALSO** (both... and...; again) **DECREASE** (lose; damage> sarcastic; caustic; cutting> mean; shabby), 损之又损， *(sǔn zhī yòu sǔn,)*

4. **USE** (<v> take <p> according to; because of <adj> so as to <conj> and) **TO** (until; > extremely; most) **IN** (at, to, from, by, than, out of) **NOTHING** (nil; without) **DO** (act as; be, mean; support). 以至于无为。 *(yǐ zhì yú wú wéi.)*

5. **NOTHING** (nil, without) **DO** <conj.> **AND** (yet, but) **NO** (not) **DO** (act as; be, mean; support). 无为而不为。 *(wú wéi ér bù wéi.)*

6. [1] **TAKE** (get; seek; adopt) **LAND UNDER HEAVEN** (the world), **ORDINARY** (normal; constant; invariable; usually) **USE** (<v> take <p> according to; because of <adj> so as to <conj> and) **NOTHING** (nil; without) **MATTER** (affair; work; responsibility; involvement), 取天下常以无事， *(qǔ tiān xià cháng yǐ wú shì,)*

---

1   D.C. Lau translates these last three lines as "It is always through not meddling that the empire is won. Should you meddle, then you are not equal to the task of winning the empire". Naturally, mine being more literal is much more terse.

7. **AND** (to reach; up to; in time for) **HIS** (its, he, it, that; such) **HAVE** (exist) **MATTER** (affair; work; responsibility; involvement), 及其有事， *(jí qí yǒu shì,)*

8. **NO** (not) **FOOT** (leg; enough; full; as much as) **USE** (<v> take <p> according to; because of <adj> so as to <conj> and) **TAKE** (get; seek; adopt) **LAND UNDER HEAVEN** (the world). 不足以取天下。 *(bù zú yǐ qǔ tiān xià.)*

CHAPTER 49

The wise person is without ordinary intention.
Takes the common people's intention as his intention.
With kindness, I am also kind.
Without kindness, I am also kind, of integrity kind.
With trust, I also trust.
Without trust, I also trust, of integrity trust.
How does the wise person exist, all under heaven, breathing in?
Becoming all under heaven, simple and natural his intention.
All the multitude explain with their knowledge;
The wise person, all of the child.

1. **SAGE** (holy; sacred) **HUMAN** (man; people) **NOTHING** (without; not) **ORDINARY** (normal; constant; often) **HEART** (mind; feeling; intention; center, core). 圣人无常心。 *(shèng rén wú cháng xīn.)*

2. **USE** (<v> take <p> according to; because of <adj> so as to <conj> and) **COMMON PEOPLE** **HEART** (mind; feeling; intention; center) **DO** (act; act as; serve as; be; mean) **HEART** (mind; feeling; intention; center, core). 以百姓心为心。 *(yǐ bǎi xìng xīn wéi xīn.)*

3. **GOOD** (perfect; kind) (者) **I** (we) **GOOD** (perfect; kind) **OF**. 善者吾善之。 *(shàn zhě wú shàn zhī.)*

4. **NO** (not) **GOOD** (perfect; kind)(者) **I** (we) **ALSO** (too) **GOOD** (perfect; kind) **OF** **VIRTUE** (moral character; heart) **GOOD** (perfect; kind). 不善者吾亦善之德善。 *(bù shàn zhě wú yì shàn zhī dé shàn.)*

5. **TRUE** (trust; faith; believe)(者) **I** (we) **TRUE** (trust; faith; believe) **OF**. 信者吾信之。 *(xìn zhě wú xìn zhī.)*

6. **NO** (not) **TRUE** (trust; faith; believe) (者) **I** (we) **ALSO** (too) **TRUE** (trust; faith; believe) **OF**, **VIRTUE** (moral character; heart) **TRUE** (trust; faith; believe). 不信者吾亦信之、德信。 *(bù xìn zhě wú yì xìn zhī, dé xìn.)*

7. **SAGE** (holy; sacred) **HUMAN** (man; people) **EXIST** (be living) **LAND UNDER HEAVEN** **INHALE** **HERE** (herein; (usu. negative questioning) how; why)? 圣人在天下歙歙焉， *(shèng rén zài tiān xià shè shè yān,)*

8. **DO** (act; act as; serve as; be; mean) **LAND UNDER HEAVEN** **MUDDY** (turbid; simple and natural; unsophisticated; whole) **HIS** (its, he, it, that; such) **HEART** (mind; feeling; intention; center, core). 为天下浑其心。 *(wéi tiān xià hún qí xīn.)*

9. **COMMON PEOPLE** **ALL** (each and every) **POUR** (concentrate; fix; annotate; explain with) **HIS** (her; its; their; they; that; such) **WHAT ONE SEES AND HEARS** (knowledge; information; one who spies for sb. else). 百姓皆注其耳目， *(bǎi xìng jiē zhù qí ěr mù,)*

10. **SAGE** (holy; sacred) **HUMAN** (man; people) **ALL** (each and every) **CHILD OF**. 圣人皆孩之。 *(shèng rén jiē hái zhī.)*

CHAPTER 50

In birth we join death.
Of life, follow three in ten.
Of death, follow three in ten.
Of people, aroused by life, in death trapped, also three in ten.
Why is this so?
Because they favor life.
It's well known, those good at conserving life,
Traveling on land never meet fierce tigers,
Joining the army never the first to fight.
Of the ferocious, no place to thrust its horns.
Of the tiger, no place to apply its claw.
Of the weapon, no place to allow the knife edge.
Why is this so?
Because he is not in death trapped

1. **BE BORN** **ENTER** (join; conform to; agree with) **DIE** (extremely; deadly; fixed; rigid). 出生入死。 *(chū shēng rù sǐ.)*

2. **GIVE BIRTH TO** (grow; existence; life) **OF** **ON FOOT** (only; follower; believer; person), **TEN** **HAVE** **THREE**. 生之徒，十有三。 *(shēng zhī tú, shí yǒu sān.)*

3. **DIE** (extremely; deadly; fixed; rigid) **OF** **ON FOOT** (only; follower; believer; person), **TEN** **HAVE** **THREE**. 死之徒，十有三。 *(sǐ zhī tú, shí yǒu sān.)*

64

4. **HUMAN** (man; people) **OF** **GIVE BIRTH TO** (grow; existence; life), **MOVE** (stir; act; change; arouse) **OF** **IN** (at, to, from, by, than, out of) **A FATAL POSITION** (deathtrap), **ALSO** (too) **TEN HAVE THREE**. 人之生，动之于死地，亦十有三。 *(rén zhī shēng, dòng zhī yú sǐ dì, yì shí yǒu sān.)*

5. **HUSBAND** (man) **CARRY** (what, how, why, which) **HAPPENING** (reason; cause; on purpose; hence)? 夫何故？ *(fū hé gù?)*

6. **USE** (<v> take <p> according to; because of <adj> so as to <conj> and) **HIS** (her, its, their; he, she, it, they; that; such) **GIVE BIRTH TO** (grow; existence; life) **GIVE BIRTH** to (grow; existence; life) **OF THICK** (deep; large; generous; favor; stress). 以其生生之厚。 *(yǐ qí shēng shēng zhī hòu.)*

7. **LID** (cover; shell <frml> approximately; for; because; in fact) **HEAR** (news; famous; smell) **GOOD** (satisfactory) **ABSORB** (conserve one's health) **GIVE BIRTH TO** (grow; existence; life)(者)， 盖闻善摄生者， *(gài wén shàn shè shēng zhě,)*

8. **LAND** (six) **GO** (travel, do, be current) **NO** (not) **MEET** (chance; opportunity) **OMINOUS** (crop failure; fierce; murder) **TIGER** (brave; vigorous), 陆行不遇凶虎， *(liù xíng bù yù xiōng hǔ,)*

9. **ENTER** (join; be admitted into) **ARMY** (troops) **NO** (not) **BY** (indicates passive-voice clauses; <literary> to cover; to meet with) **THE FIRST OF THE TEN HEAVENLY STEMS** (first; shell; armor) **WEAPONS** (private; army). 入军不被甲兵。 *(rù jūn bù bèi jiǎ bīng.)*

10. **OMINOUS** (crop failure; fierce; murder) **NOTHING** (without; not) **PLACE THROW** (drop; project; cast; go to; join; agree with) **HIS** (its, he, it, that; such) **HORN** (bugle; the shape of a horn). 凶无所投其角。 *(xiōng wú suǒ tóu qí jiǎo.)*

11. **TIGER** (brave; vigorous) **NOTHING** (without; not) **PLACE USE** (apply <frml> hence) **HIS** (her, its, their; he, she, it, they; that; such) **CLAW** (talon). 虎无所用其爪。 *(hǔ wú suǒ yòng qí zhuǎ.)*

12. **WEAPONS** (private; army) **NOTHING** (without; not) **PLACE HOLD** (contain; tolerate; permit; allow) **HIS** (her, its, their; he, she, it, they; that; such) **THE EDGE OF A KNIFE** (sword). 兵无所容其刃。 *(bīng wú suǒ róng qí rèn.)*

13. **HUSBAND** (man) **CARRY** (what, how, why, which) **HAPPENING** (reason; cause; on purpose; hence)? 夫何故？ *(fū hé gù?)*

14. **USE** (<v> take <p> according to; because of <adj> so as to <conj> and) **HIS** (her, its, their; he, she, it, they; that; such) **NOTHING** (without; not) **A FATAL POSITION** (deathtrap). 以其无死地。 *(yǐ qí wú sǐ dì.)*

CHAPTER 51

The way gives birth, virtue rears, things give shape,
　　power accomplishes.
Accordingly, everything respects the way and values virtue.
Of the way respected, of virtue valued,
　　man not of decree, but normal, naturally.
Hence, of the way born, of virtue reared.
Of long duration, of giving birth.
Of well balanced, of malicious.
Of supporting, of overturning.
It gives birth yet claims not,
It acts yet relies upon not,
It is the elder yet rules not.
This is called profound virtue.

1. **ROAD** (way, principle; speak; think) **GIVE BIRTH TO** (grow; existence; life) **OF**, **VIRTUE** (moral character; heart) **RAISE DOMESTIC ANIMALS OF**, **THING** (matter; the outside world) **FORM** (body; entity; appear) **OF**, **POWER** (influence; momentum; circumstances) **ACCOMPLISH** (become; result) of. 道生之，德畜之，物形之，势成之。 *(dào shēng zhī, dé chù zhī, wù xíng zhī, shì chéng zhī.)*

2. <grm> **IS** (yes <frml> this; that) **USE** (<v> take <p> according to; because of <adj> so as to <conj> and) **TEN THOUSAND** (a very great number; myriad) **THING** (matter; the outside world) **NO ONE** (nothing; none; no; not; don't) **NO** (not) **SENIOR** (respect; venerate) **ROAD** (way, principle; speak; think), <conj.> **AND** (yet, but) **EXPENSIVE** (precious; noble) **VIRTUE** (moral character; heart). 是以万物莫不尊道，而贵德。 *(shì yǐ wàn wù mò bù zūn dào, ér guì dé.)*

3. **ROAD** (way, principle; speak; think) **OF** **SENIOR** (respect; venerate), **VIRTUE** (moral character; heart) **OF** **EXPENSIVE** (precious; noble), **HUSBAND** (man) **NO ONE** (nothing; none; no; not; don't) **OF** **LIFE** (lot; fate; destiny; order; assign) <conj.> **AND** (yet, but) **ORDINARY** (normal; constant; often) **NATURAL** (free from affectation). 道之尊，德之贵，夫莫之命而常自然。 *(dào zhī zūn, dé zhī guì, fū mò zhī mìng ér cháng zì rán.)*

4. **HAPPENING** (reason; cause; on purpose; hence) **ROAD** (way, principle; speak; think) **GIVE BIRTH TO** (grow; existence; life) **OF**, **VIRTUE** (moral character; heart) **RAISE DOMESTIC ANIMALS OF**. 故道生之，德畜之。 *(gù dào shēng zhī, dé chù zhī.)*

5. **OLDER** (develop_ long; of long duration; regularly; strong point) **OF** **GIVE BIRTH TO** (rear; raise; bring up; educate) **OF**. 长之育之。 *(cháng zhī yù zhī.)*

6. **PAVILION** (kiosk> well balanced; in the middle; even) **OF** **POISON** (kill with poison; malicious; cruel; fierce) **OF**. 亭之毒之。 *(tíng zhī dú zhī.)*

7. **SUPPORT** (raise; keep; grow; foster) **OF** **COVER** (overturn; upset) **OF**. 养之覆之。 *(yǎng zhī fù zhī.)*

8. **GIVE BIRTH TO** (grow; existence; life) <conj.> **AND** (yet, but) **NO** (not) **HAVE** (exist), 生而不有， *(shēng ér bù yǒu,)*

9. **DO** (act; act as; serve as; be; mean) <conj.> **AND** (yet, but) **NO** (not) **RELY ON** (depend on). 为而不恃， *(wéi ér bù shì,)*

10. **OLDER** (develop_ long; of long duration; regularly; strong point) <conj.> **AND** (yet, but) **NO** (not) **SLAUGHTER** (butcher; govern; rule). 长而不宰。 *(cháng ér bù zǎi.)*

11. <grm> **IS** (yes <frml> this; that) **SAY** (call; name; meaning; sense) **BLACK** (dark; profound) **VIRTUE** (moral character; heart). 是谓玄德。 *(shì wèi xuán dé.)*

CHAPTER 52

All under heaven had a beginning;
    consider the origin of all under heaven.
Already having its origin, use this to know its seed.
Already knowing its seed, return to observe the origin.
Rising beyond oneself, not nearly almost.
Squeeze exchange, shut the gates; to the end, oneself diligent.
Open the exchange, aid that involvement;
    to the end, oneself no relief.
Seeing the small is called clarity,
    abide by yielding is called powerful.
Use the light, and again return to clarity,
    not offer oneself misfortune.
This serves as practicing the constant.

1. **LAND UNDER HEAVEN** **HAVE** (exist) **BEGINNING** (start> only then), **THINK** (believe; consider) **LAND UNDER HEAVEN** **MOTHER** (female (animal); origin; parent). 天下有始，以为天下母。 *(tiān xià yǒu shǐ, yǐ wéi tiān xià mǔ.)*

2.   **ALREADY** (<conj.> since; both... and...) **GET** (obtain, gain > satisfied_need; must) **HIS** (its; their; they; that) **MOTHER** **USE** (<v> take <p> according to; because of <adj> so as to <conj> and) **KNOW** (realize; tell) **HIS** (its; their; they; that) **SON** (child; person; seed). 既得其母，以知其子。 *(jì dé qí mǔ, yǐ zhī qí zǐ.)*

3.   **ALREADY** (<conj.> since; both... and...) **KNOW** (realize; tell; knowledge) **HIS** (its; their; they; that) **SON** (child; person; seed), **DUPLICATE** (again) **GUARD** (defend; keep watch; observe; abide by; close to; near) **HIS** (its; their; they; that) **MOTHER**, 既知其子，复守其母， *(jì zhī qí zǐ, fù shǒu qí mǔ,)*

4.   **SINK** (rise beyond; disappear; hide; die) **BODY** (life; oneself; personally) **NO** (not) **DANGER** (nearly almost). 没身不殆。 *(méi shēn bù dài.)*

5.   **FILL IN** (squeeze in; stuff_a place of strategic importance) **HIS** (its; their; they; that) **EXCHANGE** (convert; add (water, etc), **SHUT** (close; stop up; obstruct) **HIS** (its; their; they; that)**ENTRANCE** (door; gate; valve), **END** (death; eventually; after all; whole; all) **BODY** (life; oneself; personally) **NO** (not))**DILIGENT** (frequently). 塞其兑，闭其门，终身不勤。 *(sāi qí duì, bì qí mén, zhōng shēn bù qín.)*

6.   **OPEN** (start) **HIS** (its; their; they; that) **EXCHANGE** (convert; add (water, etc), **CROSS A RIVER** (aid; help) **HIS** (its; their; they; that) **MATTER** (affair; thing; involvement), **END** (death; eventually; after all; whole; all) **BODY** (life; oneself; personally) **NO** (not) **RESCUE** (save; salvage; help; relieve; succor). 开其兑，济其事，终身不救。 *(kāi qí duì, jì qí shì, zhōng shēn bù jiù.)*

7.   **SEE** (appear, become visible) **HIS** (its; their; they; that) **SMALL** (little; for a while; young) **SAY** (call) **BRIGHT** (light; clear; open; honest; understand), **GUARD** (defend; keep watch; observe; abide by; close to; near) **SOFT** (supple; flexible; soften; gentle; yielding; mild) **SAY** (call) **STRIVE** (strong; powerful; better_unyielding). 见其小曰明，守柔曰强。 *(jiàn qí xiǎo yuē míng, shǒu róu yuē jiàng.)*

8.   **USE** (apply <frml> hence) **HIS** (its; their; they; that) **LIGHT** (ray; brightness... naked; alone), **DUPLICATE** (again) **GO BACK TO** (return; give back to; come together) **HIS** (its; their; they; that) **BRIGHT** (light; clear; open; honest; understand), **NOTHING** (without; not) **OFFER AS A GIFT** (lose; leave behind; keep back; not give) **BODY** (life; oneself; personally) **CALAMITY** (disaster; misfortune). 用其光，复归其明，无遗身殃。 *(yòng qí guāng, fù guī qí míng, wú yí shēn yāng.)*

9.   <grm> **IS** (yes <frml> this; that) **DO** (act; act as; serve as; be; mean) **PRACTICE** (review; be used to; habit) **ORDINARY** (normal; constant; often). 是为习常。 *(shì wéi xí cháng.)*

CHAPTER 53

Were I mindful yet had knowledge,
Going in the great way, alone bestow this respect.
The great way is very smooth, yet people are fond of paths.
The government is very removed,
   the fields very overgrown, the storehouses very empty.
Colorful clothes, culture, belted swords,
   satisfied of drink, food, wealth and goods to spare.
This is called in praise of robbery.
This does not conform to the way either!

1. **SEND** (tell to do; use; employ) **I** (we) **BE SITUATED BETWEEN** (take seriously
   <frml> upright) **RIGHT** (correct; so; like that) **HAVE** (exist) **KNOW** (realize;
   tell; knowledge), 使我介然有知， *(shǐ wǒ jiè rán yǒu zhī,)*

2. **GO** (travel, do, be current) **IN** (at, to, from, by, than, out of) **BIG** (great;
   fully) **ROAD** (way, principle; speak; think), **ONLY** (alone) **CARRY OUT**
   (hand out; impose) <grm> **IS** (yes <frml> this; that) **FEAR** (respect).
   行于大道，唯施是畏。 *(xíng yú dà dào, wéi shī shì wèi.)*

3. **BIG** (great; fully) **ROAD** (way, principle; speak; think) **VERY**
   (extremely; more than) **SMOOTH** (safe; exterminate <old>
   foreigner), <conj.> **AND** (yet, but) **HUMAN** (man; people) **GOOD** (be
   easy_like; be fond of) **PATH** (track; way; means> straightaway) 大
   道甚夷，而人好径。 *(dà dào shén yí, ér rén hǎo jìng.)*

4. **GOVERNMENT** (dynasty; facing; towards) **VERY** (extremely; more than)
   GET RID OF (except; besides <forma> steps to a house; doorsteps), **FIELD**
   (farmland; cropland) **VERY** (extremely; more than) **OVER GROWN WITH**
   WEEDS (grassland; mixed and disordered), **STOREHOUSE** (warehouse)
   VERY (extremely; more than) **VOID** (emptiness). 朝甚除， 田甚
   芜，仓甚虚。 *(cháo shén chú, tián shén wú, cāng shén xū.)*

5. **CLOTHES** (dress; serve; obey; be accustomed to) **LANGUAGE** (culture;
   civil) **COLOR** (colored silk), **BELT** (zone; take; bring; carry) **SHARP**
   WEAPON (good tool) **SWORD** (saber), **BE DISGUSTED WITH** (be tired of;
   be satisfied) **DRINK** (a decoction of Chinese medicine) **BRING FOOD**
   TO (feed), **WEALTH** (money) **GOODS** (commodity; money; idiot) **HAVE**
   (exist) **SURPLUS** (more than; over). 服文彩， 带利剑， 厌饮食，
   财货有余。 *(fú wén cǎi, dài lì jiàn, yàn yǐn shí, cái huò yǒu yú.)*

6. <grm> **IS** (yes <frml> this; that) **SAY** (call; name; meaning; sense) **STEEL** (rob;
   thief) **EXAGGERATE** (overstate; boast; praise). 是谓盗夸。 *(shì wèi dào kuā.)*

7. **WRONG** (not conform to) **ROAD** (way, principle; speak; think) **ALSO** (either) **ZĀI** (exclamatory or interrog. part.). 非道也哉。 *(fēi dào yě zāi.)*

CHAPTER 54

What is well established cannot be pulled out.
What is well established cannot be neglected.
Descendants using ceremonial offering of sacrifice,
    to ancestors never ceases.
Of cultivating in the body, its virtue true.
Of cultivating in the family, its virtue abundant.
Of cultivating in the village, its virtue long.
Of cultivating in the nation, its virtue abundant.
Of cultivating in all under heaven, its virtue universal.
Hence,
Use the body to observe the body,
Use the family to observe the family,
Use the village to observe the village,
Use the nation to observe the nation,
Use all under heaven to observe all under heaven.
How can we know all under heaven is like that?
By using this.

1. **GOOD** (satisfactory) **BUILD** (construct; set up; establish; advocate) (者) **NO** (not) **PULL OUT** (suck out; choose). 善建者不拔。 *(shàn jiàn zhě bù bá.)*

2. **GOOD** (satisfactory) **BUILD** (construct; set up; establish; advocate> embrace ; hug; cherish) (者) **NO** (not) **TAKE OFF** (cast off; escape from <frml> neglect> if). 善抱者不脱。 *(shàn bào zhě bù tuō.)*

3. **CHILDREN AND GRANDCHILDREN** (descendants) **USE** (<v> take <p> according to; because of <adj> so as to <conj> and) **HOLD A MEMORIAL CEREMONY FOR** (offer a sacrifice to) **OFFER SACRIFICES TO THE GODS** (or to spirits of the dead) **NO** (not) **STOP** (cease). 子孙以祭祀不辍。 *(zǐ sūn yǐ jì sì bù chuò.)*

4. **EMBELLISH** (repair; write; construct; cultivate; prune <frml> long) **OF** **IN** (at, to, from, by, than, out of) **BODY** (life; oneself; personally) **HIS** (its; their; they; that) **VIRTUE** (moral character; heart) **BE** (therefore, only then, your) **TRUE** (real; genuine). 修之于身其德乃真。 *(xiū zhī yú shēn qí dé nǎi zhēn.)*

5. **EMBELLISH** (repair; write; construct; cultivate; prune <fml> long) **OF** **IN** (at, to, from, by, than, out of) **FAMILY** (home; a certain trade; a school) **HIS** (its; their; they; that) **VIRTUE** (moral character; heart) **BE** (therefore, only then, your) **EXTRA** (surplus; after <frml> I). 修之于家其德乃余。 *(xiū zhī yú jiā qí dé nǎi yú.)*

6. **EMBELLISH** (repair; write; construct; cultivate; prune <fml> long) **OF** **IN** (at, to, from, by, than, out of) **COUNTRY** (village; home town) **HIS** (its; their; they; that) **VIRTUE** (moral character; heart) **BE** (therefore, only then, your) **OLDER** (develop_ long; regularly; strong point). 修之于乡其德乃长。 *(xiū zhī yú xiāng qí dé nǎi cháng.)*

7. **EMBELLISH** (repair; write; construct; cultivate; prune <fml> long) **OF** **IN** (at, to, from, by, than, out of) **NATION** (state; country) **HIS** (its; their; they; that) **VIRTUE** (moral character; heart) **BE** (therefore, only then, your) **ABUNDANT** (plentiful; great; fine-looking; handsome). 修之于邦其德乃丰。 *(xiū zhī yú bāng qí dé nǎi fēng.)*

8. **EMBELLISH** (repair; write; construct; cultivate; prune <fml> long) **OF** **IN** (at, to, from, by, than, out of) **LAND UNDER HEAVEN** **HIS** (its; their; they; that) **VIRTUE** (moral character; heart) **BE** (therefore, only then, your) **GENERAL** (universal). 修之于天下其德乃普。 *(xiū zhī yú tiān xià qí dé nǎi pǔ.)*

9. **REASON** (cause; on purpose; hence) 故 *(gù)*

10. **USE** (<v> take <p> according to; because of <adj> so as to <conj> and) **BODY** (life; oneself; personally) **LOOK AT** (watch; observe; sight; view) **BODY** (life; oneself; personally), 以身观身， *(yǐ shēn guān shēn,)*

11. **USE** (<v> take <p> according to; because of <adj> so as to <conj> and) **FAMILY** (home; a school of thought) **LOOK AT** (watch; observe; sight; view) **FAMILY** (home; a school of thought), 以家观家， *(yǐ jiā guān jiā,)*

12. **USE** (<v> take <p> according to; because of <adj> so as to <conj> and) **COUNTRY** (village; home town) **LOOK AT** (watch; observe; sight; view) **COUNTRY** (village; home town), 以乡观乡， *(yǐ xiāng guān xiāng,)*

13. **USE** (<v> take <p> according to; because of <adj> so as to <conj> and) **NATION** (state; country) **LOOK AT** (watch; observe; sight; view) **NATION** (state; country), 以邦观邦， *(yǐ bāng guān bāng,)*

14. **USE** (<v> take <p> according to; because of <adj> so as to <conj> and) **LAND UNDER HEAVEN** **LOOK AT** (watch; observe; sight; view) **LAND UNDER HEAVEN**. 以天下观天下。 *(yǐ tiān xià guān tiān xià.)*

15. **I** (we) **WHO** (why) **KNOW** (realize) **LAND UNDER HEAVEN** **CORRECT** (so; like that <frml conj> but; nevertheless) **ZĀI** (exclamatory or interrog. part.)? 吾何以知天下然哉？ *(wú hé yǐ zhī tiān xià rán zāi?)*

16.   **USE** (<v> take <p> according to; because of <adj> so as to <conj> and) **THIS**. 以此。 *(yǐ cǐ.)*

Chapter 55

Deeply contained integrity is comparable to a child's sincerity.
Poison insects don't sting it,
   fierce beasts don't seize it, birds don't grab it.
Its bones are weak, its muscle supple, yet its hold is firm.
It doesn't know the joining of female and male,
   yet its work and spirit perfect.
Endlessly it can howl,
   yet not become exhausted, of harmony, also the most.
Knowing harmony is called the constant.
Knowing the constant is called clear and honest.
A beneficial life is called lucky.
Mind employing life energy is called striving.
The powerful ruling the old is called not of the way.
That which is not of the way ends early.

1.   **KEEP IN THE MOUTH** (contain; nurse; cherish; harbour) **VIRTUE** (moral character; heart) **OF** **THICK** (deep; large; generous; favor; stress) **COMPARE** (compete_associate with; be near) **IN** (at, to, from, by, than, out of) **RED** (loyal; sincere; single-hearted; bare) **SON** (child; ancient for virtuous man; seed; small thing). 含德之厚比于赤子。 *(hán dé zhī hòu bǐ yú chì zǐ.)*

2.   **POISON** (kill with poison; malicious; cruel; fierce) **INSECT** (worm) **NO** (not) **STING**, **FIERCE** (violent; energetic; suddenly) **BEAST** (animal) **NO** (not) **OCCUPY** (seize; rely on; evidence), **SEIZE** (grab) **BIRD** **NO** (not) **ROLL ROUND WITH HAND**. 毒虫不螫，猛兽不据，攫鸟不抟。 *(dú chóng bù shì, měng shòu bù jū, jué niǎo bù tuán.)*

3.   **BONE** **WEAK** (inferior <frml> lose through death) **MUSCLE** **SOFT** (supple) <conj.> **AND** (yet, but) **HOLD** (grasp) **SOLID** (firm <frml> in the first place, originally, admittedly). 骨弱筋柔而握固。 *(gǔ ruò jīn róu ér wò gù.)*

4.   **HAVE NOT** (did not) **KNOW** (realize) **FEMALE MALE** **OF** **SHUT** (join; combine) <conj.> **AND** (yet, but) **COMPLETE** (whole; make perfect) **DO** (make; rise; get up; write; compose; become), **REFINED** (choice; essence) **OF** **TO** (until; > extremely; most) **ALSO** (too). 未知牝牡之合而全作，精之至也。 *(wèi zhī pìn mǔ zhī gě ér quán zuò, jīng zhī zhì yě.)*

72

5. END (death; eventually; after all; whole; all) SUN (day; daily) NAME (sign _howl; yell) <conj.> AND (yet, but) NO (not) AH (exclamatory part.), GENTLE (kind; harmonious; peace> and) OF TO (until; > extremely; most) ALSO (too). 终日号而不嗄，和之至也。 *(zhōng rì háo ér bù á, hé zhī zhì yě.)*

6. KNOW (realize) GENTLE (kind; harmonious; peace> and) SAY (call; name) ORDINARY (normal; constant; often). 知和曰常。 *(zhī hé yuē cháng.)*

7. KNOW (realize) ORDINARY (normal; constant; often) SAY (call; name) BRIGHT (light; clear; open; honest; understand). 知常曰明。 *(zhī cháng yuē míng.)*

8. BENEFIT (profit; advantage; increase; increasingly) GIVE BIRTH TO (grow; existence; life) SAY (call; name) AUSPICIOUS (propitious; lucky). 益生曰祥。 *(yì shēng yuē xiáng.)*

9. HEART (mind; feeling; intention; center, core) SEND (tell sb. to do sth.; use; cause; enable) GAS (air; breath; spirit; enrage) SAY (call; name) STRIVE (strong; powerful; better _ unyielding). 心使气曰强。 *(xīn shǐ qì yuē jiàng.)*

10. THING (matter; the outside world) STRONG (robust; grand; make better) STANDARD (norm; rule > imitate; follow) OLD (aged; of long standing; old; for a long time; always) SAY (call; name; meaning; sense) OF NO (not) ROAD (way, principle; speak; think), 物壮则老，谓之不道。 *(wù zhuàng zé lǎo, wèi zhī bù dào.)*

11. NO (not) ROAD (way, principle; speak; think) EARLY MORNING (long ago; as early as; for a long time; early; in advance) STOP (cease; end; already; > thereafter; afterwards; too). 不道早已。 *(bù dào zǎo yǐ.)*

CHAPTER 56

Knowing doesn't speak; speaking doesn't know.
Subdue its sharpness, untie its tangles,
Soften its brightness, be the same as dust,
This is called profound sameness.
For this reason,
Unobtainable and intimate,
Unobtainable and distant
Unobtainable and favorable
Unobtainable and fearful
Unobtainable and noble
Unobtainable and humble
For this reason all under heaven value it.

1. **KNOW** (realize) (者) **NO** (not) **SPEECH** (word; say; talk), **SPEECH** (word; say; talk) (者) **NO** (not) **KNOW** (realize). 知者不言，言者不知。 *(zhī zhě bù yán, yán zhě bù zhī.)*

2. **DEFEAT** (frustrate; subdue; lower) **HIS** (its; their; they; that) **SHARP** (keenr; fighting spirit), **SEPARATE** (divide; untie; understand) **HIS** (its; their; they; that) **CONFUSED** (tangled; disorderly). 挫其锐，解其纷， *(cuò qí ruì, jiě qí fēn,)*

3. **GENTLE** (kind; harmonious; peace> and) **HIS** (its; their; they; that) **LIGHT** (ray; brightness... naked; alone), **SAME** (similar; together) **HIS** (its; their; they; that) **DUST** (dirt; this world). 和其光，同其尘， *(hé qí guāng, tóng qí chén,)*

4. <grm> **IS** (yes <frml> this; that) **SAY** (call; name; meaning; sense) **BLACK** (dark; profound) **SAME** (similar; together). 是谓玄同。 *(shì wèi xuán tong.)*

5. **REASON** (cause; on purpose; hence) 故 *(gù)*

6. **NO** (not) **CAN** **GET** <conj.> **AND** (yet, but) **PARENT** (close; intimate; oneself). 不可得而亲。 *(bù kě dé ér qīn.)*

7. **NO** (not) **CAN** **GET** <conj.> **AND** (yet, but) **THIN** (sparse; scattered). 不可得而疏。 *(bù kě dé ér shū.)*

8. **NO** (not) **CAN** **GET** <conj.> **AND** (yet, but) **SHARP** (favorable; advantage). 不可得而利。 *(bù kě dé ér lì.)*

9. **NO** (not) **CAN** **GET** <conj.> **AND** (yet, but) **EVIL** (harm; calamity; impair; kill). 不可得而害。 *(bù kě dé ér hài.)*

10. **NO** (not) **CAN** **GET** <conj.> **AND** (yet, but) **EXPENSIVE** (precious; noble). 不可得而贵。 *(bù kě dé ér guì.)*

11. **NO** (not) **CAN** **GET** <conj.> **AND** (yet, but) **INEXPENSIVE** (cheap; lowly; humble). 不可得而贱。 *(bù kě dé ér jiàn.)*

12. **REASON** (cause; on purpose; hence) **DO** (act; act as; serve as; be; mean) **LAND UNDER HEAVEN** **EXPENSIVE** (precious; noble). 故为天下贵。 *(gù wéi tiān xià guì.)*

CHAPTER 57

Use honesty to govern the country,
Use surprise when using weapons,
Use non responsibility when seeking all under heaven.
How do I know so? Because of this.
The wider spread the taboos, the poorer the people.
The sharper their tools, the more a country's confusion grows.
The more clever they are, the more strange things appear.
The more laws multiply, the more conspicuous the robbers.
For this reason, the holy person says,
I do nothing and the people change themselves.
I love stillness and the people straighten themselves.
I am without responsibility and the people thrive themselves.
I am without desire and the people simplify themselves.

1. **USE** (<v> take <p> according to; because of <adj> so as to <conj>
   and) **STRAIGHT** (upright; main; honest) **RULE** (govern; manage; peace)
   COUNTRY (state; of our country), 以正治国， *(yǐ zhēng zhì guó.)*

2. **USE** (<v> take <p> according to; because of <adj> so as to <conj>
   and) **STRANGE** (rare; surprise; wonder) **USE** (apply <frml> hence)
   WEAPONS (private; army), 以奇用兵， *(yǐ jī yòng bīng.)*

3. **USE** (<v> take <p> according to; because of <adj> so as to <conj> and)
   NOTHING (without; not) **MATTER** (affair; thing; responsibility) **TAKE** (get; seek;
   adopt) **LAND UNDER HEAVEN**. 以无事取天下。 *(yǐ wú shì qǔ tiān xià.)*

4. **I** (we) **WHO** (why) **KNOW** (realize; tell) **HIS** (its; their; they; that) **CORRECT** (so;
   like that <formal conj> but; nevertheless) **ZĀI** (exclamatory or interrog.
   part.)? **USE** (<v> take <p> according to; because of <adj> so as to <conj>
   and) **THIS**. 吾何以知其然哉？以此。 *(wú hé yǐ zhī qí rán zāi? yǐ cǐ.)*

5. **LAND UNDER HEAVEN** **MUCH** (more; too many; excessive) **TABOO** (avoid
   as taboo; avoid as harmful) <conj.> **AND** (yet, but) **THE PEOPLE** (civilian)
   FULL (overflowing; more) **POOR** (deficient; garrulous; loquacious).
   天下多忌讳而民弥贫。 *(tiān xià duō jì huì ér mín mí pín.)*

6. **THE PEOPLE** (civilian) **MUCH** (more; too many; excessive) **SHARP**
   WEAPON (good tool) **COUNTRY** (state; nation) **GROW** (multiply;
   more> spurt; burst) **DIM** (confused; muddled; lose consciousness;
   faint). 民多利器国家滋昏。 *(mín duō lì qì guó jiā zī hūn.)*

7. **HUMAN** (man; people) **MUCH** (more; excessive) **ABILITY** (trick) **CLEVER** (deceitful; artful) **STRANGE** (rare; surprise) **THING** (matter; the outside world as distinct from oneself) **DRIP** (trickle) **GET UP** (remove; pull; appear). 人多伎巧奇物泫起。 *(rén duō jì qiǎo jī wù xuàn qǐ.)*

8. **METHOD** (law; follow; model after) **COMMAND** (decree; make; cause) **GROW** (multiply; more> spurt; burst) **CLEAR** (evident; conspicuous) **ROBBERS** (bandits) **MUCH** (more; too many; excessive) **HAVE** (exist). 法令滋彰盗贼多有。 *(fǎ lìng zī zhāng dào zéi duō yǒu.)*

9. **REASON** (cause; on purpose; hence) **SAGE** (holy; sacred) **HUMAN** (man; people) **SAY** (cloud). 故圣人云 *(gù shèng rén yún)*

10. **I** (we) **NOTHING** (without; not) **DO** (act; act as; serve as; be; mean; support) <conj.> **AND** (yet, but) **THE PEOPLE** (civilian) **SELF** (oneself; certainly) **CHANGE** (turn; transform; convert; influence). 我无为而民自化。 *(wǒ wú wéi ér mín zì huā.)*

11. **I** (we) **GOOD** (be easy_like; be fond of) **STILL** (quiet; calm) <conj.> **AND** (yet, but) **THE PEOPLE** (civilian) **SELF** (oneself; certainly) **STRAIGHT** (upright; main; honest). 我好静而民自正。 *(wǒ hǎo jìng ér mín zì zhēng.)*

12. **I** (we) **NOTHING** (without; not) **MATTER** (affair; thing; involvement) <conj.> **AND** (yet, but) **THE PEOPLE** (civilian) **SELF** (oneself; certainly) **RICH** (wealthy; abundant). 我无事而民自富。 *(wǒ wú shì ér mín zì fù.)*

13. **I** (we) **NOTHING** (without; not) **DESIRE** (wish; want; about to) <conj.> **AND** (yet, but) **THE PEOPLE** (civilian) **SELF** (oneself; certainly) **SIMPLE** (plain). 我无欲而民自朴。 *(wǒ wú yù ér mín zì pò.)*

CHAPTER 58

When its politics are boring, its people are honest.
When its politics are scrutinized, its people are imperfect.
Misfortune, yet of good fortune its resting place
Good fortune, yet of misfortune its hiding place
Who knows such extremes? It's not mainstream.
Mainstream turns to strange, Good turns to evil.
The people have been long confused.
Thus, the wise are upright, yet not cuttingly so.
Honest, yet not stabbingly so.
Straightforward, yet not wantonly so.
Honorable yet not gloriously so.

1. **HIS** (its; their; they; that) **POLITICS** (affairs of a family or organization) **BORED** (depressed; stuffy), **HIS** (its; their; they; that) **THE PEOPLE** (civilian) **PURE** (honest). 其政闷闷，其民淳淳。 *(qí zhèng mēn mēn, qí mín chún chún.)*

2. **HIS** (its; their; they; that) **POLITICS** (affairs of a family or organization) **EXAMINE** (scrutinize; look into), **HIS** (its; their; they; that) **THE PEOPLE** (civilian) **LACK** (incomplete; be absent; vacancy). 其政察察，其民缺缺。 *(qí zhèng chá chá, qí mín quē quē.)*

3. **MISFORTUNES** (disaster; ruin) **STILL** (yet; esteem, set great store by) **GOOD FORTUNE** (happiness) **OF PLACE LEAN ON OR AGAINST** (reply on> biased, partial). 祸尚福之所倚。 *(huò shàng fú zhī suǒ yǐ.)*

4. **GOOD FORTUNE** (happiness) **STILL** (yet; esteem, set great store by) **MISFORTUNES** (disaster; ruin) **OF PLACE BEND OVER** (lie prostrate; subside). 福尚祸之所伏。 *(fú shàng huò zhī suǒ fú.)*

5. **WHO KNOW** (realize; tell) **HIS** (its; their; they; that) **EXTREME** (pole; extremely; utmost), **HIS** (its; their; they; that) **NOTHING** (without; not) **STRAIGHT** (upright; main; in the middle). 孰知其极，其无正。 *(shú zhī qí jí, qí wú zhēng.)*

6. **STRAIGHT** (upright; main; in the middle) **DUPLICATE** (answer; again) **DO** (act; act as; serve as; be; mean; support) **STRANGE** (rare; surprise), **GOOD** (satisfactory) **DUPLICATE** (answer; again) **DO** (act; act as; serve as; be; mean; support) **DEMON** (evil spirit; bewitching). 正复为奇，善复为妖。 *(zhēng fù wéi jī, shàn fù wéi yāo.)*

7. **HUMAN** (man; people) **OF BE CONFUSED** (be lost; perplex; fascinate; enchant) **HIS** (its; their; they; that) **SUN** (day; daily) **SOLID** (firm <frml> in the first place, originally, admittedly) **FOR A LONG TIME** (long; of a specified duration). 人之迷其日固久。 *(rén zhī mí qí rì gù jiǔ.)*

8. <grm> **IS** (yes <frml> this; that) **USE** (<v> take <p> according to; because of <adj> so as to <conj> and) **SAGE** (holy; sacred) **HUMAN** (man; people) **SQUARE** (upright; honest; direction; side; method) <conj.> **AND** (yet, but) **NO** (not) **CUT**. 是以圣人方而不割。 *(shì yǐ shèng rén fāng ér bù gē.)*

9. **HONEST** <conj.> **AND** (yet, but) **NO** (not) **CUT** (stab). 廉而不刿。 *(lián ér bù guì.)*

10. **STRAIGHT** (perpendicular; just; frank; stiff; directly; simply) <conj.> **AND** (yet, but) **NO** (not) **WANTON** (unbridled; > shop). 直而不肆。 *(zhí ér bù sì.)*

11. **LIGHT** (brightness, honor; glory; smooth; … naked; alone) <conj.> **AND** (yet, but) **NO** (not) **LOOK INTO THE DISTANCE FROM A HIGH PLACE**. 光而不耀。 *(guāng ér bù yào.)*

CHAPTER 59

For managing people's daily affairs, there is nothing like frugality.
Only the frugal man is said to serve from the start.
Serving from the start he is said to deeply accumulate virtue.
Deeply accumulating virtue, as a rule he is said to be limitless.
Being limitless, as a rule no one knows his utmost point.
No one knowing his utmost point, he can have the country.
Having the origin of the country, he can long endure.
This is called deep roots, solid foundation,
Long life, enduringly watchful of the way.

1.   **RULE** (govern; manage; peace) **HUMAN** (man; people) **MATTER** (affair; thing; involvement) **SKY** (heaven; day; nature) **NO ONE** (nothing) **LIKE** (seem; as if) **STINGY** (miserly). 治人事天莫若嗇。 *(zhì rén shì tiān mò ruò sè.)*

2.   **HUSBAND** (man) **ONLY** (alone) **STINGY** (miserly) \<grm\> **IS** (yes \<frml\> this; that) **SAY** (call; name; meaning; sense) **EARLY MORNING** (long ago; early; in advance) **CLOTHES** (dress; serve; obey; be accustomed to). 夫唯嗇是謂早服。 *(fū wéi sè shì wèi zǎo fú.)*

3.   **EARLY MORNING** (long ago; early; in advance) **CLOTHES** (dress; serve; obey; be accustomed to) **SAY** (call; name; meaning; sense) **OF** **WEIGHT** (heavy; important; deep) **STORE UP** (accumulate, amass) **VIRTUE** (moral character; heart). 早服謂之重積德。 *(zǎo fú wèi zhī chóng jī dé.)*

4.   **WEIGHT** (heavy; important; deep) **STORE UP** (accumulate, amass) **VIRTUE** (moral character; heart) **STANDARD** (norm; rule > imitate; follow) **NOTHING** (without; not) **BE UNABLE TO**. 重積德則无不克。 *(chóng jī dé zé wú bù kè.)*

5.   **NOTHING** (without; not) **BE UNABLE TO** **STANDARD** (norm; rule > imitate; follow) **NO ONE** (nothing) **KNOW** (realize; tell) **HIS** (its; their; they; that) **UTMOST POINT** (extreme; pole; extremely). 无不克则莫知其极。 *(wú bù kè zé mò zhī qí jí.)*

6.   **NO ONE** (nothing) **KNOW** (realize; tell) **HIS** (its; their; they; that) **UTMOST POINT** (extreme; pole; extremely) **CAN** (may) **HAVE** (exist) **COUNTRY** (state; nation). 莫知其极可以有国。 *(mò zhī qí jí kě yǐ yǒu guó.)*

7.   **HAVE** (exist) **COUNTRY** (state; nation) **OF** **MOTHER** (origin) **CAN** (may) **OLDER** (elder; chief_ long; of long duration; strong point) **FOR A LONG TIME** (long; of a specified duration). 有国之母可以长久。 *(yǒu guó zhī mǔ kě yǐ cháng jiǔ.)*

8.   \<grm\> **IS** (yes \<frml\> this; that) **SAY** (call; name; meaning; sense) **DEEP** (difficult; profound; intimate; dark) **ROOT** (base; cause; origin) **SOLID** (firm\> originally) **FOUNDATION** (root), 是谓深根固柢， *(shì wèi shēn gēn gù dǐ,)*

9. **LONG LIFE** **FOR A LONG TIME** (long; of a specified duration) **LOOK AT** (regard; watch; inspect;) **OF** **ROAD** (way, principle; speak; think). 长生久视之道。 *(cháng shēng jiǔ shì zhī dào.)*

CHAPTER 60

Govern a big country as if boiling a small fish.
So that the way is present for all under heaven,
Its spirit is not magical.
Not only that its spirit is not magical,
Its magic does not hinder the people.
Not only that its magic does not hinder the people,
The wise person does not hinder the people.
Neither assists in hindering,
Therefore, each ascribes virtue to the other.

1. **RULE** (govern; order; peace; > government; cure; control) **BIG** (great; fully) **COUNTRY** **LIKE** (as if, seem) **BOIL** **SMALL** **FRESH** (bright; delicious; aquatic foods). 治大国若烹小鲜。 *(zhì dà guó ruò pēng xiǎo xiān.)*

2. **USE** (<v> take <p> according to; because of <adj> so as to <conj> and) **ROAD** (way, principle; speak; think) **ARRIVE** (be present) **LAND UNDER HEAVEN**, 以道莅天下， *(yǐ dào lì tiān xià,)*

3. **HIS** (its; their; they; that) **GHOST** (spirit; dirty trick; terrible> clever; smart) **NO** (not) **GOD** (supernatural; magical; smart). 其鬼不神。 *(qí guǐ bù shén.)*

4. **WRONG** (not conform to <infrml> must) **HIS** (its; their; they; that) **GHOST** (spirit; dirty trick; terrible> clever; smart) **NO** (not) **GOD** (supernatural; magical; smart), 非其鬼不神， *(fēi qí guǐ bù shén,)*

5. **HIS** (its; their; they; that) **GOD** (supernatural; magical; smart) **NO** (not) **WOUND** (develop an aversion to sth.; distress; hinder) **HUMAN** (man; people). 其神不伤人。 *(qí shén bù shāng rén.)*

6. **WRONG** (not conform to <infrml> must) **HIS** (its; their; they; that) **GOD** (spirit; mind; smart) **NO** (not) **WOUND** (develop an aversion to sth.; distress; hinder) **HUMAN** (man; people), 非其神不伤人， *(fēi qí shén bù shāng rén,)*

7. **SAGE** (holy; sacred) **HUMAN** (man; people) **ALSO** (too) **NO** (not) **WOUND** (develop an aversion to sth.; distress; hinder) **HUMAN** (man; people). 圣人亦不伤人。 *(shèng rén yì bù shāng rén.)*

8. **HUSBAND** (man) **TWO** (both; either) **NO** (not) **APPEARANCE** (<frml> assist_mutually) **WOUND** (develop an aversion to sth.; distress; hinder), 夫两不相伤， *(fū liǎng bù xiāng shāng,)*

9. **REASON** (cause; on purpose; hence) **VIRTUE** (moral character; heart) **HAND OVER** (give up; meet; join) **GO BACK TO** (return; give back to; come together) **HERE** (herein; (usu. negative questioning) how; why). 故德交归焉。 *(gù dé jiāo guī yān.)*

CHAPTER 61

The larger spreads below where all under heaven meet.
Of all under heaven,
    the female normally uses stillness to overcome the male.
Using stillness she supports the lower position.
For this reason, the larger,
    using the lower position, normally takes in the smaller,
The smaller, using the lower position, normally takes in the larger.
Hence, perhaps the low takes in, perhaps the low yet taken in.⊠
The larger only wishes concurrently to raise the people.
The smaller only wishes to join in the affairs of the people.
Both each satisfying the position they want,
The larger fittingly serves the lower position.

1. **BIG** (great; fully) **COUNTRY** (者) **BELOW** (down; under; lower; inferior) **FLOW** (drifting; spread; circulate), **LAND UNDER HEAVEN OF HAND OVER** (give up; meet; join). 大国者下流，天下之交。 *(dà guó zhě xià liú, tiān xià zhī jiāo.)*

2. **LAND UNDER HEAVEN OF FEMALE** (of some birds and animals), **FEMALE** (of some birds and animals) **ORDINARY** (normal; constant; often) **USE** (<v> take <p> according to; because of <adj> so as to <conj> and) **STILL** (quiet; calm) **VICTORY** (surpass; wonderful; be equal to) **MALE**. 天下之牝，牝常以静胜牡。 *(tiān xià zhī pìn, pìn cháng yǐ jìng shèng mǔ.)*

3. **USE** (<v> take <p> according to; because of <adj> so as to <conj> and) **STILL** (quiet; calm) **DO** (act; act as; serve as; be; mean; support) **BELOW** (down; under; lower; inferior). 以静为下。 *(yǐ jìng wéi xià.)*

4. **REASON** (cause; on purpose; hence) **BIG** (great; fully) **COUNTRY** **USE** (<v> take <p> according to; because of <adj> so as to <conj> and) **BELOW** (down; under; lower; inferior) **SMALL** **COUNTRY**, **STANDARD** (norm; rule > imitate; follow) **TAKE** (get; seek; adopt) **SMALL** **COUNTRY**. 故大国以下小国，则取小国。 *(gù dà guó yǐ xià xiǎo guó, zé qǔ xiǎo guó.)*

5. **SMALL** **COUNTRY** **USE** (<v> take <p> according to; because of <adj> so as to <conj> and) **BELOW** (down; under; lower; inferior) **BIG** (great; fully) **COUNTRY**, **STANDARD** (norm; rule > imitate; follow) **TAKE** (get; seek; adopt) **BIG** (great; fully) **COUNTRY**. 小国以下大国，则取大国。 *(xiǎo guó yǐ xià dà guó, zé qǔ dà guó.)*

6. **REASON** (cause; on purpose; hence) **PERHAPS** (or; either...or...; > someone) **BELOW** (down; under; lower; inferior) **USE** (<v> take <p> according to; because of <adj> so as to <conj> and) **TAKE** (get; seek; adopt), **PERHAPS** (or; either...or...; > someone) **BELOW** (down; under; lower; inferior) <conj.> **AND** (yet, but) **TAKE** (get; seek; adopt). 故或下以取，或下而取。 *(gù huò xià yǐ qǔ, huò xià ér qǔ.)*

7. **BIG** (great; fully) **COUNTRY** **MERELY** (however; only) **DESIRE** (wish; want; about to) **DOUBLE** (simultaneously) **RAISE** **DOMESTIC ANIMALS** **HUMAN** (man; people). 大国不过欲兼畜人。 *(dà guó bù guò yù jiān chù rén.)*

8. **SMALL** **COUNTRY** **MERELY** (however; only) **DESIRE** (wish; want; about to) **ENTER** (join; agree with) **MATTER** (affair; thing; involvement) **HUMAN** (man; people). 小国不过欲入事人。 *(xiǎo guó bù guò yù rù shì rén.)*

9. **HUSBAND** (man) **TWO** (both; either; some) (者) **EACH** (every; various; different) **GET** (obtain, gain > satisfied_need; must) **PLACE** **DESIRE** (wish; want; about to), 夫两者各得所欲 *(fū liǎng zhě gè dé suǒ yù)*

10. **BIG** (great; fully) (者) **SUITABLE** (appropriate; fitting; should) **DO** (act; act as; serve as; be; mean; support) **BELOW** (down; under; lower; inferior). 大者宜为下。 *(dà zhě yí wéi xià.)*

CHAPTER 62

The way of all things is profound and difficult to understand.
Of the perfect person,
    it is precious; of the imperfect person, it is protective.
Beautiful speech can bring worldly honor.
Beautiful behavior can augment people.
For people not good, why abandon them?
Hence, the son of heaven (emperor)
    establishes three commonalities,
Even though surrounded by jade and presented with horses,
Not equal to receiving the way.
Of old, why was this way so valued?
Was it not said that by using it one got what one sought.
By using it, one avoids the evils of hardship.
Hence, all under heaven value it.

1. **ROAD** (way, principle; speak; think) (者) **ALL THINGS ON EARTH OF PROFOUND** (difficult to understand> oersted). 道者万物之奥。 *(dào zhě wàn wù zhī ào.)*

2. **GOOD** (satisfactory) **HUMAN** (man; people) **OF TREASURE** (precious), **NO** (not) **GOOD** (satisfactory) **HUMAN** (man; people) **OF PLACE PROTECT** (maintain; preserve). 善人之宝，不善人之所保。 *(shàn rén zhī bǎo, bù shàn rén zhī suǒ bǎo.)*

3. **BEAUTIFUL** (good) **SPEECH** (word; say; talk) **CAN** (may) **MARKET** (city) **SENIOR** (respect; venerate). 美言可以市尊。 *(měi yán kě yǐ shì zūn.)*

4. **BEAUTIFUL** (good) **GO** (prevail; do; behavior; O.K.) **CAN** (may) **ADD** (plus; increase; augment) **HUMAN** (man; people). 美行可以加人。 *(měi xíng kě yǐ jiā rén.)*

5. **HUMAN** (man; people) **OF NO** (not) **GOOD** (satisfactory), **WHO** (why) **THROW AWAY** (discard; abandon) **OF HAVE** (exist). 人之不善，何弃之有。 *(rén zhī bù shàn, hé qì zhī yǒu.)*

6. **REASON** (cause; on purpose; hence) **STAND** (set up) **THE SON OF HEAVEN** (the emperor), **PLACE** (put; establish) **THREE** (more than two; several; many) **PUBLIC** (common; equitable; impartial), 故立天子、置三公， *(gù lì tiān zǐ, zhì sān gōng,)*

7. **THOUGH** (although) **HAVE** (exist) **ENCIRCLE** (arch; push) **PIECE OF JADE**   **USE** (<v> take <p> according to; because of <adj> so as to <conj> and) **EARLIER** (first) **A TEAM OF FOUR   HORSES**, 虽有拱璧以先驷马， *(suī yǒu gǒng bì yǐ xiān sì mǎ,)*

8. **NO** (not) **EQUAL TO** (not as good as; inferior to) **SIT** (take a sit; travel, have its back towards) **ADVANCE** (enter; receive; eat; take) **THIS   ROAD** (way, principle; speak; think). 不如坐进此道。 *(bù rú zuò jìn cǐ dào.)*

9. **ANCIENT** (age-old) **OF** <conj.> **SO** (therefore; as a result) **EXPENSIVE** (precious; noble) **THIS   ROAD** (way, principle; speak; think) (者) **WHO** (why). 古之所以贵此道者何。 *(gǔ zhī suǒ yǐ guì cǐ dào zhě hé.)*

10. **NO** (not) **SAY** (call; name) **BEG** (request; seek; try; demand) **USE** (<v> take <p> according to; because of <adj> so as to <conj> and) **GET** (obtain, gain > satisfied_need; must), 不曰：求以得， *(bù yuē, qiú yǐ dé,)*

11. **HAVE** (exist) **CRIME** (blame; pain; hardship) **USE** (<v> take <p> according to; because of <adj> so as to <conj> and) **EXCUSE** (exempt; avoid) **EVIL** (heretical; irregular; unhealthy environment)? 有罪以免邪？ *(yǒu zuì yǐ miǎn xié?)*

12. **REASON** (cause; on purpose; hence) **DO** (act; act as; serve as; be; mean; support) **LAND UNDER HEAVEN   EXPENSIVE** (precious; noble). 故为天下贵。 *(gù wéi tiān xià guì.)*

CHAPTER 63

Do without doing,
Be involved without being involved.
Taste without tasting.
Make the great small and the many few,
Respond to resentment using kindness.
Plan difficulty out from its easy.
Do the great out from its small.
All difficulties under heaven must arise from the easy.
All that is great under heaven must arise from the small.
Accordingly, the wise man, in the end, doesn't support greatness,
For this reason he is able to accomplish greatness.
The man that softly promises, certainly few trust.
The excessively easy, certainly excessively difficult.
Accordingly, the wise man, still of difficulty,
For this reason, in the end, without difficulty.

1. **DO** (act; act as; serve as; be; mean; support) **NOTHING** (without; not) **DO** (act; act as; serve as; be; mean; support), 为无为， *(wéi wú wéi.)*

2. **MATTER** (affair; thing; involvement) **NOTHING** (without; not) **MATTER** (affair; thing; involvement), 事无事， *(shì wú shì,)*

3. **TASTE** (flavor; smell; interest) **NOTHING** (without; not) **TASTE** (flavor; smell; interest). 味无味。 *(wèi wú wèi.)*

4. **BIG** (large; great; major) **SMALL** (little; petty; minor) **MANY** (much; more; excessive; too much) **FEW** (little, lack), 大小多少， *(dà xiǎo duō shǎo,)*

5. **REPORT** (announce; newspaper) **RESENTMENT** (blame; complain) **USE** (<v> take <p> according to; because of <adj> so as to <conj> and) **VIRTUE** (moral character; kindness, heart). 报怨以德。 *(bào yuàn yǐ dé.)*

6. **PICTURE** (drawing; plan; attempt; intent) **DIFFICULT** (hard; troublesome; put somebody into a difficult position; hardly possible; bad) **IN** (at, to, from, by, than, out of) **HIS** (its; their; they; that) **EASY** (amiable), 图难于其易， *(tú nán yú qí yì,)*

7. **DO** (act; act as; serve as; be; mean; support) **BIG** (large; great; major) **IN** (at, to, from, by, than, out of) **HIS** (its; their; they; that) **THIN** (in small particles; fine; careful). 为大于其细。 *(wéi dà yú qí xì.)*

8. **LAND UNDER HEAVEN** **DIFFICULT** (hard; troublesome; put sb. into a difficult position) **MATTER** (affair; thing; involvement) **CERTAINLY** (must) **DO** (make; rise; get up; write; compose; become) **IN** (at, to, from, by, than, out of) **EASY** (amiable). 天下难事必作于易。 *(tiān xià nán shì bì zuò yú yì.)*

9. **LAND UNDER HEAVEN** **BIG** (large; great; major) **MATTER** (affair; thing; involvement) **CERTAINLY** (must) **DO** (make; rise; get up; write; compose; become) **IN** (at, to, from, by, than, out of) **THIN** (in small particles; fine; careful). 天下大事必作于细。 *(tiān xià dà shì bì zuò yú xì.)*

10. <grm> **IS** (yes <frml> this; that) **USE** (<v> take <p> according to; because of <adj> so as to <conj> and) **SAGE** (holy; sacred) **HUMAN** (man; people) **END** (death; eventually; after all; whole; all) **NO** (not) **STAND FOR** (*wèi* <prep> support: for object, cause or purpose) **BIG** (large; great; major), 是以圣人终不为大， *(shì yǐ shèng rén zhōng bù wéi dà,)*

11. **REASON** (cause; on purpose; hence) **CAN** (be able to) **ACCOMPLISH** (become; result) **HIS** (its; their; they; that) **BIG** (large; great; major), 故能成其大。 *(gù néng chéng qí dà.)*

12. **HUSBAND** (man) **LIGHT** (softly) **PROMISE** (yes) **CERTAINLY** (must) **FEW** (scant; tasteless; widowed) **TRUE** (trust; faith; believe). 夫轻诺必寡信。 *(fū qīng nuò bì guǎ xìn.)*

13. **MUCH** (more; too many; excessive) **EASY** (amiable) **CERTAINLY** (must) **MUCH** (more; too many; excessive) **DIFFICULT** (hard; troublesome; put sb. into a difficult position), 多易必多难。 *(duō yì bì duō nán.)*

14.   <grm> **IS** (yes <frml> this; that) **USE** (<v> take <p> according to; because of <adj> so as to <conj> and) **SAGE** (holy; sacred) **HUMAN** (man; people) **JUST AS** (like; still; as if) **DIFFICULT** (hard; troublesome; put sb. into a difficult position) **OF**, 是以圣人犹难之， *(shì yǐ shèng rén yóu nán zhī,)*

15. **REASON** (cause; on purpose; hence) **END** (death; eventually; after all; whole; all) **NOTHING** (without; not) **DIFFICULT** (hard; troublesome; put sb. into a difficult position) **ALREADY** (indeed; really; how). 故终无难矣。 *(gù zhōng wú nán yǐ.)*

CHAPTER 64

Its peace easily manages, Its presence easily plans,
Its fragility easily melts, Its timeliness easily scatters,
Acts without existing, Governs without disorder.
A tree barely embraceable grows from a fine tip.
A terrace nine layers high rises from piled earth.
A thousand mile journey begins below the feet.
Of doing we fail, Of holding on we lose.

Taking this, the wise do nothing, hence never fail,
Hold nothing, hence never lose.
People in their affairs always accomplish some, yet fail.
Being as careful at the end as the beginning as a rule never fails.
Taking this, the wise person desires non desire,
And does not value difficult to obtain goods.
Learns non learning and turns around people's excesses,
As well as assists all things naturally, and never boldly act.

1. **HIS** (its; their; they; that) **PEACEFUL** (quiet; calm) **EASY** (amiable) **HOLD** (grasp; support), **HIS** (its; their; they; that) **HAVE NOT** (did not) **SIGN** (omen; portent, foretell) **EASY** (amiable) **STRATAGEM** (plan; work for; seek; plot; consult.) 其安易持，其未兆易谋。 *(qí ān yì chí, qí wèi zhào yì móu.)*

2. **HIS** (its; their; they; that) **FRAGILE** (brittle; crisp; clear > neat) **EASY** (amiable) **MELT**, **HIS** (its; their; they; that) **MINUTE** (tiny) **EASY** (amiable) **BREAK-UP** (come loose). 其脆易泮，其微易散。 *(qí cuì yì pàn, qí wēi yì sàn.)*

3. **DO** (act; act as; serve as; be; mean; support) **OF** **IN** (at, to, from, by, than, out of) **HAVE NOT** (did not) **HAVE** (exist), **RULE** (govern; order; peace; > government; control) **OF** **IN** (at, to, from, by, than, out of) **HAVE NOT** (did not) **IN A MESS** (disorder; chaos). 为之于未有，治之于未乱。 *(wéi zhī yú wèi yǒu, zhì zhī yú wèi luàn.)*

4. **SO BIG THAT ONE CAN JUST GET ONE'S ARMS AROUND** **OF** **TREE** (timber; wooden; coffin) **GIVE BIRTH TO** (grow; existence; life) **IN** (at, to, from, by, than, out of) **FINE LONG HAIR** (writing brush) **END** (nonessentials; dust). 合抱之木生于毫末。 *(hé bào zhī mù shēng yú háo mò.)*

5. **NINE** **LAYER** (tier; floor) **OF** **PLATFORM** (stage; terrace) **GET UP** (remove; pull; appear) **IN** (at, to, from, by, than, out of) **PILE UP** (accumulate; continuous; involve) **SOIL** (earth; land; ground; local; native; homemade; unenlightened; opium). 九层之台起于累土。 *(jiǔ céng zhī tái qǐ yú léi tǔ.)*

6. **A THOUSAND** li (a long distance) **OF** **GO** (travel, do, be current) **BEGINNING** (start> only then) **IN** (at, to, from, by, than, out of) **FOOT** (leg; enough; full; as much as) **BELOW** (down; under; lower; inferior). 千里之行始于足下。 *(qiān lǐ zhī xíng shǐ yú zú xià.)*

7. **DO** (act; act as; serve as; be; mean; support)(者) **BE DEFEATED** (lose; beat; fail; decay) **OF**, **HOLD** (manage; stick to, carry out; observe) (者) **LOSE** (miss; let slip; mistake) **OF**. 为者败之，执者失之。 *(wéi zhě bài zhī, zhí zhě shī zhī.)*

8. <grm> **IS** (yes <frml> this; that) **USE** (<v> take <p> according to; because of <adj> so as to <conj> and) **SAGE** (holy; sacred) **HUMAN** (man; people), **NOTHING** (without; not) **DO** (act; act as; serve as; be; mean; support) **REASON** (cause; on purpose; hence) **NOTHING** (without; not) **BE DEFEATED** (lose; beat; fail; decay), 是以圣人无为故无败 *(shì yǐ shèng rén wú wéi gù wú bài)*

9. **NOTHING** (without; not) **HOLD** (manage; stick to, carry out; observe) **REASON** (cause; on purpose; hence) **NOTHING** (without; not) **LOSE** (miss; let slip; mistake). 无执故无失。 *(wú zhí gù wú shī.)*

10. **THE PEOPLE** (civilian) **OF** **GO IN FOR** (be engaged in; deal with) **ORDINARY** (normal; constant; often) **IN** (at, to, from, by, than, out of) **SEVERAL** (some) **ACCOMPLISH** (become; result) <conj.> **AND** (yet, but) **BE DEFEATED** (lose; beat; fail; decay) **OF**. 民之从事常于几成而败之。 *(mín zhī cóng shì cháng yú jǐ chéng ér bài zhī.)*

11. **CAREFUL** (cautious) **END** (death; eventually; whole; all) **IN COMPLIANCE WITH** (like; as if; can compare with) **BEGINNING** (start> only then) **STANDARD** (norm; rule > imitate; follow) **NOTHING** (without; not) **BE DEFEATED** (lose; beat; fail) **MATTER** (affair; thing; involvement). 慎终如始则无败事。 *(shèn zhōng rú shǐ zé wú bài shì.)*

12.   \<grm> **IS** (yes \<frml> this; that) **USE** (\<v> take \<p> according to; because of \<adj> so as to \<conj> and) **SAGE** (holy; sacred) **HUMAN** (man; people) **DESIRE** (wish; want; about to) **NO** (not) **DESIRE** (wish; want; about to), 是以圣人欲不欲, *(shì yǐ shèng rén yù bù yù,)*

13. **NO** (not) **EXPENSIVE** (precious; noble) **HARD TO COME BY** (rare) **OF** **GOODS** (commodity; money; idiot). 不贵难得之货。*(bù guì nán dé zhī huò.)*

14. **STUDY** (imitate; knowledge) **NO** (not) **STUDY** (imitate; knowledge), **DUPLICATE** (turn around, answer, recover) **MANY** (numerous; crowd; multitude) **HUMAN** (man; people) **OF** **PLACE** **CROSS** (past; through; over; exceed), 学 不学，复众人之所过，*(xué bù xué, fù zhòng rén zhī suǒ guò,)*

15. **USE** (\<v> take \<p> according to; because of \<adj> so as to \<conj> and) **ASSIST** (complement; supplement) **ALL THINGS ON EARTH** **OF AT EASE** (natural; free from affectation) \<conj.> **AND** (yet, but) **NO** (not) **BOLD** (dare; be certain) **DO** (act; act as; serve as; be; mean; support). 以辅 万物之自然而不敢为。*(yǐ fǔ wàn wù zhī zì rán ér bù gǎn wéi.)*

CHAPTER 65

Of ancients adept in the way, none ever use it to enlighten people,
They will use it in order to fool them.
People are difficult to govern because they are too intelligent.
Therefore,
    using intelligence to govern the country injures the country.
Not using intelligence to govern the country blesses the country.
Know these both and investigate their patterns.
Always investigate the patterns.
That is called profound moral character(.)
Moral character, profound indeed, distant indeed!
To the outside world, contrary indeed.
Then, and only then, reaching great conformity.

1.   **ANCIENT** (age-old) **OF** **GOOD** (satisfactory; be adept in) **DO** (act; act as; serve as; be; mean; support) **ROAD** (way, principle; speak; think) (者), **WRONG** (not conform to \<infrml> must) **USE** (\<v> take \<p> according to; because of \<adj> so as to \<conj> and) **BRIGHT** (light; clear; open; honest; understand) **THE PEOPLE** (civilian), 古之善为 道者，非以明民，*(gǔ zhī shàn wéi dào zhě, fēi yǐ míng mín,)*

2.   **SUPPORT** (bring; handle, will> lead, command) **USE** (<v> take
<p> according to; because of <adj> so as to <conj> and) **FOOLISH**
(stupid; make a fool of; fool) **OF**. 将以愚之。 *(jiāng yǐ yú zhī.)*

3.   **THE PEOPLE** (civilian) **OF** **DIFFICULT** (hard; troublesome) **RULE** (govern;
order; peace; > government; control), **USE** (<v> take <p> according
to; because of <adj> so as to <conj> and) **HIS** (its; their; they; that)
WISDOM (intelligence, resourcefulness; wit) **MUCH** (more; too many;
excessive). 民之难治，以其智多。 *(mín zhī nán zhì, yǐ qí zhì duō.)*

4.   **REASON** (cause; on purpose; hence) **USE** (<v> take <p> according
to; because of <adj> so as to <conj> and) **WISDOM** (intelligence,
resourcefulness; wit) **RULE** (govern; order; peace; > government;
control) **COUNTRY**, **COUNTRY OF** **INJURE** (harm; murder> thief; sly;
deceitful). 故以智治国，国之贼。 *(gù yǐ zhì zhì guó, guó zhī zéi.)*

5.   **NO** (not) **USE**´(<v> take <p> according to; because of <adj> so as to <conj>
and) **WISDOM** (intelligence, resourcefulness; wit) **RULE** (govern; order;
peace; > government; control) **COUNTRY**, **COUNTRY OF** **GOOD FORTUNE**
(happiness). 不以智治国，国之福。 *(bù yǐ zhì zhì guó, guó zhī fú.)*

6.   **KNOW** (realize; tell) **THIS** **TWO** (both; either; some) (者), **ALSO**
(too) **CHECK** (examine; investigate; procrastinate) **TYPE** (style,
pattern). 知此两者，亦稽式。 *(zhī cǐ liǎng zhě, yì jī shì.)*

7.   **ORDINARY** (normal; constant; often) **KNOW** (realize;
tell) **CHECK** (examine; investigate; procrastinate) **TYPE**
(style, pattern), 常知稽式， *(cháng zhī jī shì,)*

8.   <grm> **IS** (yes <frml> this; that) **SAY** (call; name;
meaning; sense) **BLACK** (dark; profound) **VIRTUE** (moral
character; heart). 是谓玄德。 *(shì wèi xuán dé.)*

9.   **BLACK** (dark; profound) **VIRTUE** (moral character; heart) **DEEP** (difficult;
profound; intimate; dark) **ALREADY** (indeed; really; how), **FAR** (distant;
remote) **ALREADY** (indeed; really; how) **GIVE** (get along with <conj.>
and) **MATTER** (affair; thing; responsibility) **TURN OVER** (in an opposite
direction; in reverse; inside out) **ALREADY** (indeed; really; how). 玄德
深矣、远矣！与物反矣。 *(xuán dé shēn yǐ, yuǎn yǐ, yú wù fǎn yǐ.)*

10.   <adv.> **THEN** (after that; afterwards) **BE** (therefore, only then,
your) **TO** (until; > extremely; most) **BIG** (large; great; major)
IN THE SAME DIRECTION AS (with; along; arrange; suitable; in
sequence). 然后乃至大顺。 *(rán hòu nǎi zhì dà shun.)*

CHAPTER 66

The river and sea can serve as king for a hundred valleys,
Using to their adeptness in being below.
Hence, they can support a hundred valleys as king.
Accordingly, a wise person,
Desiring to be above the people must, using speech, be below.
Desiring to be ahead of the people must, using life, be behind.
Accordingly, a wise person,
Dwells above, yet the people are not weighed down,
Dwells ahead, yet the people are not impaired.
Accordingly,
  all under heaven cheerfully push forward, yet never tire.
Using such non contention,
Is the reason, under heaven, nothing can contend with it.

1.   **RIVER SEA** (big lake) **OF** <conj.> **SO** (therefore; as a result) **CAN** (be able
     to) **DO** (act; act as; serve as; be; mean; support) **HUNDRED** (numerous;
     all kinds of) **VALLEY** (grain) **KING** (grand; great)(者), 海之所以
     能为百谷王者， *(hǎi zhī suǒ yǐ néng wéi bǎi gǔ wáng zhě,)*

2.   **USE** (<v> take <p> according to; because of <adj> so as to <conj> and)
     HIS (its; their; they; that) **GOOD** (satisfactory; be adept in) **BELOW** (down;
     under; lower; inferior) **OF**, 以其善下之， *(yǐ qí shàn xià zhī,)*

3.   **REASON** (cause; on purpose; hence) **CAN** (be able to) **DO** (act; act as; serve
     as; be; mean; support) **HUNDRED** (numerous; all kinds of) **VALLEY** (grain)
     KING (grand; great). 故能为百谷王。 *(gù néng wéi bǎi gǔ wáng.)*

4.   <grm> **IS** (yes <frml> this; that) **USE** (<v> take <p> according
     to; because of <adj> so as to <conj> and) **SAGE** (holy; sacred)
     HUMAN (man; people) 是以圣人 *(shì yǐ shèng rén)*

5.   **DESIRE** (wish; want; about to) **UPPER** (higher; superior) **THE PEOPLE** (civilian),
     CERTAINLY (must) **USE** (<v> take <p> according to; because of <adj> so
     as to <conj> and) **SPEECH** (word; say; talk) **BELOW** (down; under; lower;
     inferior) **OF**. 欲上民，必以言下之。 *(yù shàng mín, bì yǐ yán xià zhī.)*

6.   **DESIRE** (wish; want; about to) **EARLIER** (first) **THE PEOPLE** (civilian),
     CERTAINLY (must) **USE** (<v> take <p> according to; because of <adj>
     so as to <conj> and) **BODY** (life; oneself; personally) **BACK** (after) **OF**.
     欲先民，必以身后之。 *(yù xiān mín, bì yǐ shēn hòu zhī.)*

89

7.   <grm> IS (yes <frml> this; that) USE (<v> take <p> according to; because of <adj> so as to <conj> and) SAGE (holy; sacred) HUMAN (man; people) 是以圣人 *(shì yǐ shèng rén)*

8.   GET ALONG (with sb., manage <frml > dwell; live_place) UPPER (higher; superior) <conj.> AND (yet, but) THE PEOPLE (civilian) NO (not) WEIGHT (heavy; important; deep), 处上而民不重, *(chǔ shàng ér mín bù chóng,)*

9.   GET ALONG (with sb., manage <frml > dwell; live_place) FRONT (forward; before) <conj.> AND (yet, but) THE PEOPLE (civilian) NO (not) EVIL (harm; calamity; impair; kill). 处前而民不害。 *(chǔ qián ér mín bù hài.)*

10.   <grm> IS (yes <frml> this; that) USE (<v> take <p> according to; because of <adj> so as to <conj> and) LAND UNDER HEAVEN HAPPY (cheerful, music) PUSH (shove; grind; cut) <conj.> AND (yet, but) NO (not) BE DISGUSTED WITH (be tired of; be satisfied). 是以天下乐推而不厌。 *(shì yǐ tiān xià lè tuī ér bù yàn.)*

11.   USE (<v> take <p> according to; because of <adj> so as to <conj> and) HIS (its; their; they; that) NO (not) CONTEND (vie; strive; argue), 以其不争, *(yǐ qí bù zhēng,)*

12.   REASON (cause; on purpose; hence) LAND UNDER HEAVEN NO ONE (nothing) CAN (be able to) PARTICIPATE IN (give; get along with, and) OF CONTEND (vie; strive; argue). 故天下莫能与之争。 *(gù tiān xià mò néng yú zhī zhēng.)*

CHAPTER 67

Under heaven, all say my way is great resembling nothing.
Man is only great by reason of resembling nothing.
If it resembled anything,
    long ago indeed, it would trifle as would man.
I have three treasures of which I hold and protect:
The first I call kindness,
The second I call thrift,
The third I call not daring to act before all under heaven.
Being kind, I can be brave,
Being thrifty, I can spread out,
Not daring to act before all under heaven acts,
    I can succeed steadily.
Now, abandoning kindness for daring,
Abandoning thrift for spreading out,
Abandoning the rear for the front,
Death!
Man using kindness normally succeeds,
    according to rules admittedly.
Heaven leads in rescuing using kindness of defense.

1. **LAND UNDER HEAVEN** **ALL** (each and every) **SAY** (call; name; meaning; sense) **I** (we) **ROAD** (way, principle; speak; think) **BIG** (large; great; major) **SIMILAR** (like; seem; appear) **NO** (not) **RESEMBLE** (be like). 天下皆谓我道大似不肖。 *(tiān xià jiē wèi wǒ dào dà sì bù xiào.)*

2. **HUSBAND** (man) **ONLY** (alone) **BIG** (large; great; major) **REASON** (cause; on purpose; hence) **SIMILAR** (like; seem; appear) **NO** (not) **RESEMBLE** (be like). 夫唯大故似不肖。 *(fū wéi dà gù sì bù xiào.)*

3. **LIKE** (as if, seem> if; > you) **RESEMBLE** (be like), **FOR A LONG TIME** (long; of a specified duration) **ALREADY** (indeed; really; how)! **HIS** (its; their; they; that) **THIN** (thin and soft; fine; trifling) **ALSO** (too) **HUSBAND** (man). 若肖，久矣！其细也夫。 *(ruò xiào, jiǔ yǐ! qí xì yě fū.)*

4. **I** (we) **HAVE** (exist) **THREE** (more than two; several; many) **TREASURE** (precious) **HOLD** (grasp; support) <conj.> **AND** (yet, but) **PROTECT** (maintain; preserve) **OF**: 我有三宝持而保之： *(wǒ yǒu sān bǎo chí ér bǎo zhī:)*

5. **ONE** **SAY** (call; name) **KIND** (loving; mother), 一曰慈， *(yī yuē cí,)*

6. **TWO** **SAY** (call; name) **THRIFTY** (frugal), 二曰俭， *(èr yuē jiǎn,)*

7. **THREE** **SAY** (call; name) **NO** (not) **BOLD** (dare; be certain) **DO** (act; act as; serve as; be; mean; support) **LAND UNDER HEAVEN** **EARLIER** (first, ancestor). 三曰不敢为天下先。 *(sān yuē bù gǎn wéi tiān xià xiān.)*

8. **KIND** (loving; mother) **REASON** (cause; on purpose; hence) **CAN** (be able to) **BRAVE** (valiant), 慈故能勇， *(cí gù néng yǒng,)*

9. **THRIFTY** (frugal) **REASON** (cause; on purpose; hence) **CAN** (be able to) **WIDE** (vast; expand; spread), 俭故能广， *(jiǎn gù néng guǎng,)*

10. **NO** (not) **BOLD** (dare; be certain) **DO** (act; act as; be; mean) **LAND UNDER HEAVEN** **EARLIER** (first, ancestor) **REASON** (cause; hence) **CAN** (be able to) **ACCOMPLISH** (become; result) **SHARP WEAPON** (good tool) **OLDER** (develop; increase_long). 不敢为天下先故能成器长。 *(bù gǎn wéi tiān xià xiān gù néng chéng qì cháng.)*

11. **MODERN** (present-day; now) **GIVE UP** (abandon; give alms) **KIND** (loving; mother) **JUST** (for the time being; even; both...and....) **BRAVE** (valiant), 今舍慈且勇， *(jūn shè cí qiě yǒng,)*

12. **GIVE UP** (abandon; give alms) **THRIFTY** (frugal) **JUST** (for the time being; even; both...and....) **WIDE** (vast; expand; spread), 舍俭且广， *(shè jiǎn qiě guǎng,)*

13. **GIVE UP** (abandon; give alms) **BACK** (after) **JUST** (for the time being; even; both...and....) **EARLIER** (first, ancestor), 舍后且先， *(shè hòu qiě xiān,)*

14. **DIE** (extremely; deadly; fixed; rigid) **ALREADY** (indeed; really; how)! 死矣！ *(sǐ yǐ!)*

15. **HUSBAND** (man) **KIND** (loving; mother) **USE** (take; so as to_and) **WAR** (fight) **STANDARD** (norm; rule > imitate; follow) **VICTORY** (success; surpass), **USE** (<v> take <p> according to; because of <adj> so as to <conj> and) **RULES** (regulations) **SOLID** (firm> originally > admittedly; no doubt). 夫慈以战则胜，以守则固。 *(fū cí yǐ zhàn zé shèng, yǐ shǒu zé gù.)*

16. **SKY** (heaven; day; season; nature; God) **SUPPORT** (bring; handle, will> lead) **RESCUE** (save; help) **OF** **USE** (<v> take <p> according to; because of <adj> so as to <conj> and) **KIND** (loving; mother) **DEFEND** (guard; protect) **OF**. 天将救之以慈卫之。 *(tiān jiāng jiù zhī yǐ cí wèi zhī.)*

CHAPTER 68

One adept in being a scholar is not militant.
One adept in battle is not enraged.
One adept in victory over enemies does not participate.
This is called the moral character of not contending.
This is called employing the ability of the people.
This is called matching of Nature's ancient utmost.

1. **GOOD** (satisfactory; be adept in) **DO** (act; act as; serve as; be;
   mean; support) **BACHELOR** (scholar; person) (者) **NO** (not) **MILITARY**
   (valiant, fierce). 善为士者不武。 *(shàn wéi shì zhě bù wǔ.)*

2. **GOOD** (satisfactory; be adept in) **WAR** (warfare; battle; fight) (者) **NO**
   (not) **ANGER** (rage, fury). 善战者不怒。 *(shàn zhàn zhě bù nù.)*

3. **GOOD** (satisfactory; be adept in) **VICTORY** (success; surpass; be superior
   to) **ENEMY** (oppose, match, equal) (者) **NO** (not) **TAKE PART IN** (give, get
   along with, help> and). 善胜敌者不与。 *(shàn shèng dí zhě bù yú.)*

4. **GOOD** (satisfactory; be adept in) **USE** (apply <frml> hence) **HUMAN** (man;
   people) (者) **DO** (act; act as; serve as; be; mean; support) **OF BELOW** (under;
   lower; inferior). 善用人者为之下。 *(shàn yòng rén zhě wéi zhī xià.)*

5. <grm> **IS** (yes <frml> this; that) **SAY** (call; name; meaning;
   sense) **NO** (not) **CONTEND** (vie; strive; argue) **OF VIRTUE** (moral
   character; heart). 是谓不争之德。 *(shì wèi bù zhēng zhī dé.)*

6. <grm> **IS** (yes <frml> this; that) **SAY** (call; name; meaning;
   sense) **USE** (apply <frml> hence) **HUMAN** (man; people) **OF POWER**
   (strength, ability). 是谓用人之力。 *(shì wèi yòng rén zhī lì.)*

7. <grm> **IS** (yes <frml> this; that) **SAY** (call; name; meaning; sense)
   JOIN IN MARRIAGE (mate (animals), mix, match, deserve) **SKY** (heaven;
   day; season; nature; God) **ANCIENT** (age-old) **OF EXTREME** (pole,
   utmost). 是谓配天古之极。 *(shì wèi pèi tiān gǔ zhī jí.)*

CHAPTER 69

Those who use weapons have a saying:
We dare not act as hosts, but act as visitors.
We dare not advance an inch, but withdraw a foot.
This is called going without going.
Grabbing without an arm.
Casting aside without opposing.
Taking charge without weapons.
Of misfortunes, none is greater than rashly opposing.
Rashly opposing nearly lost me treasure.
Therefore contending militantly, adds sorrow to victory.

1. **USE** (apply <frml> hence) **WEAPONS** (private; army) **HAVE** (exist)
    SPEECH (word; say; talk): 用兵有言： *(yòng bīng yǒu yán:)*

2. **I** (we) **NO** (not) **BOLD** (dare; be certain) **DO** (act; act as; serve as;
    be; mean; support) **HOST** (owner) <conj.> **AND** (yet, but) **DO** (act;
    act as; serve as; be; mean; support) **VISITOR** (traveler; customer).
    吾不敢为主而为客。 *(wú bù gǎn wéi zhǔ ér wéi kè.)*

3. **NO** (not) **BOLD** (dare; be certain) **ADVANCE** (enter; receive; eat;
    take) **AN INCH** (3 cm, very short; small) <conj.> **AND** (yet, but)
    BACK (retreat; cause to move back; remove) **A FOOT** (33 cm., (foot,
    ruler). 不敢进寸而退尺。 *(bù gǎn jìn cùn ér tuì chǐ.)*

4. <grm> **IS** (yes <frml> this; that) **SAY** (call; name; meaning; sense)
    GO (travel, do, be current) **NOTHING** (without; not) **GO** (travel,
    do, be current). 是谓行无行。 *(shì wèi xíng wú xíng.)*

5. **REJECT** (resist; seize; grab; push up one's sleeves) **NOTHING**
    (without; not) **ARM** (upper arm). 攘无臂。 *(rǎng wú bì.)*

6. **THROW** (toss; cast; throw away; cast aside) **NOTHING** (without;
    not) **ENEMY** (oppose, match, equal). 扔无敌。 *(rēng wú dí.)*

7. **HOLD** (manage; stick to, carry out; observe) **NOTHING** (without;
    not) **WEAPONS** (private; army). 执无兵。 *(zhí wú bīng.)*

8. **MISFORTUNES** (disaster; ruin) **NO ONE** (nothing) **BIG** (large; great;
    major) **IN** (at, to, from, by, than, out of) **LIGHT** (gently, rashly) **ENEMY**
    (oppose, match, equal). 祸莫大于轻敌。 *(huò mò dà yú qīng dí.)*

9. **LIGHT** (gently, rashly) **ENEMY** (oppose, match, equal) **A SMALL TABLE**
    (nearly, almost_how many; some) **OBSEQUIES** (funeral_lose) **I**
    (we) **TREASURE**. 轻敌几丧吾宝。 *(qīng dí jǐ sàng wú bǎo.)*

10. **REASON** (cause; on purpose; hence) **RESIST** (contend with, be a match for) **WEAPONS** (private; army) **EACH OTHER** (mutually assist) **ADD** (plus, increase, put in) **SORROW** (grief; mourning; pity) (者) **VICTORY** (success; surpass; be superior to) **ALREADY** (indeed; really; how). 故 抗兵相加哀者胜矣。 *(gù kàng bīng xiāng jiā āi zhě shèng yǐ.)*

CHAPTER 70

Our words are very easy to know, very easy to do.
Under heaven none can know, none can do.
Speech has its faction, involvement has its sovereign.
Man alone is without knowing, and because of this I don't know.
Knowing self is rare, following self is noble.
Because of this,
    the sage wears coarse cloth and yearns for noble character.

1. **I** (we) **SPEECH** (word; say; talk) **VERY** (extremely; more than) **EASY** (amiable) **KNOW** (realize; tell), **VERY** (extremely; more than) **EASY** (amiable) **GO** (travel, do, be current). 吾言甚易知、甚易行。 *(wú yán shén yì zhī, shén yì xíng.)*

2. **LAND UNDER HEAVEN** **NO ONE** (nothing) **CAN** (be able to) **KNOW** (realize; tell), **NO ONE** (nothing) **CAN** (be able to) **GO** (travel, do, be current). 天 下莫能知、莫能行。 *(tiān xià mò néng zhī, mò néng xíng.)*

3. **SPEECH** (word; say; talk) **HAVE** (exist) **ANCESTOR** (clan; purpose, faction), **MATTER** (affair; involvement; work; responsibility) **HAVE** (exist) **MONARCH** (sovereign, supreme ruler; gentleman). 言有宗、事有君。 *(yán yǒu zōng, shì yǒu jūn.)*

4. **HUSBAND** (man) **ONLY** (alone) **NOTHING** (without; not) **KNOW** (realize; tell), <grm> **IS** (yes <frml> this; that) **USE** (<v> take <p> according to; because of <adj> so as to <conj> and) **I** (we; self) **NO** (not) **KNOW** (realize; tell). 夫唯无知，是以我不知。 *(fū wéi wú zhī, shì yǐ wǒ bù zhī.)*

5. **KNOW** (realize; tell) **I** (we; self) (者) **HOPE** (rare, scarce, uncommon), **STANDARD** (norm; rule > imitate; follow) **I** (we; self) **EXPENSIVE** (precious; noble). 知我者希，则我者贵。 *(zhī wǒ zhě xī, zé wǒ zhě guì.)*

6. <grm> **IS** (yes <frml> this; that) **USE** (<v> take <p> according to; because of <adj> so as to <conj> and) **SAGE** (holy; sacred) **HUMAN** (man; people) **BY** (indicates passive-voice clauses; <literary> to cover; to meet with) **COARSE CLOTH** (dull brown) **MIND** (keep in mind, yearn for) **JADE** (of a person: pure; fair). 是以圣人被褐怀玉 *(shì yǐ shèng rén pī hè huái yù.)*

CHAPTER 71

Realizing I don't' know is better;
    not knowing this knowing is dis-ease.
Man alone faults this dis-ease; this so as not to be ill.
The sacred person is not ill, taking his dis-ease as illness.
Man alone has this dis-ease;
    this is because to him there is no illness.

1. **KNOW** (realize; tell) **NO** (not) **KNOW** (realize; tell) **UPPER** (up; higher; superior; better), **NO** (not) **KNOW** (realize; tell) **KNOW** (realize; tell) **DISEASE** (fault; defect). 知不知上，不知知病。 *(zhī bù zhī shàng, bù zhī zhī bìng.)*

2. **HUSBAND** (man) **ONLY** (alone) **DISEASE** (fault; defect) **DISEASE** (fault; defect), <grm> **IS** (yes <frml> this; that) **USE** (<v> take <p> according to; because of <adj> so as to <conj> and) **NO** (not) **DISEASE** (fault; defect). 夫唯病病，是以不病。 *(fū wéi bìng bìng, shì yǐ bù bìng.)*

3. **SAGE** (holy; sacred) **HUMAN** (man; people) **NO** (not) **DISEASE** (fault; defect), **USE** (<v> take <p> according to; because of <adj> so as to <conj> and) **HIS** (its, he, it, that; such) **DISEASE** (fault; defect) **DISEASE** (fault; defect). 圣人不病，以其病病。 *(shèng rén bù bìng, yǐ qí bìng bìng.)*

4. **HUSBAND** (man) **ONLY** (alone) **DISEASE** (fault; defect) **DISEASE** (fault; defect), <grm> **IS** (yes <frml> this; that) **USE** (<v> take <p> according to; because of <adj> so as to <conj> and) **NO** (not) **DISEASE** (fault; defect). 夫唯病病，是以不病。 *(fū wéi bìng bìng, shì yǐ bù bìng.)*

CHAPTER 72

When the people don't fear power,
Normally great power arrives.
Without meddling with their dwelling place,
Without detesting their existence.
Man alone doesn't detest,
Because of this not detested.
Because of this the wise person,
Knows himself without seeing himself.
Loves himself without valuing himself.
Hence, gets rid of one and seeks the other.

1. **THE PEOPLE** (civilian) **NO** (not) **FEAR** (respect) **POWER** (impressive strength), 民不畏威， *(mín bù wèi wēi,)*

2. **STANDARD** (norm; rule > imitate; follow) **BIG** (large; great; major) **POWER** (impressive strength) **TO** (until; > extremely; most). 则大威至。 *(zé dà wēi zhì.)*

3. **NOTHING** (without; not) **BE IMPROPERLY FAMILIAR WITH** **HIS** (her; its; that; such) **PLACE** **DWELL** (live; store up), 无狎其所居， *(wú xiá qí suǒ jū,)*

4. **NOTHING** (without; not) **BE DISGUSTED WITH** (detest; be bored with)) **HIS** (her; its; that; such) **PLACE** **GIVE BIRTH TO** (grow; existence; life). 无厌其所生。 *(wú yàn qí suǒ shēng.)*

5. **HUSBAND** (man) **ONLY** (alone, yes) **NO** (not) **BE DISGUSTED WITH** (detest; be bored with)), 夫唯不厌， *(fū wéi bù yàn,)*

6. \<grm\> **IS** (yes \<frml\> this; that) **USE** (\<v\> take \<p\> according to; because of \<adj\> so as to \<conj\> and) **NO** (not) **BE DISGUSTED WITH** (detest; be bored with)). 是以不厌。 *(shì yǐ bù yàn.)*

7. \<grm\> **IS** (yes \<frml\> this; that) **USE** (\<v\> take \<p\> according to; because of \<adj\> so as to \<conj\> and) **SAGE** (holy; sacred) **HUMAN** (man; people). 是以圣人 *(shì yǐ shèng rén)*

8. **SELF** (oneself; certainly) **KNOW** (realize; inform; knowledge) **NO** (not) **SELF** (oneself; certainly) **SEE** (appear, become visible). 自知不自见。 *(zì zhī bù zì jiàn.)*

9. **SELF** (oneself; certainly) **LOVE** (like; treasure) **NO** (not) **SELF** (oneself; certainly) **EXPENSIVE** (precious; noble). 自爱不自贵。 *(zì ài bù zì guì.)*

10. **REASON** (cause; on purpose; hence) **GO** (remove) **THAT** (those; the other; another) **TAKE** (get; seek; adopt) **THIS**. 故去彼取此。 *(gù qù bǐ qǔ cǐ.)*

CHAPTER 73

Brave certainty rules in killing
Brave hesitation rules in living
These both either benefit or harm
Nature's ruthlessness, who knows its cause.
Nature's way never contending, yet adept in victory.
Never speaking, yet adept in answering
Never sent for, yet there from the beginning.
Simply so[1], yet adept in planning
<u>Nature's net is</u> vast and thin, yet never misses.

---
[1]   Line 8's first character is missing in the standard text. Fortunately it exists in the

1. **BRAVE** (valiant) **IN** (at, to, from, by, than, out of) **BOLD** (dare; be certain) **STANDARD** (norm; rule > imitate; follow) **KILL** (weaken). 勇于敢则杀。 *(yǒng yú gǎn zé shā.)*

2. **BRAVE** (valiant) **IN** (at, to, from, by, than, out of) **NO** (not) **BOLD** (dare; be certain) **STANDARD** (norm; rule > imitate; follow) **LIVE** (alive; living). 勇于不敢则活。 *(yǒng yú bù gǎn zé huó.)*

3. **THIS** **TWO** (both; either; some) (者) **PERHAPS** (or; either...or...; > someone) **SHARP** (favorable; advantage; profit) **PERHAPS** (or; either...or...; > someone) **EVIL** (injurious; do harm to; impair; kill). 此两者或利或害。 *(cǐ liǎng zhě huò lì huò hài.)*

4. **SKY** (heaven; day; season; nature; God) **OF** **PLACE** (indicate passive construction, agent of action) **LOATHE** (dislike; hate_fierce; ferocious) **WHO** (which, what) **KNOW** (realize; inform; knowledge) **HIS** (her; its; that; such) **REASON** (cause; on purpose; hence). 天之所恶孰知其故。 *(tiān zhī suǒ ě shú zhī qí gù.)*

5. **SKY** (heaven; day; season; nature; God) **OF** **ROAD** (way, principle; speak; think) **NO** (not) **CONTEND** (vie; strive; argue) <conj.> **AND** (yet, but) **GOOD** (satisfactory; be adept in) **VICTORY** (success; surpass; be superior to). 天之道不争而善胜。 *(tiān zhī dào bù zhēng ér shàn shèng.)*

6. **NO** (not) **SPEECH** (word; say; talk) <conj.> **AND** (yet, but) **GOOD** (satisfactory; be adept in) **ANSWER** (respond; agree (to do sth.); should). 不言而善应。 *(bù yán ér shàn yīng.)*

7. **NO** (not) **CALL TOGETHER** (convene; summon) <conj.> **AND** (yet, but) **FROM THE BEGINNING** (in the first place; originally). 不召而自来。 *(bù shào ér zì lái.)*

8. **ONE** (single; odd; only; alone; simple) **RIGHT** (correct; so; like that) <conj.> **AND** (yet, but, however) **GOOD** (satisfactory; be adept in) **STRATAGEM** (plan; scheme; plot). 单然而善谋。 *(chán rán ér shàn móu.)*

9. **SKY** (heaven; day; season; nature; God) **NET** (network; catch with a net) **EXTENSIVE** (vast) **DREDGE** (thin; sparse; distant) <conj.> **AND** (yet, but) **NO** (not) **LOSE** (miss; let slip; fail). 天网恢恢疏而不失。 *(tiān wǎng huī huī shū ér bù shī.)*

Mang Wang Tui text, so I used it here. The next character, 然, is not in the Mang Wand Tui but is in the standard. Both characters 'harmonize' so I used both.

CHAPTER 74

When people don't respect death, why use the fear of death?
If we could cause people to always respect death and be in wonder,
And we caught and killed them, who would dare?
Always have the killer manage the killing,
A man taking the place of the killer killing,
Is said to be taking the place of the great craftsman.
A man taking the place of the great craftsman
  rarely never hurts his own hands.

1. **THE PEOPLE** (civilian) **NO** (not) **FEAR** (respect) **DIE** (extremely; deadly; fixed; rigid), **HOW** (why, to no avail) **USE** (<v> take <p> according to; because of <adj> so as to <conj> and) **DIE** (extremely; deadly; fixed; rigid) **FEAR** (dread) **OF**. 民不畏死，奈何以死惧之。*(mín bù wèi sǐ, nài hé yǐ sǐ jù zhī.)*

2. **LIKE** (as if, seem> if; > you) **SEND** (tell sb. to do sth.; use; cause; enable) **THE PEOPLE** (civilian) **ORDINARY** (normal; constant; often) **FEAR** (respect) **DIE** (extremely; deadly; fixed; rigid), <conj.> **AND** (yet, but) **DO** (act; act as; serve as; be; mean; support) **STRANGE** (rare; surprise) (者)[1], 若使民常畏死，而为奇者，*(ruò shǐ mín cháng wèi sǐ, ér wéi jī zhě,)*

3. **I** (we) **NEED** (must, get > satisfied > be ready > catch) <conj.> **AND** (yet, but) **KILL** (weaken) **OF**, **WHO** **BOLD** (dare; be certain). 吾得执而杀之，孰敢。*(wú dé zhí ér shā zhī, shú gǎn.)*

4. **ORDINARY** (normal; constant; often; always) **HAVE** (exist) **TAKE CHARGE OF** (attend to; manage) **KILL** (weaken) (者) **KILL** (weaken). 常有司杀者杀。*(cháng yǒu sī shā zhě shā.)*

5. **HUSBAND** (man) **ERA** (generation> be in place of; acting) **TAKE CHARGE OF** (attend to; manage) **KILL** (weaken) (者) **KILL** (weaken), 夫代司杀者杀，*(fū dài sī shā zhě shā,)*

6. <grm> **IS** (yes <frml> this; that) **SAY** (mean) **ERA** (generation> be in place of; acting) **BIG** (large; great; major) **CRAFTSMAN**. 是谓代大匠□。*(shì wèi dài dà jiàng [].)*

7. **HUSBAND** (man) **ERA** (generation> be in place of; acting) **BIG** (large; great; major) **CRAFTSMAN** (artisan) (者), **HOPE** (rare) **HAVE** (exist) **NO** (not) **WOUND** (hurt; hinder) **HIS** (her; its; that; such) **HAND** (have in one's hand; hold; handy) **ALREADY** (indeed; really; how). 夫代大匠□者，希有不伤其手矣。*(fū dài dà jiàng [] zhě, xī yǒu bù shāng qí shǒu yǐ.)*

---

[1] 者 (zhě) used after an adjective or verb as a substitute for a person or a thing.

CHAPTER 75

The people are hungry because taxes eat much,
That is why they are hungry.
The people are difficult to govern because of their expectations,
That is why they are difficult to govern.
The people take death lightly because they seek life's flavor,
That is why they take death lightly.
Only the man without use for life is worthy of a noble life.

1. **THE PEOPLE** (civilian) **OF** **BE HUNGRY** (starve; famish; famine; crop failure) **USE** (\<v\> take \<p\> according to; because of \<adj\> so as to \<conj\> and) **HIS** (her; its; that; such) **UPPER** (up; higher; superior) **EAT** (food; feed) **TAX** **OF** **MUCH** (more; too many; excessive), 民之饥以其上食税之多， *(mín zhī jī yǐ qí shàng shí shuì zhī duō,)*

2. \<grm\> **IS** (yes \<frml\> this; that) **USE** (\<v\> take \<p\> according to; because of \<adj\> so as to \<conj\> and) **BE HUNGRY** (starve; famish; famine; crop failure). 是以饥。 *(shì yǐ jī.)*

3. **THE PEOPLE** (civilian) **OF** **DIFFICULT** (hard; troublesome) **RULE** (govern; order; peace; > government; control) **USE** (\<v\> take \<p\> according to; because of \<adj\> so as to \<conj\> and) **HIS** (her; its; that; such) **UPPER** (up; higher; superior) **OF** **HAVE** (exist) **DO** (act; act as; serve as; be; mean; support), 民之难治以其上之有为， *(mín zhī nán zhì yǐ qí shàng zhī yǒu wéi,)*

4. \<grm\> **IS** (yes \<frml\> this; that) **USE** (\<v\> take \<p\> according to; because of \<adj\> so as to \<conj\> and) **DIFFICULT** (hard; troublesome) **RULE** (govern; order; peace; > government; control). 是以难治。 *(shì yǐ nán zhì.)*

5. **THE PEOPLE** (civilian) **OF LIGHT** (softly, un-important, gently) **DIE** (extremely; deadly; fixed; rigid) **USE** (\<v\> take \<p\> according to; because of \<adj\> so as to \<conj\> and) **HIS** (her; its; that; such) **BEG** (request; seek; try; demand) **GIVE BIRTH TO** (grow; existence; life) **OF** **THICK** (deep; large; generous; rich in flavor), 民之轻死以其求生之厚， *(mín zhī qīng sǐ yǐ qí qiú shēng zhī hòu,)*

6. \<grm\> **IS** (yes \<frml\> this; that) **USE** (\<v\> take \<p\> according to; because of \<adj\> so as to \<conj\> and) **LIGHT** (softly, un-important, gently) **DIE** (extremely; deadly; fixed; rigid). 是以轻死。 *(shì yǐ qīng sǐ.)*

7.   HUSBAND (man) ONLY (alone) NOTHING (without; not) USE (<v> take
     <p> according to; because of <adj> so as to <conj> and) GIVE
     BIRTH TO (grow; existence; life) DO (act; act as; serve as; be; mean;
     support) (者), <grm> IS (yes <frml> this; that) VIRTUOUS (worthy,
     able) IN (at, to, from, by, than, out of) EXPENSIVE (precious; noble)
     GIVE BIRTH TO (grow; existence; life). 夫唯无以生为者，是贤
     于贵生。 (fū wéi wú yǐ shēng wéi zhě, shì xián yú guì shēng.)

CHAPTER 76

Of people, existence weak and delicate,
Their death hard and unyielding.
Of plants, existence soft and yielding,
Their death withered and haggard.
Therefore the hard and unyielding, of death only,
The weak and fragile, of life only.
The use of powerful weapons, normally destroys,
The strong tree normally breaks.
The big and powerful dwell below,
The weak and fragile dwell above.

1.   HUMAN (man; people) OF   GIVE BIRTH TO (grow; existence; life) ALSO
     (either) WEAK (delicate), 人之生也柔弱， (rén zhī shēng yě róu ruò,)

2.   HIS (her; its; that; such) DIE (extremely; deadly; fixed; rigid) ALSO
     (too) HARD (firm; strong; firmly; resolutely) STRIVE (strong; powerful;
     better_unyielding). 其死也坚强。 (qí sǐ yě jiān qiáng.)

3.   GRASS (careless; hasty) TREE (timber; wooden; coffin) OF   GIVE BIRTH TO
     (grow; existence; life) ALSO (too) SOFT (supple; yielding) FRAGILE (brittle;
     crisp; clear > neat), 草木之生也柔脆， (cǎo mù zhī shēng yě róu cuì,)

4.   HIS (her; its; that; such) DIE (extremely; deadly; fixed; rigid)
     WITHERED (haggard). 其死也枯槁。 (qí sǐ yě kū gǎo.)

5.   REASON (cause; on purpose; hence) HARD (firm; strong; firmly;
     resolutely) STRIVE (strong; powerful; better_unyielding) (者) DIE
     (extremely; deadly; fixed; rigid) OF   ON FOOT (only; follower; believer;
     person), 故坚强者死之徒， (gù jiān qiáng zhě sǐ zhī tú,)

6.   WEAK (delicate) (者) GIVE BIRTH TO (grow; existence; life) OF   ON FOOT (only;
     follower; believer; person). 柔弱者生之徒。 (róu ruò zhě shēng zhī tú.)

7. <grm> **IS** (yes <frml> this; that) **USE** (<v> take <p> according to; because of <adj> so as to <conj> and) **WEAPONS** (private; army) **STRIVE** (strong; powerful; better_unyielding) **STANDARD** (norm; rule > imitate; follow) **EXTINGUISH** (submerge; destroy), 是以兵强则灭， *(shì yǐ bīng jiàng zé miè,)*

8. **TREE** (timber; wooden; coffin) **STRIVE** (strong; powerful; better_unyielding) **STANDARD** (norm; rule > imitate; follow) **BREAK** (lose; bend; turn back_ turn over). 木强则折。 *(mù jiàng zé shé.)*

9. **BIG AND POWERFUL** (formidable) **GET ALONG** (with sb., manage <frml > dwell; live_place) **BELOW** (down; under; underneath; lower; inferior), 强大处下， *(qiáng dà chǔ xià,)*

10. **WEAK** (delicate) **GET ALONG** (with sb., manage <frml > dwell; live_place) **UPPER** (higher; superior). 柔弱处上。 *(róu ruò chǔ shàng.)*

CHAPTER 77

The way of nature is like a stretching bow.
The high restrains, the lower lifts.
The surplus decreases, the insufficient benefits.
The way of nature decreases surplus yet benefits the insufficient.
The way of man, as a rule however,
    decreases the insufficient so as to give to the surplus.
Who can have a surplus and give to all under heaven?
Only those who have the way.
The holy person uses this to serve, yet does not rely on,
Meritorious deeds result, yet not dwelled within.
Such absence of desire appears able and virtuous - how odd!.

1. **SKY** (heaven; day; season; nature; God) **OF** **ROAD** (way, principle; speak; think) **HIS** (her; its; that; such) **JUST AS** (like; still; as if) **OPEN** (spread; stretch) **BOW-SHAPED** **TAKE PART IN** (give, get along with, help> and). 天之道其犹张弓与。 *(tiān zhī dào qí yóu zhāng gōng yú.)*

2. **TALL** (high; above the average) (者) **RESTRAIN** (repress; curb) **OF**, **BELOW** (down; under; underneath; lower; inferior) (者) **LIFT** (raise; hold up; act; deed; move) **OF**. 高者抑之，下者举之。 *(gāo zhě yì zhī, xià zhě jǔ zhī.)*

3. **HAVE** (exist) **EXTRA** (surplus; after <frml> I) (者) **DECREASE** (lose; damage> sarcastic> mean; shabby) **OF** **NO** (not) **FOOT** (leg; enough; full; as much as) (者) **REPAIR** (fill; supply; nourish> benefit) **OF**. 有余者损之，不足者补之。 *(yǒu yú zhě sǔn zhī, bù zú zhě bǔ zhī.)*

4. **SKY** (heaven; day; season; nature; God) **OF** **ROAD** (way, principle; speak; think), **DECREASE** (lose; damage> sarcastic> mean; shabby) **HAVE** (exist) **EXTRA** (surplus; after <frml> I) <conj.> **AND** (yet, but) **REPAIR** (fill; supply; nourish> benefit) **NO** (not) **FOOT** (leg; enough; full; as much as). 天之道，损有余而补不足。 *(tiān zhī dào, sǔn yǒu yú ér bǔ bù zú.)*

5. **HUMAN** (man; people) **OF** **ROAD** (way, principle; speak; think), **STANDARD** (norm; rule > imitate; follow) **NO** (not) **RIGHT** (correct; so; like that> but), **DECREASE** (lose; damage> sarcastic> mean; shabby) **NO** (not) **FOOT** (leg; enough; full; as much as) **USE** (<v> take <p> according to; because of <adj> so as to <conj> and) **GIVE** (receive; esteem; believe in; wait upon) **HAVE** (exist) **EXTRA** (surplus; after <frml> I). 人之道，则不然，损不足以奉有余。 *(rén zhī dào, zé bù rán, sǔn bù zú yǐ fèng yǒu yú.)*

6. **WHO** (which; what) **CAN** (be able to) **HAVE** (exist) **SURPLUS** (spare; remaining; beyond <frml> I) **USE** (<v> take <p> according to; because of <adj> so as to <conj> and) **GIVE** (receive; esteem; believe in; wait upon) **LAND UNDER HEAVEN**, 孰能有余以奉天下， *(shú néng yǒu yú yǐ fèng tiān xià,)*

7. **ONLY** (alone) **HAVE** (exist) **ROAD** (way, principle; speak; think) (者). 唯有道者。 *(wéi yǒu dào zhě.)*

8. <grm> **IS** (yes <frml> this; that) **USE** (<v> take <p> according to; because of <adj> so as to <conj> and) **SAGE** (holy; sacred) **HUMAN** (man; people) **DO** (act; act as; serve as; be; mean; support) <conj.> **AND** (yet, but) **NO** (not) **RELY ON** (depend on), 是以圣人为而不恃， *(shì yǐ shèng rén wéi ér bù shì,)*

9. **MERIT** (achievement) **ACCOMPLISH** (become; result) <conj.> **AND** (yet, but) **NO** (not) **GET ALONG** (with sb., manage <frml > dwell; live_place). 功成而不处。 *(gōng chéng ér bù chù.)*

10. **HIS** (her; its; that; such) **NO** (not) **DESIRE** (wish; want; about to) **SEE** (appear, become visible) **VIRTUOUS** (worthy, able) **EVIL** (heretical; irregular; unhealthy environment)! 其不欲见贤邪！ *(qí bù yù jiàn xián xié!)*

CHAPTER 78

Under heaven, nothing is more yielding and weak than water.
Yet for attacking the hard and strong nothing can surpass,
Because of its nothing-ness and ease.
Of weakness and loss through death, superior to strength.
Of flexible, superior to firm
Under heaven, none do not know; none can do.
Because of this, the holy person says,
Receiving the humiliation of the country
     means mastering the country.
Receiving the country's misfortune serves all under heaven great.
Straight and honest words seem inside out.

1. **LAND UNDER HEAVEN** **NO ONE** (nothing) **WEAK** (delicate) **IN**
   (at, to, from, by, than, out of) **WATER** (river; lakes, seas). 天
   下莫柔弱于水。 *(tiān xià mò róu ruò yú shuǐ.)*

2. <conj.> **AND** (yet, but) **ATTACK** **HARD** (firm; strong; firmly; resolutely)
   STRIVE (strong; powerful; better_unyielding) (者), **NO ONE** (nothing)
   OF **CAN** (be able to) **VICTORY** (success; surpass; be superior to). 而攻
   坚强者，莫之能胜， *(ér gōng jiān qiáng zhě, mò zhī néng shèng,)*

3. **USE** (take; because of; so as to; and) **HIS** (her; its; that; such) **NOTHING**
   (without; not) **USE** (<v> take <p> according to; because of <adj> so as to
   <conj> and) **EASY** (amiable) **OF**. 以其无以易之。 *(yǐ qí wú yǐ yì zhī.)*

4. **WEAK** (feeble; young> lose through death) **OF** **VICTORY**
   (success; surpass; be superior to) **STRIVE** (strong; powerful;
   better_unyielding), 弱之胜强， *(ruò zhī shèng jiàng.)*

5. **SOFT** (supple; yielding) **OF** **VICTORY** (success; surpass; be superior to)
   FIRM (strong; indomitable, just). 柔之胜刚。 *(róu zhī shèng gāng.)*

6. **LAND UNDER HEAVEN** **NO ONE** (none, nothing) **NO** (not) **KNOW** (realize; inform;
   knowledge) **NO ONE** (none, nothing) **CAN** (be able to) **GO** (travel, do, be
   current). 天下莫不知莫能行。 *(tiān xià mò bù zhī mò néng xíng.)*

7. <grm> **IS** (yes <frml> this; that) **USE** (<v> take <p> according to;
   because of <adj> so as to <conj> and) **SAGE** (holy; sacred) **HUMAN**
   (man; people) **SAY** (cloud), 是以圣人云， *(shì yǐ shèng rén yún,)*

8. **RECEIVING** (accept; suffer; endure; bear) **COUNTRY** **OF** **DIRTY** (humiliation)
   <grm> **IS** (yes <frml> this; that) **CALL** (meaning) **THE COUNTRY** **HOST** (master,
   owner). 受国之垢是谓社稷主。 *(shòu guó zhī gòu shì wèi shè jì zhǔ.)*

9. **RECEIVING** (accept; suffer; endure; bear) **COUNTRY** **OMINOUS** (inauspicious) <grm> **IS** (yes <frml> this; that) **DO** (act; act as; serve as; be; mean; support) **LAND UNDER HEAVEN** **KING** (monarch; great). 受国不祥
是为天下王。 *(shòu guó bù xiáng shì wéi tiān xià wáng.)*

10. **STRAIGHT** (situated in the middle; honest) **SPEECH** (word; say; talk) **LIKE** (seem; as if) **TURN OVER** (in an opposite direction; inside out; return, on the contrary). 正言若反。 *(zhēng yán ruò fǎn.)*

CHAPTER 79

With great resentment must exist lingering resentment.
Such peace, passable, serves perfectly.
That is because the wise person holds this queer contract,
Yet doesn't punish the people.
Having kindness takes charge of the contract,
Not having kindness take charge of the penetration.
Nature's way is without match,
Constantly helping the charitable person.

1. **GENTLE** (together with; and) **BIG** (large; great; major) **RESENTMENT** (blame; complain) **CERTAINLY** (must) **HAVE** (exist) **EXTRA** (surplus; remaining; after) **RESENTMENT** (blame; complain). 和
大怨必有余怨。 *(hé dà yuàn bì yǒu yú yuàn.)*

2. **PEACEFUL** (quiet; calm) **CAN** (may <informal> passable; not bad) **THINK** (believe; consider that) **GOOD** (satisfactory; be adept in, perfect). 安可以为善。 *(ān kě yǐ wéi shàn.)*

3. <grm> **IS** (yes <frml> this; that) **USE** (<v> take <p> according to; because of <adj> so as to <conj> and) **SAGE** (holy; sacred) **HUMAN** (man; people) **HOLD** (manage; stick to, carry out; observe) **LEFT** (east; heretical; wrong; different) **ENGRAVE** (carve; agree; contract), 是以圣人执左契， *(shì yǐ shèng rén zhí zuǒ qì,)*

4. <conj.> **AND** (yet, but) **NO** (not) **DUTY** (responsibility) **IN** (at, to, from, by, than, out of) **HUMAN** (man; people). 而不责于人。 *(ér bù zé yú rén.)*

5. **HAVE** **VIRTUE** (moral character; mind; kindness) **TAKE CHARGE OF** (attend to; manage) **ENGRAVE** (carve; contract; deed; agree; get along well), 有德司契， *(yǒu dé sī qì,)*

6. **NOTHING** (nil; not have; without) **VIRTUE** (moral character; heart; mind; kindness) **TAKE CHARGE OF** (attend to; manage) **THOROUGH** (penetrating). 无德司彻。 *(wú dé sī chè.)*

7. **SKY** (heaven, nature; God) **ROAD** (way, path, speak) **NOTHING** (nil; without; not) **PARENT** (relative; match; intimate), 天道无亲， *(tiān dào wú qīn,)*

8. **ORDINARY** (normal; constant) **GIVE** (offer; help; and, together with) **PHILANTHROPIST** (charitable person; well doer). 常与善人。*(cháng yú shàn rén.)*

CHAPTER 80

Small country, few people.
Enable the existence of various tools, yet never need them.
Enable the people attach importance to death,
    yet not travel around.
Although there exists boats and carriages,
    there is no place to ride them.
Although there exists weapons, there is no place to deploy them.
Enable the people to again use the knotted rope.
Find their food sweet, their clothes beautiful.
Peaceful in their lives, happy in their customs.
Neighboring countries mutually seen in the distance,
Of chicken and dog sounds mutually heard.
People until death not mutually come and go.

1. **SMALL** (little; minor) **COUNTRY** (state, nation) **FEW** (scant; tasteless; widowed) **PEOPLE**. 小国寡民。*(xiǎo guó guǎ mín.)*

2. **SEND** (employ; enable) **HAVE** (exist) **ASSORTED** (varied, miscellaneous; ten) **ELDEST BROTHER** (uncle) **OF TOOL** (ware; capacity) <conj.> **AND** (yet, but) **NOT NEED**. 使有什伯之器而不用。*(shǐ yǒu shén bó zhī qì ér bù yòng.)*

3. **SEND** (employ; enable) **PEOPLE HEAVY** (important; value; deep; heavy; attach importance to) **DEATH** <conj.> **AND** (yet, but) **NO** (not) **FAR** (distant) **MOVE FROM ONE PLACE TO ANOTHER**. 使民重死而不远徙。*(shǐ mín chóng sǐ ér bù yuǎn xǐ.)*

4. **ALTHOUGH HAVE** (exist) **BOAT CARRIAGE** (territory; public) **NIL** (without) **PLACE RIDE** (take advantage of <frml> multiply) **OF**. 虽有舟舆无所乘之。*(suī yǒu zhōu yú wú suǒ chéng zhī.)*

5. **ALTHOUGH HAVE** (exist) **FIRST** (armor) **WEAPONS NIL** (without) **PLACE LAY OUT** (put on display) **OF**. 虽有甲兵无所陈之。*(suī yǒu jiǎ bīng wú suǒ chén zhī.)*

6. **SEND** (employ; enable) **PEOPLE** **DUPLICATE** (recover; resume; again) **TIE** (knit; knot) **ROPE** <conj.> **AND** (yet, but) **USE** **OF**. 使民复结绳而用之。 *(shǐ mín fù jiē shéng ér yòng zhī.)*

7. **SWEET** **THEIR** **FOOD**, **BEAUTIFUL** (good) **THEIR** **CLOTHES** (dress). 甘其食、美其服、 *(gān qí shí, měi qí fú,)*

8. **PEACEFUL** (quiet; tranquil; calm) **THEIR** **DWELL** (live, residence), **HAPPY** (enjoy) **THEIR** **CUSTOM** (convention; common; secular). 安其居、乐其俗。 *(ān qí jū, lè qí sú.)*

9. **NEIGHBOR** (neighboring; near; adjacent) **COUNTRY** (state, nation) **EACH OTHER** (mutually) **GAZE INTO THE DISTANCE** (look over; call on; visit), 邻国相望, *(lín guó xiāng wàng,)*

10. **CHICKEN** **DOG** **OF** **SOUND** (voice; make a sound) **EACH OTHER** (mutually) **HEAR** (news; story; well-known). 鸡犬之声相闻。 *(jī quǎn zhī shēng xiāng wén.)*

11. **PEOPLE** **TO** (until; extremely; most) **OLD** (of long standing; tough; always) **DIE** (extremely; implacable) **NO** (not) **EACH OTHER** (mutually) **COME AND GO** (contact; dealings; intercourse). 民至老死不相往来。 *(mín zhì lǎo sǐ bù xiāng wǎng lái.)*

CHAPTER 81

True speech isn't beautiful
Beautiful speech isn't true.
Expertise doesn't debate.
Debate isn't expertise.
Knowing isn't wealth
Wealth doesn't know.
The holy person doesn't accumulate.
Already, considers people's personal healing his own.
Already, so as to support people's personal healing more.
Nature's way benefits, and yet doesn't harm.
The holy person's way acts, and yet doesn't contend.

1. **TRUE** (trust; word) **SPEECH** (word) **NO** (not) **BEAUTIFUL** (pretty; good). 信言不美。 *(xìn yán bù měi.)*

2. **BEAUTIFUL** (pretty; good) **SPEECH** (word) **NO** (not) **TRUE** (trust; word). 美言不信。 *(měi yán bù xìn.)*

3. **GOOD** (kind; be expert in; be adept in) (者) **NO** (not) **ARGUE** (dispute; debate). 善者不辩。 *(shàn zhě bù biàn.)*

4. **ARGUE** (dispute; debate) (者) **NO** (not) **GOOD** (kind; be expert in; be adept in). 辩者不善。 *(biàn zhě bù shàn.)*

5. **KNOW** (realize; be aware of) (者) **NO** (not) **RICH** (abundant; plentiful; win; gain). 知者不博。 *(zhī zhě bù bó.)*

6. **RICH** (abundant; plentiful; win; gain) (者) **NO** (not) **KNOW** (realize; be aware of). 博者不知。 *(bó zhě bù zhī.)*

7. **SAGE** (holy; sacred) **HUMAN** (man; people) (者) **NO** (not) **AMASS** (store up; accumulate). 圣人不积。 *(shèng rén bù jī.)*

8. **ALREADY** (<conj.> since; both... and...) **THINK** (consider) **HUMAN** (man; people) **ONESELF** (personal) **HEAL** (recover; become; well; better) **HAVE** (exist). 既以为人己愈有。 *(jì yǐ wéi rén jǐ yù yǒu.)*

9. **ALREADY** (<conj.> since; both... and...) **USE** (<v> take <p> according to; because of <adj> so as to <conj> and) <conj.> **GIVE** (get along with; support <conj.> and; together with) **HUMAN** (man; people) **ONESELF** (personal) **HEAL** (recover; become; well; better) **MORE** (excessive). 既以与人己愈多。 *(jì yǐ yú rén jǐ yù duō.)*

10. **SKY** (heaven; weather; nature) **OF WAY SHARP** (benefit, advantage, profit) <conj.> **AND** (yet, but) **NO** (not) **EVIL** (harm; destructive). 天之道利而不害。 *(tiān zhī dào lì ér bù hài.)*

11. **SAGE** (holy; sacred) **HUMAN** (man; people) **OF WAY DO** (act; serve as; be, mean; support) <conj.> **AND** (yet, but) **NO** (not) **CONTEND** (argue). 圣人之道为而不争。 *(shèng rén zhī dào wéi ér bù zhēng.)*

Commentary[1]

FORMAT ISSUES

The *italicized phrases* are from my translations on the preceding pages. Most of the SMALL CAPED words and phrases are links to D.C. Lau's translation. Links to the Internet or to other posts I've made are in this form. To read these commentaries (1 -81) and follow those links, go to Centertao.org/tao-te-ching/carl.

CORRELATIONS

The journey that the death of my brother launched in me finally culminated in the "**correlations**" twenty years later. I often refer to these in my commentaries. I find the correlation process an even more succinct way of getting beyond the 'language barrier' than the Tao Te Ching. To learn more about this process, go to Centertao.org/essays/correlations.

1.

Here I am again, back at chapter one. I comment on each chapter as I cycled through the Tao Te Ching. My view deepens a bit each time, which goes to show how important the 'eye of the beholder' really is in understanding it. As I see it, one's intuitive knowing is key to whatever cognitive understanding one is able to ponder or express.

It is helpful to remember that even the most authentic translations carry interpretive and commentary baggage from the intervening millennia when it was 'originally written.' When was it originally written? Or more likely, wasn't it derived from a oral transmission dating far back into prehistory. This is just another reason why it is essential to realize that 'the eye of the beholder' is the major bridge to understanding.

---

1   I've written so much commentary over the years, that this time around I intended to post only short (and hopefully pithy) observations. However, as you will see, that plan soon fell apart. Perhaps next time... On the other hand, chapter 1 suffered from excessive California casual, so I replaced it with my most recent take on it. Yep, I see a second edition already on the way..

Normally without desire and *normally having desire* are two sides of a complementary coin. In a very real way, the more I throw myself at one, the more that energizes the other side. Naturally, this is very hard to write about or describe. *Without desire and having desire* feel so opposite. The opposites we sense are hoodwinks of our biology. Neurons make mountains out of molecular molehills. The most practical thing I can say here is how being partial to one side merely encourages the other side to ramp up its reaction.

Speaking of reaction: Can you see how Newton's "for every action, there is an equal and opposite reaction" applies to so much more than physics. Personally, I notice giving to one side sets up a war zone within. I contend with myself. My ideal of what should be so battles against what is so. The ideals I cooked up for how to improve my life always backfire in the end... except my ideal to downplay my ideals. Paradoxically, that works beautifully just as chapter 1 suggests.

The name possible to express runs counter to the constant name. Without description, the universe began. Our practice of labeling (naming) things we observe in the world create a schism, which rips us from the whole. One name begins two, begets three and to on to infinity... it is without end or resolution. That means without peace..

2.

I find that insight comes not from any answers that a translation (or anything else) offers, but rather from the questions it (or experience) evokes. Questions, puzzlement, mystery all turn the light of Consciousness on, while answers just put it to sleep. That's all right though; sleep feels good too.

Of course, as this chapter suggests, answers and questions *give birth to each other*. In light of this, how shall I proceed? Sit as loose to life as possible is the advice this chapter gives. If both sides of everything are so intimately intertwined (inseparable) holding out for one side or the other feels like an unrelenting struggle. Therefore, *considering this, the wise person manages without doing anything...* This defies common sense naturally. Yet, it is the only way that actually works. I'd paraphrase it this *give birth to each other* process as '*All under heaven realize common sense as common sense, there is folly already*'.

3.

When my mind goes blank, I'm tempted to look back at how I (or another) interpreted a chapter. I've learned, however, to take a deep breath, just wait, and let 'IT COME TO ME NATURALLY'. I've found that I am always happier with my most recent 'take' than anything previous, which helps makes trusting this contemporaneous approach to the Tao Te Ching easier. Besides, this approach surely suits any attempt to deal with *the indescribable teaching*. (That's my excuse and I'm sticking to it.) Come to think of it, this approach also suits any attempt to deal with life... 'the indescribable experience'!

I prefer using *aspirations* rather than will. *Aspirations* arise from a future thinking ability highly developed in humans. Our *aspirations* become the idealistic laden fantasies to which we cling. Or as they say, "the best laid plans..." We perpetually leap forward to *aspirations* in lieu of '*returning to observe the origin*'. The illusion is so powerful it takes *forever* to realize the promise is never realized, even if and when we realize an *aspiration*. The promise we feel (nature's biological hoodwink) is that we will be happy once we satiate our desire. The Taoist (and Buddhist) view sees it otherwise.

D.C. Lau uses 'will' instead in his translation. 'Will' though is far more mysterious in my view. Animals have 'will'. Perhaps 'will' is another name for the survival instinct. We can survive and prosper without *aspirations*, but not without 'will'.

Oh there is so much that begs Comment in this chapter! But I KNOW WHEN TO STOP AND MEET NO DANGER ... right?

4.

I suppose the phrase *the way flushes* is another way to express the idea of 'letting go'. It is good to have another way to say that. 'Let go' has become a little worn out - in my mind anyway. Besides that, what a beautiful way to put it! *Flush it!*

When did the idea of 'less is more' come into popular usage? Probably, as our culture became cluttered and FULL TO THE BRIM BY with material (i.e., things as well as knowledge).

Subdue that sharpness… etc., speaks to me about dealing with the 'death hold' life places on consciousness. Biology needs us to be sharp enough to differential this *dust* from that *dust*. The downside of that is becoming trapped in the differences - this is good *dust*, that is bad *dust*. Yet, to paraphrase Shakespeare, *dust* by any other name is still *dust* (although, I doubt that is what he was driving at). Note: The *same as that dust* here is also KNOWN AS MYSTERIOUS SAMENESS.

Finally, there is a hint here about something I've come to take very seriously. Namely, not to trust anything I THINK THAT I KNOW. In tracing back the cause and effect of anything of which I'm aware, I ultimately end in an IMAGE THAT IS WITHOUT SUBSTANCE. I cherish the freedom OF NOT KNOWING ANYTHING. Although, I admit it feels a little weird. I suspect my biology wants it otherwise. Well, it has had decades to have its way, now it is 'my' turn. Whose turn?

5.

I use this and chapter 2 (i.e., BEAUTIFUL, UGLY, GOOD, BAD) as 'tell' chapters. How a translation deals with them tells me how true to 'the tao' they are. The views expressed in both fly in the face of humanistic values. The God idea appeals to people for 'he' gives the *impartial* cold universe a warm benevolent face lift. 'He' also gives us a stand-up FATHER figure to follow. God makes a perfect tribal elder. 'He' is benevolent and a champion of *goodness* and *beauty*.

That's enough sarcasm already, and how *unlike keeping to the middle*. On the other hand, a fellow has got to have some fun. Taoist views certainly aren't easy to swallow for anyone who feels a need to choose sides, cherish dogma, or believe anything really.

6.

'*The entrance of the profound female*' brings to my mind a sense of what preceded the big bang. What was before something? *Nothing*. Not just nothing, but a *great way resembling nothing*. The 'cool' thing about this ('cool' <u>corrlates</u> with mystery) is that 'it' is still here. I can't imagine consciousness not sensing that most fundamental reality, yet I can't imagine biology evolving a creature's ability to be aware of this mystery, at least consciously. What I see in religion – all religion – is a symptom of our underlying consciousness of *the profound female*, yet also a more mundane and socially relevant expression of the mystery we sense. A so called 'taoist' point of view, as expressed in the Tao Te Ching, is a valiant attempt to snuggle up to that mystery.

It is in that spirit, the attempt to get closer to the root
of reality, that its terse and obscure turn of phrase finds
the greatest value. Mull it over. Let the mind sit on it,
and like an egg something will hatch eventually.

7.

Here again we see the emotionally confounding truth of
how we only really 'get' what we 'give up'. Christ put it this
way: 'Whosoever shall seek to save his life shall lose it; and
whosoever shall lose his life shall preserve it.' We (and all
life) feels an innate need to hold on, to contend, yet we can
only KNOW CONTENTMENT when we let go. A harmonious
life rests in the delicate balance between competition
and cooperation with ourselves, others, and nature.

Scripture is mostly biased towards the cooperation side of
the equation. I think, however, not because cooperation
is the greater *virtue*. Rather, civilization's core purpose

has always been to tip the scales in our favor vis-à-vis
our competition with nature. Thus, balance for humanity
requires tipping the scales in favor of cooperation in order to
merely return us to the middle — the happy middle. All that
stands in our way is our species' exceptional *cleverness*.

8.

Also, *water is somewhat like the way* in that it *serve the lower
position*. Given our hierarchical biology (nature), the lower
position is also a *place the multitude loathe to dwell*. That
is, unless everyone is down there to keep us company.

Why do we so easily become ungrounded and complicate the
simple? Personally, it always comes down to biting off more
than I can chew. Just spiting 'it' out works well, it is just bringing
myself to spit 'it' out that's difficult. Of course, that's all right
for EVEN THE SAGE TREATS SOME THINGS AS DIFFICULT. If that is
true for the sage, doesn't that let everyone else off the hook?

Now for a look at those rules of thumb:

•   *In being, good is earth*: I could also read that as 'being
grounded is good'. The foundation is most important. If that is
wobbly everything built upon it inherits that instability. That
is why I finally had to examine the words with which I think
(see correlations). Of course, now everything is wobbly 😊

•   *In intention, good is depth and benevolence:* The actual
Chinese word here, *xin* (心), translates as mind, emotion, heart,
feeling, intention, core, etc. I wonder if we don't tend to put
much more stock in 'thinking' than 'feeling'? As I see it, it is
the 'feelings' at our core that directs and drives our 'thinking'.
Benevolent emotions results in benevolent thoughts and
actions. Disturbed emotions result in disturbed thoughts and
actions. Who determines the emotions we feel? Personally,
I've never decided to feel a particular emotion, emotions
well up from deep inside and visit my awareness. However,
I do have a hand in fanning or dampening those flames.

- *In speech, good is truth:* I know (viscerally) that truth works best. I reckon it is the promise of short-term gain that pushes us to bend the truth. In the end, the unintended consequences of that are long-term loss. That's a BY-PATH as I see it. I much prefer the other way: short-term loss, with the 'unintended consequence' of long-term gain. Now, that's a buy low - sell high strategy that works!

- *In honesty, good is order:* Be honest up to the point where order is impaired. Then be silent. The Japanese are very skilled in this, which often drives Westerns nuts. As for me, I've found this advice exceptionally useful.

- *In work, good is ability:* As my mother always said, "I don't care what you do, just do it well". Ability comes from paying as close attention to the work I'm doing at the moment. That ties right in with this last point.

- *In action, good is present:* Being present, moment to moment makes all action sacred action. The "Bhagavad Gita" refers to this as 'consecrated action'. It is the core principle in yoga. 'Yoking' one's attention (presence of mind, watchfulness, mindfulness, etc.) to the task at hand. Personally, this is my holy grail of consciousness. Talk about biting off more than I can chew!

9.

Why do we feel the need to *hold surplus, maintain a fighting spirit (vigor), keep treasures to fill a room*, and chalk up *meritorious deeds?* All these fit a common M.O. (modus operandi) - an unremitting quest for perfection. Why? It is as though we are driven to fill an essentially bottomless pit; a VOID we don't feel is bottomless. On the other hand, when we feel the full emptiness of the 'perfect' moment there is nothing left to do or get, and no where to go. We are *content*; the 'TASK IS ACCOMPLISHED'.

So, *holding on* (and the rest) appears to be symptomatic of what we currently feel missing. Many are the ways to fill this personal void: food, sex, work, rest, friends, enemies, music, silence, art, collecting, sports, and travel. Rather than saying, 'idle hands are the devil's workshop', we should say 'empty hands are the devil's workshop'. The deeper the emptiness feels, the stronger the drive to fill it. Ironically, the more that *emptiness* is integrated in our life, the less driven to fill it we feel. I suppose you could say you become the emptiness. To paraphrase Tat Tvam Asi (That Thou Art), 'I am the void; the void is I'.

Personally, it helps knowing that this process is natural and no part needs fixing. *It is the way of nature.* In addition, it helps knowing that ALL THE MYRIAD CREATURES IN THE WORLD are in this 'ordeal of life' together. Whoopee, it's the party of life and *everything* is invited! Like any party, it has its high points and low ones. As I realize that, '*Knowing to stop*' seems to come easier. Although, I'm not really sure it has anything to do with realization. After all, the same preference for *stillness* occurs in all animals as they age.

10.

Loaded down with life, can you leave with nothing reminds me of advice Jesus gave: "Lay not up for yourselves treasures upon earth, where moth and rust doth corrupt, and where thieves break through and steal. But lay up for yourselves treasures in heaven, where neither moth nor rust doth corrupt, and where thieves do not break through nor steal. For where your treasure is, there will your heart be also".

The last sentence points to underlying causes in my view. Here, 'where your heart is' determines what treasures pull you. I suppose most would agree with that, and yet I often hear folks blame the 'treasure'. Clinging to treasure is a symptom of 'where the heart is'. The treasure isn't the cause, it's the effect. So, what causes the heart to be where it is at? Do we choose that? Every example I can recall suggests an emphatic 'no way!' Rather, it is weakness, or perhaps the fear of weakness, that drives us to hang on, to *give birth and have;* to *act and depend on;* to *be in charge and rule,* and the rest. In other words, WEAKNESS IS THE MEANS THE WAY EMPLOYS; in our case, the fear of weakness does

116

the trick. The master puppeteer, Mother Nature (MYSTERIOUS FEMALE) sure knows how to pull our strings to get life done.

Given most, if not all, of this natural process is beyond our control, why discuss it? I've found that the more I realize it is beyond my control, the easier it becomes to model THAT WHICH IS NATURALLY SO. It is an ultimate irony; only by accepting my helplessness can I *see life as flawless*; only then can I truly be who I am; only then can I avoid CONTENDING with ideals of who I should be. Although, by discussing any of this leads to the ideal of how 'it' could be. Irony upon irony, I suppose it's a wash in the end.

11.

The first three lines introduce the principle and the fourth brings it home: *'Hence, of having what is thought favorable, of nothing think as the useful.'* Appreciating the fundamental *the virtue of 'less'* is a profound challenge. We are innately (instinctively, biologically) drawn to the 'SOMETHINGS' in life. We VALUE LIFE over death, SUPERIOR or inferior, MERIT over inadequacy – in other words survival and success. Likewise, we fear failure; we want to go directly to success. We buy lottery tickets.

I find that recognizing and even embracing the 'failures and mistakes' part of life's journey makes life EASIER TO UNDERSTAND AND EASIER TO PUT INTO PRACTICE. Contending with the inevitable *spirit of the valley*, on the other hand, simply increases the difficulty. Ironically, the desire to avoid difficulty leads to difficulty. In losing I gain, in gaining I lose. Only *of the nothing think as the useful*. Now, that's what I call true justice.

12.

Our mind's *eye* gives us a superior ability to solve problems. Ironically, the source of some of our greatest problems originates in our mind's *eye*! Our expectations channel what we expect to see; our expectations drive what we think we see. Like a horse wearing blinders to avoid being spooked by things moving in its peripheral vision, conforming to cultural norms helps us avoid being spooked by what exists 'outside the box'.

This is no accident. Cultural 'blinders' are vital for large populations of people to maintain group identity, a sense of shared cultural connection. All the *blind, deaf,* hobbled and *crazy* effects are the price we pay (the trade-off, the unintended consequences). Of course, this results in some 'positive' feedback. In other words, the *blind, deaf,* hobbled and *crazy* effects we feel often narrow our cultural blinders even further. We become neurotic. To undo that damage, *the wise person acts for the belly, not the eye.*

Acting for the belly, however, need not mean renouncing those *tastes, colors, sounds, goods hard to come by*, etc. These are actually symptoms rather than causes. Why we desire the *tastes, colors, sounds, goods hard to come by* is the deeper question.

Again, we feel safer in the solidarity shared norms make possible. This physiological culture fortress keeps the wilderness at bay, initially. The downside of any fortress is that it also serves as an excellent prison. The final irony: The more we want to escape its walls, the higher the walls become. Bottom line: *With desire choosing anything, of doing I see no satisfied end.* HAVING TOO MANY DESIRES for the safety and comfort that these *five* promise become the prison. Escape is simple: *Taking this, the wise person desires non desire, And does not value difficult to obtain goods.*

Now, this begs the question... how? As they say, nature abhors a vacuum. You can't just be *without desire so as to observe its wonder,* now can you? You must replace the *five tastes, colors, sounds, goods hard to come by* with 'something else'. Alas, only by letting go of what we cling to can make room for that 'something else' for which we yearn. Usually our life's circumstances bring about the '*Loss through death, of the way 'it' uses'* required to make room. In the meantime, there is always, '*Devote effort to emptiness, sincerely watch stillness.*'

13.

I've read research that documents how both *gain* and *loss* stress the nervous system. In other words, change is stressful regardless of whether it is change we like or not. This has its limits of course; losing one's leg in an accident must certainly be more stressful than winning the lottery. Although, over the long run, one's life would likely suffer either way for lottery winners often fair poorly, physiologically speaking. However, given the choice we couldn't help but choose the lottery over the leg. Even so, I become increasingly aware of the 'equal nature' of *gain and loss, favor and disgrace* as the years roll by. This is life's *'very easy to know, very easy to do'* yet *none can know, none can do* irony.

For me, it boils down to this simple rule of thumb: The *gains* we desire set the stage for *losses* we fear and suffer. The upside is inextricably linked to its complimentary downside. Nature hoodwinks us into doggedly chasing the upside, and naively believing we can escape the downside. Much of our 'common knowledge' is anchored in the illusion that one can win in the end.

How does this relate to the aphorism, 'it is better to have loved and lost than to never have loved at all'? I find 'love' is deepest the less I need it. Need kills love. The more I need it, the more I lose it. It's easy to see where this leads – a vicious circle. Thus, the other rule of thumb: We only get what we give (i.e., give without ulterior motives of getting, of course). So, I'd rephrase that aphorism as, 'better to have given love, for what is given freely is never lost'.

I suppose I am really talking about emotional UNDERSTANDING versus the cognitive understanding. Cognitive knowing is uniquely human; it's quick, easy, and idealistic. Emotional knowing, on the other hand, is common to *all under heaven*; it's slow, *difficult*, and realistic. Does common to *all under heaven* mean a brick 'knows'? That depends on how we define 'emotional'. Perhaps, it is enough here just to recognize and accept the common ground we share with all living things. We'll save the bricks for another day.

14.

Perhaps the most remarkable thing about the Tao Te Ching is how it attempts to speak 'subjectively' to consciousness in various ways, e.g., *know, watch, listen, seems, hear, discern, think*. As awareness slows down and my mind settles into its consciousness, the more unfathomable consciousness becomes. A profound tradeoff we make in having awareness preoccupied with the thinking side of consciousness is a declining awareness of the *profound sameness* side of consciousness.

I'm having a problem keeping rhythm on fast songs. People have given me advice on what to do, but I find nothing 'works'. Perhaps the reason the advice never truly works is that we always attempt to name it. What does seem to work is being as conscious as possible of the *smooth, rarified, minute...* the *unfathomable*. That is to say, I find that I can *manage* this problem best by *holding to the ancient way*.

Now, that's easy to say and easy to do, yet when I 'try to do it', it becomes impossible, i.e., *Doing decays, grasping loses*. Not that I can cease *doing* and *grasping* mind you. Happily though, I've found that '*In desiring a little less, one must first make an effort*'. Knowing and giving into this, *the way's discipline*, helps me *manage today*. That this is not widely valued may be because when we LAY HOLD OF IT WE LOSE IT; thanks to biology, we don't realize that only through loss do we gain. This makes for life's greatest adventure - the adventure within.

Note: A character halfway through this chapter is missing in the standard (Wang Bi 226-249 AC) version. When this happens I use a character (收) from the earlier Mawangdui version (dating from 168 BC) when available (otherwise I resort to poetic license). Below, I'll past in a short description of these two versions from Wikipedia.

Mawangdui Silk Texts

Some people believe that the silk texts of the Tao Te Ching are the real book, and that the texts that have come down to us generation by generation are wrong wherever they disagree with these two earlier versions. Other people point out that the silk texts are not particularly good — in the sense that people often would not be able to make sense of them unless they had access to the texts written with the full forms of the characters. They add that Wang Bi, and other very early scholars who edited the texts that are the ancestors of the ones that came down to us by tradition, had access to many early versions of the Tao Te Ching and so were able to correct many mistakes by comparing the several versions available to them.

Most of the time the received versions of the Tao Te Ching are in substantial agreement with each other, and most of the time the text is simple and straightforward. Occasionally, however, two received versions will write homonyms with entirely different meanings at some point in a chapter. In such cases, much help can be received from a silk text that gives a third character that has a different pronunciation but is a synonym for one of the two in the received text.

In recent years several scholars have made new translations of the Tao Te Ching that are based on the silk text and ignore the received texts entirely or almost entirely. These include works by D. C. Lau, and by Robert G. Henricks. Henricks' translation does compare received versions of the Tao Te Ching with the text found in the tomb.

15.

I've always read this chapter as describing my 'original nature' (i.e., subjective, personal, mysterious). While still mysterious, today I see it describing everyone's 'original nature'. Not that I ever thought otherwise really, I just never put the two together on the same page. Probably the phrase '*Of old, the adept student was minutely subtle...*' pointed me in that subjective, personal direction. After all, I've been '*the adept student*' of the way as long as I can remember—not that I actually practice what I preach, mind you. Alas, it is often easy to confuse where we are with where we see ourselves going. Nevertheless, I felt I was hopefully (and truly) on the way there. Finally,

I've come to feel that we MYRIAD CREATURES, one and all, are there, here! Now, that's a mouthful of *profound sameness*.

It is natural to take a purely subjective view, as I use to do. On the other hand, it would be just as easy to take an opposite, purely objective view of this too. From that vantage point it could appear to describe someone 'over there' and certainly beyond normal experience. It is easy to see things either subjectively or objectively. Seeing outside (or is it inside?) those two boxes is more difficult.

If everyone '*is minutely subtle, open and deep beyond knowledge, cannot be known*,' etc., why don't we act (*prepare, blend, honest, allow*) like it in the 'real world'? Precisely because our 'original self' feels so utterly *deep beyond knowledge*'. We are instinctively driven to work around (contend, mask) the sense of weakness this causes. Life must resist entropy (the essence of weakness) to live. Life must work. The difficulty: how does one work and yet be *vanishing like ice that melts away?* Another irony here: *In the opposite direction, of the way 'it' moves. Loss through death, of the way 'it' uses..* Oh my word, *circular[1] as if without end* certainly describes it. It helps to stand back far enough from the circle to see: *Still and silent, it alone does not change. Goes round yet doesn't harm...* And then, get back to work.

16.

Today this chapter speaks to the experience of consciousness more directly than it ever has before (or so it feels like today). The *constant* feels like my mind's mirror, its consciousness neither pulled nor pushed by emotion. Returning to *root causes* is only temporary, for the emotional impact of *everything* 'out there', (THE TEAMING, MYRIAD CREATURES), waxes forth again soon enough. So, I enjoy it while I can!

Answering to one's destiny is an odd concept perhaps, especially as we feel that time moves forward. This is nature's greatest hoodwink. TURNING BACK IS HOW THE WAY MOVES,

---

1   A character is missing from the original so I had to use my poetic license:
     圓 yuan = round; circular; spherical.

but we are not biologically set up to feel that. <u>Correlations</u> allows us to peak into this. Consider these few:

Active	Passive
energy	time
future	past
illusion	real
forward	behind
clear	obscure.

It appears that what we call 'time' is actually energy moving forward through time TURNING BACK. (It's spooky enough to raise the hair on the back of one's head.) Life insists we be forward looking and active, resisting entropy every moment of life. The bio-illusion (the innate, biology based hoodwink) that drives us moving forward is a visceral sense that we will become *whole* and fulfilled once we satiate our most pressing DESIRE of the moment.

Devoting effort to emptiness and sincerely watching stillness doesn't seem to lead forward and fulfill our desires. Our difficulty lies in not knowing that *Entering the way seems like moving backwards.* And so we rush forward into the future thinking the *answer* must lie *'out there'*. Off balance, we feel even more desperate to make *'everything out there'* fulfill our desires and make *whole* our *destiny*.

Simply said, we yearn for the *constant* yet pursue *'everything out there',* none of which are *constant*. i.e., THE WAY THAT CAN BE SPOKEN OF IS NOT THE CONSTANT WAY. The more we expect *'out there'* to be *constant,* the LESS CONTENT AND MORE NUMEROUS OUR DESIRES. Certainly, all life is driven by this emotional hoodwink. However, our superior thinking mind / brain turns this emotional hoodwink into an illusion, which then feeds back upon emotion. We easily end up going around in circles... neurotic vicious circles!

THE GREAT IMAGE HAS NO SHAPE; the answer is the question. Yet we are compelled to nail down an answer. How can we ever feel secure when we settle for the answer that can be nailed down (named), or the image that has a shape? *Impartiality* is beyond reach as long as we impose a shape upon the *constant*. Never feeling secure in our *destiny*, we are then driven to hold even more tightly to '*everything*', to 'God', or whatever else we name 'it'.

17.

I'm departing a bit from the traditional interpretation again. There is a cultural tendency to 'follow the leader'. Because we've 'always seen' something a certain way in the past drives us to maintain that tradition going forward. While that's often wise, if one wishes to see 'outside the box', it helps to be not religiously bound to the view 'always seen' from inside the box. Each time I return to a chapter, I attempt to see what I've not seen before - to set 'always' aside and read between the lines. I feel the following translation /interpretation is faithful to the core meaning, though not in the traditional way. It is a matter of perspective. Anyway, you be the judge...

In Lau's version, BEST OF ALL RULERS IS BUT another word for God, in my view. LOVE, PRAISE, FEAR, AND TAKE LIBERTIES (*bullying*) are various ways people treat 'God'. On a personal level, this describes the various ways 'I' can manage 'my' life. I use 'I' and 'my' tenuously for these are nonsensical at their core (but, then what isn't?). How one manages life hinges on one's sense of responsibility, guilt, morality, desires, pride, fear, etc. This results in two sides of a MYSTERIOUS coin: some equate God (*the greatest heights*) with 'self' ('God-self'), while others see 'self' (ego) as an impediment to *the greatest heights*.

Lau's version talks of 'WHEN HIS TASK IS ACCOMPLISHED'. Accomplish what? Letting life's '*accomplishments*' happen naturally means giving up responsibility; I can't take credit, nor can I receive blame. I become an integral part of whatever happens no matter what I 'do'. I can do nothing, or rush about and meddle in everything. Yet, neither makes a difference when viewed from *the greatest heights*. What is different, however, is how I end up feeling as time unwinds events before me. Realizing that I can't truly decide (i.e., free will) is very peaceful. Indeed, I always end up doing what needs doing anyway, regardless. I only lose this *fulfilling* sense of *meritorious accomplishment* when I forget what I realize to be so. Why do I forget something so integral to KNOWING CONTENTMENT? Nature can't allow living beings to feel that content. After all, life must push back on entropy to survive.

This chapter gives good guidance for parenting, and for encounters with wild animals. Being a shadowy presence (*lying below what we realize*) works wonders. Many would probably wonder how this keeps the kids and wild animals in line? Why do they not take liberties? Kids and animals alike are able to see past cultural pretence into one's core nature. It instills respect (*praise and fear*) when all they see is a 'SHADOWY PRESENCE' (i.e., the *below what we realize*). Otherwise, they simply respond to what they see; this is often the duplicity of conflicting needs and fears we of less MATURITY struggle to maintain.

18.

The great way is wasted WHEN THERE IS NOT ENOUGH FAITH. Faith in what? Faith in THE SHAPE THAT HAS NO SHAPE, which makes faith so hard to grasp and impossible to hold. Like breathing, faith is the RETURNING TO ONE'S ROOTS moment to moment. Failing that, we cling to surrogates. So, for example, WHEN THE WAY IS LOST THERE IS VIRTUE; WHEN VIRTUE IS LOST THERE IS BENEVOLENCE; WHEN BENEVOLENCE IS LOST THERE IS RECTITUDE; WHEN RECTITUDE IS LOST THERE ARE THE RITES. Our ideals of *benevolence and justice* are merely symptoms of the insecurity felt by a lack of faith. And when *benevolence and justice* wane, we turn to rectitude and rites.

In his third law of motion, Newton says, "for every action there is an equal and opposite reaction". While not necessarily always 'opposite', I know of nothing that happens without consequences. A corollary to this is the view that 'nature abhors a vacuum'. Create a vacuum and nature will fill it. We certainly (and understandably) have great difficulty seeing this bigger picture: the consequences, the vacuum 'fillers'.

Intelligence begets great falseness is one such unforeseen and unwanted consequences, or as chapter 18 puts it, WHEN CLEVERNESS EMERGES THERE IS GREAT HYPOCRISY. Yet, few fully accept the connection between the two. Why? We value *intelligence,* which blinds us to its 'ugly' side. And why do we value *intelligence* so highly? *Intelligence* is just another surrogate for the *great way. Waste* not, want not.

Our ideals of benevolence and justice also serve tribal purposes. Shared ideals offer seemingly trustworthy common ground upon which all the tribe's member can stand. Mutual 'faith' abounds, provided everyone conforms to the current societal ideals of virtue. It works pretty well too, except for perhaps the stray heretic who suspects there's more to it than meets the eye.

The great way is wasted in other ways too, similar to the *wasting* of a sunset, or the aroma of a rose. In not 'smelling the roses along the way', we are rushing past a deeper side to life. Such perceptual losses are *wasted* opportunities to know life more deeply; IN QUALITY OF MIND IT IS DEPTH THAT MATTERS. The *great way* is always here, now; yet it is *wasted* when we leap beyond here, now. Of course, this isn't the whole view. For that, <u>correlations</u> can give a broader picture.

19.

I've always had a special fondness for this chapter. EXTERMINATE THE SAGE, BENEVOLENCE, INGENUITY turns civilization's sacred cows on their ears. Seriously pondering these ideas (without any actual *exterminate* and '*cut off*') opens a possibility for thinking outside the box. Each of us, from birth onward, is indoctrinated into civilization's story. Thus, seeing life from outside that story is no small task! Even rebellious anti-civilization points of view COMPLEMENT that story.

The main thing I see here is a report on a natural dynamic. How it works, not any prescription for what should be done (i.e., *cut off benevolence*, etc.). For example, it is due to the lack of *devout kindness* that civilization's call for *benevolence and justice* arises. Why the lack? Civilization is un-natural, narrowly speaking anyway; we evolved to live in close knit tribal groups, not as anonymous cogs in multimillion peopled populations. We live this way now because civilization provides comfort and security (and the promises of more). Let's face it, who really wants to RETURN TO THE USE OF THE KNOTTED ROPE. A few weeks camping usually satisfies that urge!

However, the comfort and security come with a cost; believing in civilization's story causes cognitive stress. The story's highest ideals can never be realized, for those ideals are merely symptoms of underlying causes, not viable destinations. Robbers exist because people value *cleverness and advantage*. Only by giving up the 'positives' (*cleverness and advantage*) can one lose the 'negatives' (*thieves*). Believing in civilization's story is essentially wanting to have it both ways, i.e., I want the *advantage*, I don't want the *thievery*. Wanting it both ways is a no-win stressful way to worry one's life away.

A final irony: The more one believes in the story, the more one wants the story to be true, the further from 'what is' one gets. The further away one's mind gets from 'what is', the more cognitive stress one feels. Although, I suspect most people take civilization's story with a grain of salt, and only embrace it when they need it. Here we see the benefit of HYPOCRISY; otherwise most of us would be jumping off bridges!

20.

I've often seen folks over the years interpret the Tao Te Ching as telling us what we 'should' (or shouldn't) do. For example, at a recent Sunday meeting, some folks said they initially took '*Cut off learning and be without worry* ' to mean that learning and knowledge were bad and something to avoid.

Now, I imagine that our social instinct drives this interpretation. When social animals all do the 'right things', the group works harmoniously, and so we feel an innate need to do 'right'. This drives our judgments, both of self and of others; it gives us the standards with which to measure individual and group behavior. So, if reading the Tao Te Ching's message in that context 'floats your boat', then nothing I say will deter you. If, on the other hand, you are worn wearisome from passing judgment (on self and on others) you might consider looking at the Taoist message as merely a description of how nature works. Not that you need to, or indeed can, do anything about it I suppose. Personally though, seeing the TTC as simply a description of nature brings me CONTENTMENT.

Thus, in my view, the rest of the chapter goes on to describe how each and every person feels, even though they may not 'think' they do. The odd thing about cognitive awareness is that we only 'know' what we 'think', and only 'think' what we 'know'. ('Think' and 'know', in this case refer only to human 'learning' awareness, not to consciousness in general.)

Society's myths and expectations are why most people wouldn't 'think' this chapter is describing them. Of course, I may be way off base here; it's just my gut feeling. Socially speaking, we generally loathe the idea of being *drowsy, foolish, and subdued*. We admire cleverness, alertness, activity, and align ourselves in that camp. We hide the *drowsy, foolish, and subdued side* of ourselves from others and ourselves as much as possible. The 'ego' you know. What's ego? A self-image driven by the survival instinct. There's nothing we can do about that survival instinct, but self-image rests upon how seriously one THINKS THAT ONE KNOWS. How seriously we 'think that we know' hinges on how much we trust WORDS and NAMES. Alas.

21.

Today this chapter speaks to me of consciousness, or the light thereof. Often the mind is interested in the objects of awareness upon which the light shines. The mystery is the light itself, and in using the light to 'inspect' the light... 'USE THE LIGHT, BUT GIVE UP THE DISCERNMENT'. It is very odd... like using the eye to see itself. The marvel of consciousness is that, unlike the impossibility of a physical eye seeing itself, consciousness can. At least it feels so, most especially when the NAMES and WORDS are put to bed. Only in that silence can I see the *indistinct and suddenly*.

'The opening of moral character allows only the way through' sure sounds awkward compared with D.C. Lau's IN HIS EVERY

MOVEMENT A MAN OF GREAT VIRTUE FOLLOWS THE WAY AND THE WAY ONLY. The difference, if there is one, lies in the view that an *opening of moral character* must be present in order to *allow the way through*. D.C. Lau's translation seems to evoke a more active approach on the part of man. The phrase, 'In his every movement' is nowhere to be found in the Chinese. For me, the literal Chinese evokes a more passive view, more like: when the window is *open* the sun shines *through*. D.C. Lau's phrasing lends a 'free will' tone to this chapter, which the original lacks.

22.

I reckon another word for 'the *One*' is 'the circle': No beginning, no end, GOES ROUND AND DOES NOT WEARY. Any place you think you are 'choosing' on the circle brings you to the other side… Oops! As a consequence, being as HESITANT AND TENTATIVE as possible helps avoid unintended consequences. This situation parallels two forks I see in the path of life: short-term pain, long-term pleasure, versus short-term pleasure, long-term pain. In each case, one *follows* the other. By choosing the former, long-term pleasure *follows* the short-term pain. Folks who prefer to 'pay upfront' tend to choose this fork. Fortunately, paying up front becomes easier as you realize those are the rules of THE WAY OF HEAVEN, i.e., balance: where each side is 'paid in full' by the other.

Folks who feel they can 'get in free' tend to choose the later, opting for the pleasure first. They feel the short cut is real; a free ride in life is possible; they can avoid the pain. I find this 'get in free' is one of life's most compelling illusions (a bio-hoodwink). What is its purpose? Perhaps it serves a 'survival of the fittest' role. Certainly, there is a survival advantage for animals that realize early on that there is more to life than meets the eye.

Another bio-hoodwink is the drive to *contend*. CONTENDING tricks us into thinking (feeling actually) that if we just win the battle and vanquish our opponent, peace will reign. Certainly, peace returns, but not through winning any battle. Peace *follows* naturally. The illusion (hoodwink) lies in feeling that winning and success bring (cause) security and peace. Sure, it will feel like we have won a skirmish here and there, and that keeps us motivated, driving us to *contend* until we achieve final success. As long as we feel success is possible we will continue to *contend*. Ironically, peace only comes after we surrender.

This is nature's way and so we struggle; life is struggle – death is peace. However, this need not be as stressful as it often is. Believing one can actually win just increases stress. The advantage animals have over us is their inability to 'believe' (i.e., NOT TO KNOW YET TO THINK THAT THEY KNOW) they can win. They can only experience this hoodwink in the moment. I find that rationally knowing that winning is illusionary offsets this illusion a little, helping me TO ACCOMPLISH MY PRIVATE ENDS.

Know that winning is illusionary aids me in 'TAKING THE LOWER POSITION' too. Although, it goes without saying that expecting to 'excel in taking the lower position' is really just putting yet another mask (a self righteous one) on the illusion of success. Taking the lower position is the opposite of action and success. STILLNESS is key. Ironically, and contrary to every fiber of common sense, profound passivity get the job done the best.

23.

Infrequent speech is natural. So what, pray tell, <u>is not</u> natural, frequent speech? We commonly think of natural as pertaining to nature. If nature is natural and our species are part of nature, how can we say some human activity isn't natural? The natural inconsistency in saying some human activity isn't natural resolves itself a little if we consider the concept of natural, especially via the Chinese translation.

Natural is translated as **zìrán** (自然): natural world; nature; naturally; in the ordinary course of events; of course; naturally. This word is made from two characters, **zì** (自): self; oneself; one's own; certainly; of course; from; since, and **rán** (然): right; correct; so; like that. Combining these, we get the following: self right; one's own so; certainly so; self so; certainly right, and so on.

To me this all adds up to say natural is how things are, just so, unqualified and without judgment. One primary purpose of language (WORDS and NAMES) is to qualify and judge things. So, in this sense, 'Infrequent speech is natural' is consistent with the larger meaning of natural. Moreover, words are not the thing, but rather symbolic shorthand for the thing. As a result, words break the connection between what is 'out there' and what is perceived 'in here'. Ironically, words and names are not what they pretend to be. (Of course, this is impossible to notice if you believe words and names real, e.g., "In the beginning was the Word, and the Word was with God, and the Word was God".)

Together in virtue, virtue happily satisfies (or, HE WHO CONFORMS TO VIRTUE IS GLADLY ACCEPTED BY VIRTUE) parallels my sense that what we see is what we want to see. Our experience of life is a reflection of what we want (or don't want) from life. One 'matches' the other. I suppose it is an identity thing, as some would say. The down side: What we identify with happily satisfies us and eventually 'takes over'. Identity with what CAN BE NAMED allows us to cling to it. As Buddha said, "The illusion of self originates and manifests itself in a cleaving (cling, adhere or stick fast) to things". Another way to put this: 'Our hates originate and manifest themselves in our loves'.

This makes the idea of being 'together in the way' liberating. After all, THE WAY THAT CAN BE SPOKEN OF IS NOT THE CONSTANT WAY. Taking this to heart (trusting it completely) pulls me to notice 'THE THREAD RUNNING THROUGH THE WAY'. Each moment of experience shares an ESSENCE with past and future moments. Trusting this, I can become the same as the way. However, either this trust is here or it's not. When it isn't, all I can do is shut up and listen for it again.

24.

I've long seen this chapter as pointing out symptoms that reveal one's deeper reality (i.e., underlying causes). For example, D.C. Lau translation says 'HE WHO BRAGS WILL HAVE NO MERIT'. This implies that bragging causes one to have *no merit*. Seeing it that way is putting the cart before the horse. Bragging is simply a way to compensate for feeling a lack of merit (a sense of self worth). In other words, we counterbalance our inner reality with external opposites. The more extreme the inner, the more extreme the external 'counterbalance' one can notice. That is, provided one knows this counterbalancing process runs the show. There's the hitch. The tendency judge a book by its cover blinds us to underlying causes.

Interestingly, the original says, '**self** (one's own, certainly) **fell** (cut down, strike, attack) (thing) **nothing** (without, not, regardless of) **merit** (achievement)'. How faithful is D.C. Lau's translation? A translation is, in part, an interpretation arising from one's own worldview. I'm guessing D.C. Lau holds the view that 'he who brags *will* have no merit'. The word *will* gives the time line, i.e., this *will* produce that. On the other hand, simply saying 'He who brags is without merit' is closer to the original and more vague as to which causes which.

Again, the original states: **self** (one's own, certainly) **fell** (cut down, strike, attack) (thing) **nothing** (without, not, regardless of) **merit** (achievement). D.C. Lau translated this as 'HE WHO BRAGS WILL HAVE NO MERIT' while last time I translated this as IN SELF ATTACK, WE ACHIEVE NOTHING. Let's break that down: When one achieves nothing, one often attacks oneself (self-blame). This is a more symptoms' point of view. The achieving nothing precedes the self-blame. Of course, if one is always attacking one's self, one will not achieve much of anything. I suppose both are true. The fundamental cause though, is a sense of lacking. This drives self-blame which in turn inhibits achievement. It can become a vicious circle leading one to seek therapy or booze!

This time I am inclined to put it this way: Cutting down one's self is without merit, or perhaps, cutting down one's self regardless of one's merit. Both sound reasonable. The former says there is no merit in demeaning yourself. The later says just the opposite in a 'positive' way. To put it another way, take the lower position regardless of any meritorious achievements.

While I rather prefer the later, 'positive' view, I went with: *Attacking your self is without merit.* This illustrates the role one's own worldview plays in 'understanding' the Tao Te Ching. At best, in truth, you only end up 'understanding' your own worldview a bit more broadly. In this case, I have two opposing ways to 'understand' it. The bottom line: I cannot learn what I do not 'know' already for the learning is a function of what is already within my current worldview. Goodness, what a radical view! It's something Chuang Tzu might have liked.

The '**stand on tiptoe** (look forward to) (thing) **not stand** (found; exist; live); **step** (stride; go beyond) (thing) **not go** (be current; prevail; do; competent) ' also raises the question of which causes which. I experience it this way: not existing in the here and now causes me to look forward; not being current causes me to go beyond. Again, this easily becomes a vicious circle. The more I look forward the less here and now I am; the less here and now I am, the more I look forward to... FOREKNOWLEDGE

We must be innately set up to see the symptoms we see, not as the symptoms they are, but as causes. I suppose this is biologically more expedient survival wise, especially for species that don't think. That way an animal need not sweat reality's details, but simply react to how reality appears. The downside for humans is that we fail to get to the bottom of 'things' and notice underlying causes. 'Thing' being the mountains we make out of the mole holes we see. Regarding what I see 'out there' as merely a symptom of something 'in here' helps me get deeper toward the bottom of 'things', and so avoid the vicious circle into which my mind can sometimes lead me.

25.

This chapter down-plays "The Tao", and reduces it to merely "tao". How? This chapter ends with, *And the way follows that which is natural and free from affectation,* or D.C. Lao put it, AND THE WAY ON THAT WHICH IS NATURALLY SO. The Chinese word for nature is *ziran*, which is a combination of two characters: (自) *zi* = *self; oneself; one's own; certainly; of course; from; since,* and (然)

ran = right; correct; so; like that. This stands in sharp contrast to how nature is often viewed in the West. We give the word a moralistic, bordering on GoDlike, quality in the West. For example, a plastic bottle isn't *natural* and artificial foods aren't *natural.*

I've always felt nature was much more profound than anything humans did or didn't do. This moralized view is symptomatic of how taken we are with our own self importance, which in turn, is symptomatic of our ideal of self, which leaves us with a deep sense of disconnection and insignificance, which is why we have religion in the first place. (Boy, that was a long sentence.) The Chinese word for nature expresses a broader view of nature. What is 'tao', but the unfolding *way* of nature?

Inquiries into reality, its nature, origin and fate, are among the earliest and continuing questions humanity asks about *the outside world.* As long as we expect an objective answer, our inquiries will continue. It is an odd thing really, like asking where a circle begins and ends. Of course, biology hoodwinks us into perceiving reality as contrasts; the greater the contrasts, the more acute the perceptions, and the more real *the outside world* feels.

Therefore, ironically, as long as we insist on answering the MYSTERY in terms that allow us to feel we have a solid answer, we can never find the answer that ultimately satisfies[1]. To paraphrase chapter 2, THUS [ANSWERS AND QUESTIONS] PRODUCE EACH OTHER, COMPLEMENT EACH OTHER, OFF-SET EACH OTHER, HARMONIZE WITH EACH OTHER, AND FOLLOW EACH OTHER.

Simply said, the answer is the question, the beginning is the end, etc. (and visa verse naturally). Of course, just saying that doesn't offer any emotional relief, but it may tell one where to look.

---

1   One symptom of not finding an answer that ultimately satisfies is the fervency with which we hold on to our beliefs, and sometimes try to convert others to these belief. After all, the belief with the most 'votes' must surely be the true one. Fervently holding on is symptomatic of the tenuousness we feel. On the other hand, when you know you 'have it', 'it' can become DARKLY VISIBLE, (AND) ONLY SEEMS AS IF IT WERE THERE.

26.

THE GENTLEMAN WHEN TRAVELING ALL DAY can at least let his guard down when he puts his 'stuff' safely away. How is the ruler able to put his stuff away? The poignant comparison here is that limited sense of responsibility allows one to rest, albeit somewhat obliviously. Children are another example of this. Becoming an adult means having an increasing sense of responsibility for what lies outside of your direct sights (experience). I doubt there is an end to this either. CIRCUMSTANCES KEEP BRINGING US TO MATURITY over our entire lifetime. I expect that if I were to live a thousand years my sense of responsibility would still be increasing.

To be clear, 'sense of responsibility' does not mean acting upon anything. If anything, it probably means 'KNOWING WHEN TO STOP'. Another word for 'sense of responsibility' would be 'breadth of awareness'. Children can be 'worry free' because their breath of awareness is nescient.

The only sane way of dealing with the DIFFICULTY of deepening sense of responsibility is stillness and the heavy. The memory of an old silver back gorilla at the zoo comes to mind. He was heavy and still - 'grounded' I'd have to say. The young juvenile gorillas were just the opposite, restless and light. Nature's model applies to us all, regardless of the species to which we belong.

27.

ONE WHO EXCELS at something reflects an underlying agenda on their part. Action follows motivation, the urge to 'do it'. This urge is energized by the need to achieve the goal to which the action is aimed. Ironically, the greater the need (DESIRE) to achieve the goal, the less likely the doer will feel he excels, and so relies on 'audience' feedback. What's more, lacking a sense of *adeptness* further energizes the urge to 'get it right', finally. The need to 'get it right' counteracts the sense of CONTENTMENT one innately dreams of feeling once success arrives. This dynamic powers the seemingly *adept* results of us all (yes, even plant and animals - though without the unique complications that imagination gives humans).

Even though the world 'out there' judges and THINKS it sees true excellence, the subjective experience is otherwise. It is an ironic process where underlying need pushes for the achievement of something, and prevents the subjective experience of anything more than fleeting moments of success for the doer. The world 'out there', in not experiencing the subjective stress that brings success, only sees the *adept* results. Feeding into our one-sided perception of *adeptness* and perfection is hierarchical instinct, which drives us to rank the apparent successes we see.

Any *essential and subtle* wisdom brought to bear here must play out in the DISCERNMENT of the doer. The doer, by transferring his fixation on the goal to the flow of doing, can find the success he seeks in that eternal moment (as long as he remains detached from any idealized goal). In other words, HAVE LITTLE THOUGHT OF SELF AND AS FEW DESIRES AS POSSIBLE.

In the process of life, mistakes are the first step toward becoming *adept*. Mistakes are commonly seen (especially by adults) as something to avoid. The folly of this is obvious; avoiding mistakes leads to a standstill frustration with life. Embracing mistakes as the essence of life's process redirects the eye away from the idealized goal and back to the *essential and subtle* moment to moment (i.e., step-by-step, A JOURNEY OF A THOUSAND MILES STARTS FROM BENEATH ONE'S FEET).

The idealized goals we pursue are outside of reality. While we can imagine a perfect world, or action, with nothing 'CHIPPED', reality comes in pairs. Mistakes <-> perfection; life <-> death; good <-> bad. (see correlations for more). 'One without the other' only exists in the wishful needs of the one's imagination. This two-fold co-generating dynamic plays itself out in *those who are adept* and *those who are not adept. Neither to value the model nor love the supporter* is unavoidable once one sees the whole picture and no longer harbors FAVORITISM.

28.

We are able to CLEVERLY OVERCOME nature through an awareness of past, future and the apparent cause and effect relationship between the two. Furthermore, our survival biology drives us to climb, reach for and achieve meaning, position, honor, to 'be somebody' seemingly without end. We have an innate gut sense that 'more is better', even when wisdom tells us otherwise. Obviously, the higher up one climbs, the further down one has to fall. The further out on a limb one reaches, the more separated from the trunk one feels.

What natural mechanisms are in place to push back against the impulse for more and more 'progress'? Certainly, other creatures also struggle for all they can get, (which usually means eat). However, natural conditions limit their success. That was once true of us, before our brain evolved enough to map out clever BY-PATHS around those natural limits. Hooray! Nothing can stop us now. The world... uh, er... no, the universe is our oyster.

Well, it doesn't always work out that way, now does it? We are also able to see how success is empty in the long run. We can see death's doorway. Nuts! The brain that brings us success also sees the failure that lurks ahead, behind, and all around. This began turning more problematic as civilization and the agricultural revolution took hold. With that came the blossoming of religion. Religion is undoubtedly humanity's way of coping with a thinking mind that 'knows' too much for its own sanity.

Does religion work? I don't suppose it really does. Religion is a symptom of a deeper disconnection; since when do symptoms cure causes? At best, religion is a palliative. For a 'cure', each mind must dig deep within its psyche until DISCERNMENT PENETRATES THE FOUR QUARTERS. Then it can feel THE TEACHING THAT USES NO WORDS, THE BENEFIT OF RESORTING TO NO ACTION. Thus then, *being a valley for all under heaven, constant virtue will be sufficient, and one can again return to simplicity* (i.e., BEING THE UNCARVED BLOCK).

Returning to simplicity, to the extent possible, fosters within me a sense of *profound sameness* wherein even THE GREATEST CUTTING DOES NOT SEVER. In other words, it may not be perfect, but it will do.

29.

Being responsibile is more about accepting and conforming to 'how it is' rather than action bent on changing 'how it is'. Chapter 65 speaks to this: MYSTERIOUS VIRTUE IS PROFOUND AND FAR-REACHING, BUT WHEN THINGS TURN BACK IT TURNS BACK WITH THEM. ONLY THEN IS COMPLETE CONFORMITY REALIZED.

Any action that flows from this bottom line is less likely cause unintended consequences. This is somewhat like a spiritual 'buy low, sell high'. 'Buy low' is TAKING THE LOWER POSITION, the 'sell high' is the natural benefit that ensues. Life offers two paths, 'short-term pain, long-term pleasure' is the buying low; 'short-term pleasure, long-term pain' is the buy high approach and is always SURE TO END IN IMMENSE LOSS. Of course, this also parallels the pay-up-front-now versus buy-on-credit-pay-later. Modern life certainly favors the later, and yet is shocked by the predictable unintended consequences.

THE EMPIRE IS A SACRED VESSEL AND NOTHING SHOULD BE DONE TO IT brings to mind the quantum paradox of <u>Schrödinger's cat</u>. Think of the empire as like a painting. You must begin and paint something, but then also KNOWING WHEN TO STOP. Knowing when to stop is key. I came into existence as 'carl' 70 years back. The empire (whether we're talking about the universe, or my home town's current era) were 'painted' before I was born. I entered the picture and now add my dollops of paint to this cosmic canvas. It was perfect as could be when I entered the scene, although in life, act I must. Here is the dilemma: how to act and yet leave well enough alone, or act without acting. Like the Schrödinger's cat paradox, I act and yet don't act. How is that possible? It all lies in the eye of the observer. That is why THINKING THAT ONE KNOWS is so fraught with self-deception.

'Hence' or 'therefore' often implies an active free will view, i.e., a sense of *because of this* I intend to do that. My experience is much more passive. The more I see the ebb-and-flow nature of existence, the more TENTATIVE AND HESITANT I become naturally. I can't help it. It is like playing whack-a-mole. You smash here and it pops up there. Nothing really changes; you just move stuff around. And in moving stuff around you create unintended consequences. The mole pops up where you least expect it. Oops! In youth and ignorance, I wasn't aware of 'it' popping up 'over there'. I thought taking care of the situation would solve the problem; end of story. DEAL WITH A THING WHILE IT IS STILL NOTHING IS BEST, works best when NOTHING is truly NOTHING.

Is this not why nothing really ever changes in human affairs, despite our dreams to the contrary? Babies born replace those who pass on. The babies must undergo the same 'learning on the job of life' that those who pass on underwent to gain whatever sense of how things really are versus how they first appear.

30.

Not of the dao, or as D.C. Lau put it, GOING AGAINST THE WAY, means what exactly? Especially when seen in context with the rest of the Tao Te Ching. For example: Chapter 73, THE NET OF HEAVEN IS CAST WIDE. THOUGH THE MESH IS NOT FINE, YET NOTHING EVER SLIPS THROUGH; chapter 34, THE WAY IS BROAD, REACHING LEFT AS WELL AS RIGHT; and especially chapter 4, I KNOW NOT WHOSE SON IT IS. IT IMAGES THE FOREFATHER OF GOD. So can one ever truly be *not of the dao,* or as D.C. Lau said, 'going against the way'? As with most things, I reckon the answer lies in the eye of the beholder.

There are two ways to 'eye' the 'way': Subjectively and objectively. This is a little odd and so requires some background. First, a subjective view of the world is, by definition, a projection of the subject - one's self. However, an objective view, in the final analysis, is also a projection of one's self (i.e., it's grounded in biology). A human point of view cannot help but reflect all the needs and fears, and all the instinctive emotions that are innate to our species. Thus, any 'objective' point of view is most likely a combination of cultural conditioning and wishful thinking, not the reality it purports to be. Fortunately, we can test how objective we are by gauging how impartial we feel at that moment. Total objectivity may even be possible at the point of complete IMPARTIALITY. Although, how would we know if we are CAPABLE OF NOT KNOWING ANYTHING WHEN OUR DISCERNMENT PENETRATES THE FOUR QUARTERS?

In light of all this, what does it mean when it says, THAT WHICH GOES AGAINST THE WAY WILL COME TO AN EARLY END? Personally, I feel I'm going 'against the way' when I loose impartiality and become driven by impulsive needs or fears. In other words, I've lost 'the big picture'; I've lost *my sense* of the way and simply react out of narrow self-interest (altruistic though they may be). My experience of 'THE WAY' has become overshadowed and drowned out by a more compelling emotion. Even so, nature, at least from a biological point of view (and thus somewhat more objective), is still pulling the strings. I am just not aware of it. Even acknowledging this possibility is difficult because I need to feel responsible and in control (free will).

For example, the need to feel in control indirectly amplifies the sense of guilt, and this intensifies feelings of 'going against the way'. Viewed biologically, however, guilt seems to be just one facet of the 'social instinct'. Interestingly, women tend to feel guilt more keenly, and so are often more responsive socially. This makes natural sense, for being potential mothers, guilt would make them more sensitive to the needs of their offspring. So, ironically, when feeling guilty we'll feel we are 'going against the way', yet the social instinct that makes those feelings possible HAPPENS TO US NATURALLY; it is 'of the way' and nothing to feel guilty about.

Chapter 36 is another example of this perplexing dynamic: IF YOU WOULD HAVE A THING SHRINK, YOU MUST FIRST STRETCH IT. In the same way, we must first experience folly to reach wisdom. While traveling through our foolish years, we are 'going against the way' in the sense that 'the way' is the furthest thing from our mind at the moment. Only later, in reflection, can we realize our BY-PATH. In short, we are always 'of the way' despite feelings to the contrary. While we are 'stretching it', the way is just all that more SHADOWY, INDISTINCT. INDISTINCT AND SHADOWY.

The lack of *using the way to assist in managing people* is easy to see at play in politics. When one party wins, they tend to ride rough shod over the losing party. While there is talk of reaching across the isle, of bipartisanship, few seem capable of doing so. This parallels: MY WORDS ARE VERY EASY TO UNDERSTAND AND VERY EASY TO PUT INTO PRACTICE, YET NO ONE IN THE WORLD CAN UNDERSTAND THEM OR PUT THEM INTO PRACTICE. The marvel of our mind is that it allows us to be detached enough TO THINK what could be possible (our ideals and wishful thinking), yet when push comes to shove, reality takes over and we behave like the animals we are. We bear a uniquely human burden: the weight of our ideals, which are invariably at odds with our actions.

31.

The *left* and *right* referred to here make translating this in context with modern culture difficult. True, correlations do provide a glimpse at possible subtle connections between *left* and *right* and life, but those may prove even more INDISTINCT AND SHADOWY. Briefly: *left* correlates loosely to death, humble, mature, listens, mysterious, sameness, follows, etc., while *right* correlates loosely to arrogant, juvenile, speaks, obvious, difference, leads, etc. To pursue this avenue, see Using Yin and Yang to Pop Preconceptions

The *left* and *right* 'rules' were cultural standards for normalcy in ancient China. Codes of behavior like this make civilizations of large populations possible. Rules, arbitrary as they may be, give a sense of emotional comfort and security. Everyone following the rules imparts a sense of mutual understanding. Sure, it is only skin deep, but skin deep is deep enough, as we seldom look beneath the surface anyway. Such cultural norms are also symptomatic of how socially insecure we truly are. We are terrified of making mistakes, of looking foolish, of shame. My, what a profoundly social animal we are.

It is natural for the *superior general* to take charge of life's most serious matters (e.g., THIS MEANS THAT IT IS MOURNING RITES THAT ARE OBSERVED). Like they say, "if you can't take the heat, get out of the kitchen". 'Taking the heat' is simply being able to boldly make decisions and lead the way. That is the stuff of leadership. Ironically, making the wise 'right' decision is not a priority (at least until after a wrong decision has been made and everyone has been led off a cliff). Only in hindsight do we know who the *superior general* was truly.

Why would one use *weapons* anyway? Weapons gain an advantage. This is clearly symptomatic of the survival instinct. Viewed broadly, words, clothes, political pull, social contacts, expertise, and such, are also *weapons* to achieve *gain or fame*. Rising above the need for *fame or gain* to the point of *superior indifference* is rare, I expect. Notice, however, it does not say absolute, perfect *indifference*. *Superior indifference* conveys a more flexible view. For example, my *indifference* now is *superior* to when I was a young man. Survival and ascendancy were high on my list of needs back then. The closer I approach the end of life, the less important that NATURALLY becomes (thankfully).

A larger view of being *victorious* must also include an inevitable and corresponding defeat. All gains and successes 'here' entail losses and failures 'elsewhere'. To paraphrase: [VICTORY AND DEFEAT] OFF-SET, PRODUCE, AND COMPLEMENT EACH OTHER. The universe is ONE whole becoming. Adding to 'this side' entails removal from 'that side'. There are no free lunches; everything is paid for in full. Any dream of bypassing that natural balance comes to naught.

So what? At least you get to enjoy the illusion of winning *victorious* success, right? In my heart of hearts, I don't think so. In every such self satisfied smile I see its opposite. That PEOPLE PREFER BY-PATHS is driven by a lack of CONTENTMENT. The 'hole' (THE VOID) is there and we rush to fill it in. In that process, we tend to notice the filling action rather than the hole that causes it and drives it. Observation-wise isn't this putting the cart before the horse? How can life ever be fully lived when that is the case? On the other hand, they say ignorance is bliss. Alas no; if it was, we would never be eager to KNOW.

32.

This chapter points out what 'should' be obvious, namely that NO ONE IN THE WORLD DARE CLAIM ITS ALLEGIANCE. If anyone truly had The Answer, The Secret, or the 'ear of God', human history would not be the record of chaotic stumbling missteps that it is. Our ability to ignore history and cling faithfully to our ideals is as remarkable as it is irrational. Clearly, claiming ourselves to be a rational species (Homo sapiens) is more a reflection of wishful thinking than fact. Separating our wishes and ideals from what actuality is perhaps biologically impossible.

For example, long ago I realized and 'accepted' the irrationality of human nature, and yet I continue to be surprised by actions which reflect irrationality. The fact that I never seem to get used to the irrationality is a little surprising, frankly. Obviously, I accept it as a fact, yet can't accept it emotionally. Doesn't this show just how irrational I am in some underlying innate hope for rationality?

Nevertheless, I CAN BE FREE FROM DANGER as long as I remember that any judgments I make stem from what I irrationally feel 'should' be. 'Names already exist' is another way of saying that we are all trapped by WORDS and names from infancy onward. While feeling a need for some things to be otherwise is innate (biological), linking words and names to that only serve to trap me there. Thus, 'man handles the realization to stop. Knowing to stop [he] can be without danger'. If I stop needy feelings from driving what I think, I can be without danger, i.e., I can avoid the 'TO THINK THAT ONE KNOWS' problem.

Admittedly, that is a tall order! Alas, emotion drives thought. Nevertheless, improvement is possible as long as I remember!... remember!... remember! what I know! Then CONTENTMENT becomes possible. I should add here that by 'remember' I don't mean repeating a string of words. Remembering what I know is an intuitive experience along the lines of Buddha's <u>Right Understanding, Right Mindfulness, Right Attentiveness, and Right Concentration</u>.

I think I once saw the idea of KNOWING WHEN TO STOP, as a warning to *stop* using words. That is reinforced, naturally, by other passages, such as ONE WHO SPEAKS DOES NOT KNOW... Today I see this as saying, that yes, the NAMELESS UNCARVED BLOCK is *restricted* by names, and yes, we can't turn back that clock. Nevertheless, it is possible to avoid making mountains out of molehills if we realize and remember that names and words are **never** the reality they appear to represent. Then it is possible TO KNOW YET TO THINK THAT ONE DOES NOT KNOW.

Taking myself less seriously means taking my thoughts less seriously. Recognizing that names and words are a means of social connection - communication - and don't actually mirror reality 'out there' helps calm mind and heart greatly. At best, word and names reflect the 'in here' of who I am, my desires and fears. Accepting this simple view can avoid much misunderstanding. Of course, one could argue that part of the underlying purpose of communication is actually misunderstanding via miscommunication. This helps keep the social pot stirred, so to speak. Otherwise, *Heaven and earth would join and let* [too much] *sweet dew fall.* Ah, but that's another story.

33.

Parsing the meaning of 'know' is a curious thing. What does saying 'HE WHO KNOWS OTHERS IS CLEVER; HE WHO KNOWS HIMSELF HAS DISCERNMENT' really mean? Personally, I've found that truly knowing others hinges on how honestly I know myself. Putting this in another context may help clarify it.

If a hunter cleverly and keenly observes an animal's habits, he objectively knows that animal well. He can then set a trap for it, train it, avoid it, and so on. That is a *knowledge of resourcefulness.* On the other hand, knowing one's self is an *honest* subjective knowing. Simply put, *knowledge*

of self is honesty. That's a tall order, for we tend to spin
what we see to fit preconceptions (our 'story').

We are driven to see ourselves in a good light, or a guilt-ridden
bad light, depending on our 'story'. Call it ego, or call it survival
instinct. This innate imperative, with its primal elements of need
and fear, drives the core elements of our 'story'. It is little wonder
that observing self impartially is so very difficult. Essentially
then, *honesty* is merely another word for IMPARTIALITY.

I would add to this chapter, 'He who is discontent with one's
lot seeks riches', which would be the counterpoint to 'HE WHO
KNOWS CONTENTMENT IS RICH'. Also, 'HE WHO LIVES OUT HIS
DAYS HAS HAD A LONG LIFE' could have the counterpoint, 'He
who lives for tomorrow has had a short life'. We certainly have
a tendency to think of and hold out for a brighter tomorrow
where our dreams can come true. Alas, holding out for what
will come is a sure way to lose what is here and now. Why do
we so easily opt for such a foolish tradeoff? I suppose because
wishing for 'later' takes less effort than seizing 'now'.

What does *not losing my place* really mean in daily life? For
one thing, if *my place* depends on something - anything
- *endurance* over time is out of the question. The external
world is constant change: IT IS ON DISASTER THAT GOOD
FORTUNE PERCHES; IT IS BENEATH GOOD FORTUNE THAT
DISASTER CROUCHES. Good fortune followed by misfortune.
So, *place* has more to do with my approach to life than any
particulars of life. If I don't lose my 'taoist' approach to life, I
can endure. *Dead, but not gone* for me means *dead* to the ebb
and flow of the particulars, but *not gone* in the approach.

The Bhagavad Gita puts it this way, "Who dwells in his inner self,
and is the same in pleasure and pain; to whom gold or stones or
earth are one, and what is pleasing or displeasing leave him in
peace; who is beyond both praise and blame, and whose mind
is steady and quiet". Honestly, I prefer the few words version:
Dead, but not gone. More words make it easier for my mind to
become trapped in the ideal. This only carries me further from

the real and increases emotional pressures to be perfect. These days I'm more than willing to settle for GREAT PERFECTION.

34.

(This '34' is really a commentary on understanding. The actual commentay for chapter 34's begins on the following page.)

I've said this before, and I must say it again. Using more words can easily obfuscate the issue at hand. This is especially true with existential matters. Understanding what is being said hinges on what one already knows at the gut level. In other words, existential matters cannot really be taught. This is not unlike that, 'you can lead a horse to water, but you can't make him drink'.

For example, I usually understand what the Tao Te Ching says when reading it in the terse original Chinese. Not that I'm fluent in Chinese – far, far from it. I imagine that I have a gut level 'taoist' worldview formed through an innate (genetic) 'taoist' disposition, life experience, and the adoption of ways to cognitively model all this from various written sources (Yoga, Buddha, Tao, Christ...). The final source, and perhaps the most effective for me, was Correlations[1]. These come closest to being a word based 'TEACHING THAT USES NO WORDS'

Overall, I find that the fewer words used to portray a core existential view, the fewer words there are to obstruct that view. Oddly then, translating the original into what must be a more wordy English version (to make grammatical sense) is the hardest part of what I'm doing here. Why bother? Is it the challenge that draws me?

The moral here: how you interpret what you see (or read) is the weakest link in existential learning. This is because your understanding is purely a reflection of what you already know. Thus, truth is not to be found 'out there', but rather 'in here'. It is not important what the 'sage' says, rather, it is how you interpret it that matters. Thus, you can EXTERMINATE

---

1 See: Centertao.org/essays/correlations

THE SAGE, DISCARD THE WISE, AND THE PEOPLE WILL BENEFIT A
HUNDREDFOLD. The only true authority is one's own self-honesty:

> WITHOUT STIRRING ABROAD
> ONE CAN KNOW THE WHOLE WORLD;
> WITHOUT LOOKING OUT OF THE WINDOW
> ONE CAN SEE THE WAY OF HEAVEN.
> THE FURTHER ONE GOES
> THE LESS ONE KNOWS.

Some agree with this right from the start. Yet for others,
truth is something found 'out there'. If you've read this far,
I imagine you lean to the former. More power to you!

34.

LEFT AS WELL AS RIGHT applies across the board: political,
religious, moral issues, yin and yang, etc. Saying, '*The great
way flows*, such as it may *left and right* is simply another
way to consider *profound sameness*. It is remarkable that we
can even see this deeper aspect of Nature considering how
unavoidably drawn we are to see reality in contrasting shades
of color (or black and white if you're colorblind). Difference is
what stimulates awareness; sameness just puts us to sleep.

'*Because of its ultimate non-self, it becomes great*' is one more
way to consider the illusion of self. What causes this illusion?
Buddha nailed it with his 'the illusion of self originates and
manifests itself in a cleaving to things'. Yet, perhaps there
is something still more fundamental happening here.

Clearly, we cling (cleave) to ideas, things, memories, beliefs,
kith and kin. Indeed, anything that can be clung to, someone
will be found to be clinging. *Meritorious accomplishment*,
clothes, mastery, desire, are just the tip of the iceberg. Why
do we cling so? Let's consider our powerful urge to cling as a
symptom and see where that leads. For example, if you saw
me clinging to a branch, you could assume I was hanging from
a tree or off the edge of a cliff. I'd be clinging to stop myself
plunging to death. The fear of falling drives me to cling.

The implication here: We cling to things and ideas[1] in order to avoid plunging down into an abyss of STILLNESS AND EMPTINESS. Our extreme reliance on WORDS and NAMES creates a highly structured field of awareness. Ensuing illusions of future, past, and present, along with the clear-cut differences we use to maintain those illusions, paints us into a perceptual corner. It feels safe there, but because the 'safe there' is only make believe, we also feel insecure there. We know the void is lurking just behind the veil of what we THINK THAT [WE] KNOW. No wonder we have difficulty.

35.

This chapter offers a teaching on what to look for in life that can bring CONTENTMENT. Well, don't they all? Perhaps, but each from a slightly different angle. Calling it a teaching is not that accurate either in the usual sense of a teaching tells you what to do. The Tao Te Ching's TEACHING is really an invitation to dig down deep into your own mind to find something (or Nothing) relevant. Simply put, one needs to bring mental rigor to this, which may explain its under-whelming popularity. Mind you, it is not that folks don't bring mental rigor to life. It is just that rigor often arise from perceived necessity. The 'fuzzy' MUDDLED nature of the Tao Te Ching doesn't really stimulate that sense of urgency.

Enjoyable things in life, like MUSIC AND FOOD, ENTICE US TO STOP and linger for a while on life's journey. However, when we become full of the music and food, we travel on. In a very real sense we are seeking that *great image* this chapter refers too. Think of this as one of biology's HOODWINKS, keeping living things on their life's journey from birth to death. If the *great image* is what we seek, how then can we *hold* it?

---

1   The irony in this example is that the self I'm protecting first originated and now manifests itself in a cleaving to things. The illusion of self I've created must now cling to that from which it originated, otherwise it fears it will plunge into a SILENT AND VOID oblivion, a death of self. It is a vicious circle of sorts. Although, you could say all of existence is as well: IT IS ON DISASTER THAT GOOD FORTUNE PERCHES; IT IS BENEATH GOOD FORTUNE THAT DISASTER CROUCHES. Okay, time to stop; I've done enough damage for one night. ;-)

The age-old view of "Thou art that," (<u>Tat Tvam Asi</u>) and the related "not this, not this" (similar to <u>negative theology</u>) are helpful. Knowing that everything you perceive is you (that thou art) is equivalent to knowing that nothing is 'it' (not this, not this). In other words, as long as you hold onto something, your hands are full and there is no way to also *hold the great image*. Only by letting go can you *hold* on (ah yes, STRAIGHTFORWARD WORDS SEEM PARADOXICAL).

The beauty of *holding the great image* (or *holding* NOTHING, if you like) is that USE WILL NEVER DRAIN IT. Everything else can certainly be EXHAUSTED BY USE. It is a little ironic how costly Nothing truly is. Costly? Sure, you must give everything to receive Nothing. That's a pretty steep price indeed!

36.

No matter how strong and active life is, it always ends in weakness and stillness (death). That is why we say, THE SUBMISSIVE AND WEAK WILL OVERCOME THE HARD AND STRONG. Yet, even at the everyday level, weakness is profoundly useful. It is the 'power' of THE MYSTERIOUS FEMALE. I see this linkage between 'power' and weakness as a <u>co-generating principle</u> of nature.

This co-generating principle is obvious in the way BEFORE AND AFTER FOLLOW EACH OTHER. Likewise, but perhaps less obvious, selfish and selfless COMPLEMENT each other, life and death HARMONIZE with each other, right and wrong PRODUCE each other, and so on. We make life more difficult than need-be by favoring one side at the expense of the other. Although, this is just the way nature (instinct) intends it to be, I might add. Why? Let's just say such hoodwinking serves interaction and evolution. Curiously, defying this instinct and DOING MY UTMOST TO ATTAIN EMPTINESS, allows *the weak to get the better of the unyielding*. This breaks up any 'emotional log jams' and helps bring on a resurgence of effort to move forward.

Feeling the importance of moving forward in life is universal. We must move forward and persevere (or at least feel we are) to feel

Right with life. Fundamentally, life meaning lies in movement. When we feel stuck, movement becomes impossible. The way of addressing this 'movement issue' is what differentiates Taoism from 'common sense'. For example, pushing for movement can often produces its opposite - feeling even more stuck. Rather than push even harder, the Taoist way does NOT CONTEND with the 'emotional log jam', but rather becomes one with it. Curiously, this allows life's movement to return naturally and effortlessly. In short, the easiest way to bring about the side desired is to RETURN to the other. Put another way, we can only truly have what we let go of. (That such going against natural inclinations works so well probably accounts for the continuous state of irony I feel.)

I translate / interpret the end of this chapter quite differently than D.C. Lau. First, I reckon it is not that 'THE FISH MUST NOT BE ALLOWED TO LEAVE THE DEEP'. Rather, *fish can't escape from the deep*. The implication of the former is that we have a choice in the matter. The later offers a view of 'THAT WHICH IS NATURALLY SO'. Next, how can one reveal 'the instruments of power', even if one wanted too? After all, 'MY WORDS ARE EASY TO UNDERSTAND...' More realistic, if still somewhat obscure, is the idea that *a state's weapons can't instruct the people*. Although it does parallel my sense that true learning can only arise from within. True ignorance can't be un-taught through external measures like 'education'. Nuts, that's not what we want to hear!

37.

I was struck today by how this chapter's point of view shifts from 'out there' to 'in here'. The MYRIAD CREATURES WILL BE TRANSFORMED OF THEIR OWN ACCORD arguably portrays lords and creatures 'out there'. Then the view shifts inward, ending with... AND IF I CEASE TO DESIRE AND REMAIN STILL, THE EMPIRE WILL BE AT PEACE OF ITS OWN ACCORD.

To me, this is a roundabout way to say that the world we see is a reflection of ourselves; perfection lies 'in here', in the eye of the beholder. If I'm right, does the round about way the Tao Te Ching puts it, hit home any more effectively than me saying that the world we see merely mirrors who we are? Not if cognitive understanding MUST NEEDS HAVE ITS BEGINNINGS in intuitive knowing. In other words, if you don't 'gut get it', nothing said will really hit home. In fact, more words can even get in the way. Of course, this is entirely antithetical to our belief that teaching conveys understanding. Yet, it agrees with my experience.

Years ago, I read about 'projection', a narrower psychiatric version of my view that the world we THINK we see is simply a reflection of our senses and emotions (needs and fears). Although, I never really 'gut got it' back then. Sure, I understood the words, but didn't really feel the reality until years later. Believing the illusion of my senses and emotion, I long failed to notice the dead obvious fact that my biology had me seeing reality as something 'out there'. It is DIFFICULT to this day to discern, moment to moment, that what appears to be 'out there' is actually 'in here'. Biology makes seeing the world with such IMPARTIALITY (a 'taoist' point of view) understandably very difficult. Nature's HOODWINK (biology) continuously boggles my mind.

How is it that 'The way normally does nothing, yet there is nothing not done'? The more I live the immediacy of each moment, the less paradoxical this view. In fact, when I am without desire and still everything gets done all the more. Actually, everything not only gets done, it gets done more efficiently and effortlessly. It turns out that any effort I feel, especially wasted effort, is a result of my desire for an ideal outcome. When I HAVE LITTLE THOUGHT OF SELF AND AS FEW DESIRES AS POSSIBLE, the outcome actually becomes the ideal! Instead of my ideals pushing for particular outcomes, CONTENTMENT helps me look upon any outcome as ideal.

Alas, need and fear (the origin of desire) traps the human mind in an illusionary world of ideals where we battle demon after evil demon. Yet what are those demons? They are only that which threatens those ideals we cherish. Talk about shooting one's self in the foot! In a way, this parallels government (and personal) finances. Money comes in through taxes and wages. Money goes out through expenditures. Limiting expenditures correlates to contentment and 'less is more', until...

BRING IT ABOUT THAT THE PEOPLE WILL RETURN
TO THE USE OF THE KNOTTED ROPE,
WILL FIND RELISH IN THEIR FOOD,
AND BEAUTY IN THEIR CLOTHES,
WILL BE CONTENT IN THEIR ABODE,
AND HAPPY IN THE WAY THEY LIVE.

Have you noticed how both the government and the people find limiting expenses extremely difficult? Some want to raise taxes, work more, or win the lottery to support more expenditure. Others want to lower taxes or work less, but never get around to limiting expenditures if they can help it. Both groups only differ in name and ideology. Neither DESIRES NOT TO BE FULL... although this is natural. After all, we are merely animals. So much so that the sole meaningful difference I see between us and other animals is our HYPOCRISY. This feels ironic and pitiful, though I'm not sure why. Perhaps this arises from the origin of the ideals—the nagging feelings of what could be, or should be.

38.

Much of this chapter supports my so-called 'symptoms' theory of reality. Briefly stated: Whatever we see or think are real in the world are actually symptoms (effects) of underlying–normally opposite–causes[1]. So, for example, the reason A MAN OF THE LOWEST VIRTUE NEVER STRAYS FROM VIRTUE [IS BECAUSE] HE IS WITHOUT VIRTUE. The whole sequence below shows a descending chain of causation: *Virtue follows loss of way; Benevolence follows loss of virtue; Justice follows loss of benevolence; Ritual follows loss of justice.* We are biologically 'hoodwinked' to deal with external symptoms and overlook underlying causes. Our innate incentive to ponder causation and WATCH THESE TEAMING CREATURES RETURN TO THEIR SEPARATE ROOTS is fairly weak. Overall, life is easier to manage when I know (REMEMBER) I'm seeing symptoms, and not 'the real thing'. Whenever I lose sight of this 'secret' I am led off onto one wild goose chases

---

1   Confounding our perception are also the projections of our own needs and fears into our thinking. What a messy affair! The best way I've found, so far, to untangle this is through **correlations**.

after another (i.e., those BY-PATHS PEOPLE PREFER). Needless to say, I treasure being as mindful of this as possible.

'ABIDING IN THE FRUIT NOT IN THE FLOWER' describes one of the more tragic sides of life. We have the greatest DIFFICULTY appreciating the fruit of this moment. Instead, we hold out for tomorrow's fruit promised in the flowers of our dreams. Naturally, instinct drives all life to keep looking ahead in the scramble for survival. The hunter-gatherer has to be always searching for his next meal. Our difficulty lies in our ability to move out of 'now' into a *foreknowledge* of tomorrow. Our mind easily *dwells in the thin*, whereas non-thinking animals have no alternative but to be grounded, *dwelling in the thick* of the present.

Civilized man, free from the daily drudgery of actually hunting and gathering, but still retaining these survival instincts to 'get on the move', channels his hunt and gather energies into shopping, working, warfare, sports, arts, business... you name it! TURNING BACK to be *in the thick* of it all is essential for apes who THINK.

Note: The term '*without doing*' (*wu wei*) used below is a core Taoist view of human conduct that lets things takes their own natural course, e.g., ONE DOES LESS AND LESS UNTIL ONE DOES NOTHING AT ALL, AND WHEN ONE DOES NOTHING AT ALL THERE IS NOTHING THAT IS UNDONE.

39.

D.C. Lao translates this chapter's final sentence as, 'NOT WISHING TO BE ONE AMONG MANY LIKE JADE, NOR TO BE ALOOF LIKE STONE.' Does this convey the meaning of the original? Compare D.C. Lao's with the literal translation of the characters and/or my translation. Although, I don't think it matters much. When you read either from a 'taoist' point of view, you will likely see a 'taoist' message, provided both are well written (i.e., grammar and such). The 'best' one will be the one that says best what you want to hear. Naturally, this holds true regardless of translation accuracy. Simply put, what we THINK we see is a result of what we want to see. Just as 'beauty is in the eye of the beholder', so also is 'meaning is in the mind of the believer.' (No wonder I have to say, in the end, MY MIND IS THAT OF A FOOL - HOW BLANK! Nevertheless...)

We used to use D.C. Lao's more readable translation at the Sunday meeting. Personally, I see 'Not wishing to be one among many like jade' as speaking to our hierarchical drive for social status. Each person feels special (i.e., the ego illusion) which ironically makes this a 'one among many' reality. This can only increase any indifference one has about 'keeping up with the Jones', and instead nudge one to 'be aloof like stone' (and perhaps gain a competitive edge in the process).

I imagine that righteous purists, of every stripe, fit this 'be aloof like stone' model. Personally, never being particularly drawn to the cultural mainstream, this 'aloof like stone' turned out to be a principle BY-PATH for me. Naturally enough, I never found contentment in being more aloof like stone, nor in longing to be one among many like jade. That makes sense, of course, because these are symptoms of underlying imbalance (i.e., symptoms reveal imbalance and/or mask imbalance, but never eliminate imbalance).

Finding a inner balance is the only way that works. Like maintaining physical balance, in a headstand for example, constant vigilance is essential. Of course, this is an 'easier said than done' ideal. Still, at least I know what to head for. Often in existential matters, merely knowing the way is more than sufficient. Knowing this, the rest takes care of itself; A JOURNEY OF A THOUSAND MILES STARTS FROM BENEATH ONE'S FEET. What happens beneath one's feet **now** is far more crucial than getting anywhere; the getting there is how WE LIVE OUT OUR DAYS.

Existence fulfills the One and grows, and so on, parallels my view that everything in *existence* rests on a symptom of something deeper. Calling 'that something' *the One* is appropriate. For one thing, as soon as you NAME 'that something', it then becomes a symptom of something *One* level deeper. *The One* is that INDISTINCT AND SHADOWY aspect that has yet to be named. I suppose this is like a house of mirrors, with *the One* obscured by the last mirror. The practical value in knowing that *existence*

154

fulfills the One and grows lies not in understanding what *the One* actually is, but rather in knowing that what ever you see is resting on a deeper base cause. The mind can only identify and name the surface, the appearance, of things. The trap lies in believing that the surface of which you are aware is the whole picture, when in fact, it is only the tip of the iceberg. The more you understand that *existence fulfills the One and grows*, the less likely you can become swept up and trapped by what you THINK THAT YOU KNOW. This sounds horribly abstract to me, but that's only because WORDS don't lend themselves to describing such matters. I suppose it is the challenge of tackling the impossible that keeps me trying and typing.

The high take low as the base. This, and so rulers call themselves solitary, scant, pathetic. I see two ways to interpret this: (1) They are *solitary, scant, pathetic* because they are kings, or (2) they are kings because they are *solitary, scant, pathetic.* For me, the base cause here is feeling *solitary, scant, pathetic.* In other words, feeling *solitary, scant, pathetic* drives one to be 'king' of something. *The high take low as the base;* the low is the foundation and the powerhouse that drive the high. As they say, "nature abhors a vacuum"; the SILENT AND VOID are the mother of all action; circumstances just nudge the outcomes.

40.

TURNING BACK IS HOW THE WAY MOVES corresponds to the correlation's derived[1] world-view that 'time returns', i.e., time moves backwards, time stays still[2]. Sure, saying that 'time returns' defies common sense and observation, but no less so than saying, 'Turning back is how the way moves', or as I translate it, *In the opposite direction, of the way 'it' moves.*

---

1   Correlations is a rigorous process of using words to define each other until they COMPLEMENT EACH OTHER in a balanced way not commonly seen.
2   What is time anyway? The experience we have in what we call 'time' is actually our experience of 'energy moving'. Clocks don't measure time; you might say that they measure energy 'within time'. If you can loosen the common sense meanings to that which you were conditioned from birth, you will experience time (or perhaps I should say eternity) differently.

Perhaps we trust common sense and observation a little too much for our own good. Surely, the purpose of evolution is not to enable living things to know how 'it' really is, or works. Evolution is all about ensuring that living things see 'reality' in such a way that drives them to compete (or cooperate) to survive. If that means USING THE WAY TO HOODWINK all us living things, then so be it.

The wonder of the Tao Te Ching is that it attempts to help us see 'it' from the other side - in reverse and inside out... to defy common sense in order to stumble into 'ultra-common sense'. The downside is that reality is often just the opposite of how it appears to be. This can be a 'little' disconcerting and takes time getting used to (if ever). The upside is that if you take 'it' seriously, you can often spot GOOD FORTUNE PERCHING AND DISASTER CROUCHING in a timely way. What more could one ask for?

That 'symptoms point of view' I'm always touting is expressed here succinctly in *Loss through death, of the way 'it' uses* and *Having is born in nothing* (or as Lau puts it: WEAKNESS IS THE MEANS THE WAY EMPLOYS, & SOMETHING FROM NOTHING). This is why judging a book by its cover is utterly misleading. It is not important what 'facts' we think see; the underlying causes are what enlightens. All our actions are merely reactions to our intuitive sense of the SILENT AND VOID. It's the cause. It drives us to do, or not do, whatever. The advantage of looking as deeply as possible using a 'symptoms point of view' is not that you'll get a clear and distinct view of what is happening. It's just the opposite, and there in lies an advantage. This helps you be more TENTATIVE, HESITANT, VACANT, AND MURKY LIKE MUDDY WATER. Only then can THE TEACHING THAT USES NO WORDS be heard.

Part of our common sense meanings are due to cultural conditioning and part due to natural instinct as I said above. Being so deeply rooted in our being, 'common sense meanings' are not about to, poof – vanish. Nor need they. Simply loosen your trust in 'common sense' enough so you can notice nature's hoodwinks.

There is a bonus too. Those weird and PARADOXICAL effects of Einstein's space-time relativity will begin to make simple sense!

41.

For nearly 50 years, I've been interpreting *the superior student* as referring to students of the *way* in relation to the Tao Te Ching. Today I broadened my view to include every attempt to study. Along with this, I must also consolidate and simplify my definition of what it means to study. Study normally means concentrating on a subject, which may eventually lead to becoming an expert in that field. This feels like an oddly narrow artifact of civilization, however.

The further back in time we look, we see that individuals 'studied' (lived) life as an all-inclusive whole, i.e., there were no experts to speak of. The way for them was truly BROAD, REACHING LEFT AS WELL AS RIGHT. Study, in this broader sense, means being as watchful as possible to notice what has yet to be seen, and therefore un-named. As D.C. Lao puts it, THE WAY CONCEALS ITSELF IN BEING NAMELESS. I think of this as studying (watching) life until I can see it beyond the names. Seeing everything as simply symptoms of deeper, subtler, concealed causes helps me reach being CAPABLE OF NOT KNOWING ANYTHING. (Now that is an ironic definition of study, eh?)

Entering the way seems like moving backwards, and so on, points to a most tragic, if subtle, aspect of life. We keep looking forward for happiness. Whenever we remain still, we soon become restless and seek out the way that seems bright, unaware that actually *the bright way seems hazy and hidden*.

This is natural of course. The hunter-gather instinct drives us to keep looking forward. That is where our next meal would be coming from, and so I don't see this as being tragic in the wild. Those ancestral 'wild' conditions played themselves out slowly, which helped maintain balance (in the wild). The fundamental focus of civilization has been to speed up our access to whatever we seek (need, desire, want, crave). This only hinders the ability to CEASE TO DESIRE AND REMAIN STILL.

In an odd way, the more we get, the less we have. Meaning, we can only truly have what we appreciate. Rushing ahead seeking *virtue, purity, smooth, and bright* is a symptom of less appreciation. This only occurs from a deeper sense of not having enough. Sure, we say, HENCE IN BEING CONTENT, ONE WILL ALWAYS HAVE ENOUGH. Isn't that actually putting the cart before the horse? Contentment comes IF AND WHEN we feel we have enough. Desire leads to a vicious circle; the more desire, the more we seek, the less we feel appreciation, which drives on desire even more. On the other hand, a *virtuous* circle would be, the less we desire, the less we seek, and the more content we feel which leads to less desire. It's no wonder, therefore, that THE SAGE DESIRES NOT TO DESIRE. I don't know if that actually breaks the vicious circle of desire, but it can't hurt, and perhaps slows it down.

42.

The literal puts it somewhat differently than D.C.Lau's translation reads. This always feels odd at first, for I've been reading D.C.Lau's translation for about 50 years now. Nevertheless, I approach this, whether D.C.Lau's or the Chinese, with an intention of having it represent something I know to be so through experience. This has not always been easy, or possible, especially in my younger days. For me, understanding the Tao Te Ching is really about understanding my own experience. This is another way of saying: the Tao Te Ching teaches you nothing you don't know already. The task is really about understanding cognitively what you know intuitively (i.e., ...SHADOWY, INDISTINCT. INDISTINCT AND SHADOWY), and the Tao Te Ching is a useful tool to that end. Now, on with this chapter...

'*The way gave birth to the whole. The whole gave birth to difference*' offers me a deeper view compared to 'THE WAY BEGETS ONE; ONE BEGETS TWO'. *One* and *two* also mean *whole* and *difference*, but *whole* and *difference* mean more to me that *one* and *two* (especially in this context).

The word '*fu*' (负) translates various ways: *carry on back; suffer; owe; betray; lose.* D.C.Lau used the CARRY ON THEIR BACKS, where as I went with *suffer*. Both meanings are equally fine; I choose *suffer* as that corresponds with Buddha's

First Noble Truth. Seeking and finding parallels in other scriptures always helps broaden and deepen the view.

Next, THERE ARE NO WORDS WHICH MEN DETEST MORE THAN 'SOLITARY', 'DESOLATE', AND 'HAPLESS', YET LORDS AND PRINCES USE THESE TO REFER TO THEMSELVES. I see this as the unintended consequences of rising to the top leadership position. The higher up one goes, the further from THE LOWER POSITION one can get, leaving one with an inevitable sense of isolation. This is a secret of sorts, in that the many at the bottom look up to the select few at the top and see mostly the 'good' side (i.e., the success, wealth, power, control, and fame they may aspire to in their dreams). On the other side of the coin, the buck stops with the MASTER at the top! That's sobering enough to make one feel *alone, few, and not of the valley.*

Generally, I think the burden of responsibility is only appreciated by those who are carrying it. Why? For one thing, it is an abstract 'burden' compared to hauling water up hill, for example, which everybody can picture doing. The burden of responsibility is a psychological and emotional burden. Indeed, taking on a physical burden often helps lighten the mental and emotional load... as does, or course, FOLLOWING THE WAY AND THE WAY ONLY!

Both *perhaps lose as well as benefit, and benefit as well as lose* and, THUS A THING IS SOMETIMES ADDED TO BY BEING DIMINISHED AND DIMINISHED BY BEING ADDED TO, conform to my experience, but in different ways. The literal may put it better for me. It is another way of saying 'there are no free rides' in nature. Everything comes with a price. There is no "sometimes" about it, although D.C.Lau's "sometimes" may be his translation of *huo* (或) which translates more directly as *perhaps*. Come to think of it, there is no "*perhaps*" about it either.

43.

The most flexible of all things under heaven surpasses the most resolute is easier to appreciate when considered from a quantum non-locality view. Although, this fits a more down to earth point of view as well. Young men, or young mountains, are *resolute* initially, but bend over in time. Time? Sure, what is more *'flexible (soft; supple; gentle; yielding; mild)'* than time? Virtually nothing... although, time[1] and the VIRTUE OF NOTHING are perhaps essentially the same 'thing' anyway.

The later part of this chapter, *Not of words teaching, Without action advantage,* voice an odd thing about *teaching* I began to notice as I home schooled my kids. *Teaching* wasn't as straightforward a process as I expected. Learning requires understanding, which I realized requires a deeper sense of knowing. Rather that 'top down', I found teaching and learning to be more of a 'bottom up' experience.

Essentially, knowing is the basis of understanding. The knowing must be 'there' before true understanding can occur. Now, are you thinking to yourself, "Aren't knowing and understanding essentially the same?" I guess they are, at least in the common meaning of these words[2].

I consider knowing to be a deep intuitive sense experienced by all living things (pretty much, although I'm not sure how that works out in nervous-system-less creatures like virus). Understanding, on the other hand, is a cognitive, language based sense experienced only by humans, as far as I know. My ducks do know they like snails... they don't understand that they do (or the why, how, when, where of it all). In an ironic way, attempting to teach with words is putting the cart somewhat before the horse.

---

1   I am not referring to 'clock time', which is more a measure of energy's role in time. Time itself is much more MYSTERIOUS, like consciousness itself. And by consciousness, I don't mean the contents (worldly clutter) of consciousness. The contents of consciousness are energy's actors; consciousness is time's stage. Or to put this another way: WHEN YOUR DISCERNMENT PENETRATES THE FOUR QUARTERS ARE YOU CAPABLE OF NOT KNOWING ANYTHING?

2   We feel these words, know and understand, are synonymous because we associate language and thinking with both words. Indeed, people have often seen thinking as a prerequisite for consciousness itself. Alas, such species-centric views are very misleading and account, in part, for why PEOPLE ARE IGNORANT. Word meaning and language reflect our understanding, and ultimately our knowing... not the other way around (whatever that means ;-)).

Let's take a closer look...
Knowing is accumulative, built upon previous knowing/s.
One must know sitting to crawl, crawling to walk, walking
to run. One must know '2' before knowing '2+2'. Knowing
also hinges on interpretation of one's experience. A fly has
a compound eye that makes the world appear a certain way.
What a fly knows of the world is determined in part by its
multi-lens interpretation. The world it knows appears different
from the world known by the snail, dog, duck, or spider.

For humans, knowing also hinges on cultural paradigms that
filter basic (biologically based) sensory input. This is a major
determinant to judgment, part of the 'where one is coming
from' side of things. All these factors combine to make any
idea of teaching via words unlikely to measure up to our ideals
and expectations. Nevertheless, we hold to the illusion that
words can convey understanding and knowing. And so, it is
little wonder that THE TEACHING THAT USES NO WORDS, THE
BENEFIT OF RESORTING TO NO ACTION, THESE ARE BEYOND THE
UNDERSTANDING OF ALL BUT A VERY FEW IN THE WORLD. Once
I began experiencing this sobering point of view, much of the
seemingly contradictory, perplexing and paradoxical aspects of
human activity become more straightforward and NATURAL.

44.

For the past 50 years I've interpreted this as generally asking me
to choose between which of two I prefer. D.C. Lau's translation
may have encouraged that a little. For example, GAIN OR LOSS,
WHICH IS A GREATER BANE? That just goes to show how once we
begin thinking a certain way, the tendency to continue thinking
that way is very strong. Thoughts (e.g., ideas, beliefs, opinions,
facts, etc.) are just another thing upon which to cleave and cling.

Buddha said, the illusion of self originates and manifests
itself in cleaving to things. After that, the survival of our
'illusion of self' (ego) gives us an ongoing incentive to
cleave to what we think. That sounds like a vicious circle
to me. By the way, doesn't the result of cleaving to what

we think construe "I think therefore I am" to mean just the opposite to what Descartes had in mind? Hmm...

Today I saw the light... maybe. Today, anyway, I may be finding a more balanced view of this chapter. The key suggestion being, *knowing when to stop*. The more we favor either, *name* or *body*, *body* or *goods*, *gain* and *loss*, the more we are setting ourselves up for danger and loss as the fifth line plainly states, *The more we hold on, the deeper the loss.*

Come to think of it, perhaps the only 'light' I see here is this: the loss we suffer is proportional to the degree we hang on. Rather than blame the circumstances that bring about the losses we morn, perhaps it is wiser to acknowledge the actual source of the pain - *the more we love, the more we hold on, the deeper the loss.* Pain is just the price we pay for that pleasure.

The meaning of *love* and pleasure often co-mingle, as we see here. *Love* is a word that dances with many meanings. A meaning of *love*, free from the connotations stated in this chapter, is easily found through correlations. This 'truer' *love* correlates to: giving, accepting, being patient... and IMPARTIALITY, STILLNESS, EMPTINESS... THE MYSTERIOUS FEMALE... *profound sameness*... CONTENTMENT... NOTHING.

45.

Among other things, this chapter takes a gentle swipe at so-called objective awareness. What does that mean? Let's return to the beginning. At birth, consciousness exists as a moment-to-moment subjective awareness (and/or visa versa?). With non-thinking animals, awareness continues to be subjective throughout life. We, on the other hand, soon associate names and words with our subjective perceptions. Subsequently, we mentally manipulate these perceptual objects in mind-space and presto, we get so-called 'objective' awareness. This enables us to THINK THAT WE KNOW.

Naming something as *straight*, for example, requires the category of *straightness* and its counter part *bendiness*. Both are needed to nail down ('know') the distinction. Likewise, if you believe *accomplishment* is real, then you can't help but believe its counterpart *incompleteness* and failure are real also. Perception becomes stuck in a vicious circle choosing one side, the other side, or a confused in-between. Alas, WORDS and NAMES make the vicious circle an inevitable characteristic of objective awareness.

Whoa, cycling circles... I'm getting dizzy! Fortunately taking the broader view helps quiet down this circle cycle. Here, *Great* comes into sight as one begins to notice how opposites produce each other (i.e., OFF-SET, COMPLIMENT, FOLLOW, HARMONIZE WITH). Naturally, you'll eventually become CAPABLE OF NOT KNOWING ANYTHING[1], and little more. Hmm... perhaps this is why few are attracted to a Taoist point of view. "Not knowing anything" is hardly an enviable or award-winning *accomplishment*.

The idea of *Great* ____(you name it)____ reminds me of the moment I saw garbage floating in a canal in Tokyo and it looked *Great* (and no, I wasn't on LSD). I mean it really looked BEAUTIFUL. That was the first time I felt GREAT PERFECTION SEEMS CHIPPED. Up until that moment, I'd always regarded garbage and pollution as something ugly and *incomplete* (being the neat-n-tidy freak that I am).

The generally held sense of *perfection* is a state of being that has an end point; something can be *accomplished* (or at least work towards). I think of *Great perfection*, Taoist style, as something

---

1   To be fair (and practical) one can't survive in society 'not knowing anything.' However, I find 'not knowing anything' to be a *Great* vacation. I find that losing trust in the certainty of differences and shifting faith over to *profound sameness* makes popping in and out of 'not knowing anything' fairly easy for the most part.

So how does one go about finding faith in '*profound sameness*'? Lose trust in the reality of words. How? I suppose the answer to that is the same as how one loses trust in anyone or anything. Mainly you become aware of the dishonesty, duplicity, and deviousness, and don't wish to play along anymore. Evidence is all around us – it's an open secret. Yet we are conditioned from birth to believe, so it is difficult to see what even a infant sees. Correlations may help a few, otherwise, your guess is as good as mine.

that lives in the eye of the beholder. It can't be made, found, achieved, meddled with, drained or destroyed. It only exists in our point of view. Finding this point of view within myself has been liberating, for it relieves me of the arbitrary and often hypocritical standards of an exceedingly intelligent species like us. I guess that only in a Taoist view of life is cleverness not all it is cracked up to be, i.e., WHEN CLEVERNESS EMERGES THERE IS GREAT HYPOCRISY.

46.

The way has two sides, as I see it here: a subjective one, and a 'objective one'. Subjective is the personal sense of harmony, or the lack of it, we feel. It all depends on circumstances. Pinned under a ton of concrete after an earthquake one would not feel THE WAY WAS PREVAILING IN THE EMPIRE (their way anyway). On the other hand, after we have eaten well, are rested, with friends and feel content, we would feel *all under heaven, have the way* . This fits the view that the world we see is just a reflection of how we feel (desires/needs and insecurities/fears).

And what about the objective one? How about, 'DARKLY VISIBLE, IT ONLY SEEMS AS IF IT WERE THERE'. Perhaps balance is the word that comes closest to describing the way objectively (for me anyway). Although, balance, as a definition of the way, is far more SHADOWY AND INDISTINCT than how I normally define balance. I think of the 'way of balance' as an 'ideal' to which nature aspires. By aspires, I mean pointed to, driven towards, pull into...etc. Balance is the center, the core around which the universe eternally revolves. Interestingly, this ideal of balance to which nature moves toward (or returns to) can also be seen as the origin of (driving force behind) our ideals of peace and harmony. After all, our consciousness, at its height of IMPARTIALITY, must certainly reflect the essential qualities of nature. How could it be otherwise?

The needs and fears of living things (desire, covetousness, discontent in humans) are biological hoodwinks to push us to act. The illusion is that only when our fears are allayed and desires sated will we feel eternal peace and harmony - be in balance. Even if we rationally know that contentment will be fleeting, our emotions say otherwise. Emotion is convinced that feeding desires make us happy. In truth, happiness is momentary, sated desire, like the Greek Hydra, is almost immediately replaced by another need or fear.

This parallels nature naturally. For example, stresses build, like desires and we have an earthquake. The ground settles, tension is relieved for a moment until stress begins to build again. Nature swings like a pendulum, back and forth through the Golden Mean of balance. Balance is immediately lost as soon as it has won. Like any ideal, the reality of balance is never realized. Indeed, the process of seeking balance is itself an unbalancing force, which serves to counterbalance balance.

47.

What if the world we see 'out there' is simply a reflection of ourselves (who we are 'in here'). That is my sense of it, and this chapter points that way. Only by knowing yourself, the 'in here', can you know the 'out there'. Put another way, what we see 'out there' is merely a reflection of what is 'in here'. Therefore, through knowing one's self, one can *know all under heaven without going out the door.*

Going here and there and everywhere is often a way of distracting yourself, avoiding the uncomfortable unknown (fear and uncertainty) you inevitably face 'in here'. How can something so straightforward and simple be so 'invisible'? I can only assume that nature doesn't want us to look 'in here' all that much. And even when we do, we tend to judge what we see 'in here' by the apparent reality we believe exists 'out there'. The irony is overwhelming at times!

THE FURTHER ONE GOES, THE LESS ONE KNOWS may parallel my recent post, <u>Why Do Idiot Savants Run Things</u>? Looking *farther* 'out there' narrows one's view. You see more of less, and less of more. If knowing is about having a sense of the MYSTERY UPON MYSTERY 'big picture', then a narrower view means knowing more about less. This is the classic, 'not seeing the forest for the trees'.

Why would one go *farther* and *farther* anyway? Going *farther* is a symptom; we go *farther* when we don't KNOW CONTENTMENT (have enough of what we desire or value). Therefore, rewording this as, "the less one knows, the *farther* one goes" may be more accurate, from a symptom's point of view anyway.

More can be *accomplished* by being patient and letting nature takes its course. Of course, this is very hard to do. A 'just get it done' instinct drives us to resolve uncertainty, settle issues and be done with it so we can go on to the next 'greener pasture'. Haste makes waste is no empty saying. To forgo the 'greener pastures' and live 'in here' now requires a truer understanding of life.

A truer understanding of life naturally arises from self-understanding. Without self-understanding what can one really know, how can one interpret experience wisely? The more one tries to go somewhere and do something to gain self-understanding, the less chance they will find it, directly anyway (yes, in the end, 'all roads lead to Rome'). Self-understanding is found within; one need *go nowhere*, do nothing.

Obviously, the next question is: What is self-understanding really? I boil that down to self-honesty and digging down into my sense of life priorities – what do I truly want out of life over the long-term? A motto of mine[1] speaks to this: 'Short-term pleasure attracts long-term pain. Short-term pain attracts long-term pleasure'. The more I know what I truly want of life, the more the later guides my moment.

48.

A regular experience of '*Until without doing; Without doing yet not undone*' happens daily for me in yoga. Each moment presents two paths, you might say. One is where 'I am doing this yoga posture' and the other is where 'I am watching this yoga posture happen'. The former is when I struggle to control the action, the

---

1 This motto goes back to my years in Japan; a time of serious self examination. I find it as true today as ever, and helps me not second guess life as much as I might otherwise perhaps.

later is where I passively allow the action to happen. The former feels like I am doing more and more, the later feels like I am DOING LESS AND LESS. The former feels like I am expressing strength, The later feels like I am expressing weakness. The later is much more peaceful, and yet the work still gets done. It is simply a matter of approach. So, why don't I always 'choose' the later path?

Simply put, life happens as a BLENDING OF THE GENERATIVE FORCES OF THE TWO paths. I suppose it is simple ignorance (a result of our ability to think) that drives us to dream of perfection, such as *without doing yet not undone*. The survival instinct drives to take charge and control life; be strong and succeed, and not settle for something that SEEMS CHIPPED. Expressing weakness is emptiness, and we know how nature abhors a vacuum. That success truly comes through weakness is the greatest of ironies, i.e., TURNING BACK IS HOW THE WAY MOVES; WEAKNESS IS THE MEANS THE WAY EMPLOYS. Accepting that these are the rules for the game of life take the edge off; success becomes failure, failure becomes success… and soon all you have left is *profound sameness*. Ha!

49.

First, consider how we interpret two core 'taoist' words, *De* and *Xin*: *De* is the *De* of *Dao De Jing* (i.e., *Tao Te Ching*) and translates all the way from *virtue, integrity, character… to… heart, mind, kindness*. The other, *Xin*, translates as *heart, mind, feeling, intention, center, core*. These words can infer different meanings now (esp. in the West) than they did a few thousand of years ago.

For example, Christian culture narrows and polarizes the meaning of *virtue* with its views on God; how different they are from the Taoist view of God! Science also narrows and polarizes definitions, like the precise distinction made between *heart* and *mind*. Overall, we continue to CUT THE UNCARVED BLOCK into smaller, more distinct pieces. This makes translating the Tao Te Ching challenging! Although, this is easier when I am as THICK LIKE THE UNCARVED BLOCK; VACANT LIKE A VALLEY; MURKY LIKE MUDDY WATER as possible. Likewise, a reader will understand this better by approaching it with a similar *Xin* (i.e., *heart, mind, feeling, intention, center, core).*

The word *Xin* (same sound as above but a different character and tone) translates as *true, confidence, trust, faith* and *believe,* and can vary widely in what it infers. Personally, I have *faith* that ducks will be ducks; likewise, I have *faith* that people will be people. This is a bottom line *faith* in the reality of 'what is', rather than *faith* in an ideal of what should ideally be. I have *trust* in people, that they will be people rather than judging them from an ideal moral standard. This is more like HAVING NO MIND OF MY OWN, BUT TAKING ON AS MY OWN THE MIND OF THE PEOPLE. Of course, it is not that straightforward in real life. I must always first go through a MUDDLED phase before I can see clearly. I find this the precondition for clarity and understanding, however INDISTINCT AND SHADOWY understanding ends up being. We can't know until we viscerally realize that we don't know. Ah yes, STRAIGHTFORWARD WORDS SEEM PARADOXICAL.

What does *true, faith* and *trust,* or any other word, truly mean? Words are like 'black boxes' that emotions go into and come out of, but the 'box' itself is cloaked in mystery. Words are like the outside of the box, we usually only look at the outside and take 'meaning' for granted. Meaning though is actually only a reflection of our own emotions (primal needs and fears) and, by extension, of how we see the world. Words are mirrors and mean nothing in themselves. Even so, we often take and use words at face value as if real in their own right.

The adage 'put your money where your mouth it' speaks to this. How kind is being kind when others are kind to you? How about when, *without kindness, I am also kind, of integrity kind?* (D.C. Lau puts it less literally and so less awkwardly as... THOSE WHO ARE NOT GOOD I ALSO TREAT AS GOOD.) Being kind to those who are not kind exemplifies the no stings attached emotion of giving, not one of exchanging or taking. We know anecdotally and through science (brain scans) that giving is more pleasurable that receiving. Revenge, passing judgment and FAVORITISM are acts of taking, and so are less pleasurable. Simply put, love feels a lot more pleasurable than hate.

So why would anyone 'choose' anything other than giving kindness and love? Why don't we all do as Christ suggested and just "turn the other cheek"? Simple, WE HAVE NO FREE WILL when it comes to choosing our feelings, our emotions! Action and reaction is the only arena in which we have choice. Yet, even this is only pseudo-choice, for our choice of actions originates in emotion. Note: If you understand all this, 'murky' it up a bit by considering *kindness* (i.e., *good, perfect, kind)* in its Taoist context, i.e., THE WHOLE WORLD RECOGNIZES THE GOOD AS THE GOOD, YET THIS IS ONLY THE BAD.

DC Lao's version may seem a little at odds with itself to some. THE SAGE HAS NO MIND OF HIS OWN. HE TAKES AS HIS OWN THE MIND OF THE PEOPLE initially agrees with the more literal, *The wise person is without ordinary intention. Takes the common people's mind as his mind.* But how does this mesh with THE SAGE IN HIS ATTEMPT TO DISTRACT THE MIND OF THE EMPIRE SEEKS URGENTLY TO MUDDLE IT? He is attempting to distract the mind of the empire, which as we see, is his own, i.e., 'he takes as his own the mind of the people'. This reminds me of I ALONE AM MUDDLED. CALM LIKE THE SEA. The Tao Te Ching is certainly a cornucopia of food for thought! No wonder I have difficulty keeping my commentary as short as I'd wish.

50.

This breakdown, THREE IN TEN WILL BE COMRADES OF LIFE, THREE IN TEN WILL BE COMRADES IN DEATH, reminds me of the Bell-Curve. No matter what the issue, there are always the extremes at either end, with the rest in the middle. It is empirically obvious that life, whether plant or animal (human type included), conforms to this curve. So? Accepting the nature of Nature is the only way I've found to find peace. My mind can conjure up all sorts of ideals that turn a blind eye to the Bell-Curve of reality. Let's face it; ideals are merely counter-balancing projections stemming from my own needs and fears. And what is need and fear really, but simply emotions originating in deficiency (i.e., ...BORN FROM

SOMETHING, AND SOMETHING FROM NOTHING). In other words, I need whatever I feel I lack, I fear loosing whatever I feel I need.

Truth be told then, I can't help feel need or fear as long as I'm alive. This makes ideals, desires, and worries inevitable, as long as I can THINK, anyway. However, expecting reality (how 'it is') to conform to my ideals (how 'it should be'), offers nothing but a life of CONTENTION. I may be slow learner, but I get it now! Although, this is like the termites around here. They are always around; I always have to be watchful enough to keep them at bay as much as possible. Sure, the work is never done, but lack of watchfulness ensures utter failure!

Of people, aroused by life, in death trapped, also three in ten. Why is this so? Because they favor life. This is true about anything we cling on to. As soon as I cling to something, I experience a virtual loss of it. The pleasure of gain and the stressful fears of loss OFF-SET EACH OTHER. Balance is maintained. Another way is to see this is from a symptoms point-of-view: Clinging to SOMETHING fills the SILENT AND VOID, or rather gives us the illusion that it does (the illusion of balance is maintained). This is a key HOODWINK in Mother Nature's toolbox of tricks.

Next, how does being *good at conserving life* differ from *favoring life?* For me, being *good at conserving life* means BEING AS CAREFUL AT THE END AS AT THE BEGINNING of each moment. Being this alive to life is *conserving life.* On the other hand, *favoring* the content of the moment attaches me to it, and it to 'me' (destroying IMPARTIALITY in the process). That to which we attach ourselves augments our 'Self'. As Buddha put it, the illusion of self originates and manifests itself in a cleaving to things. The more this illusion of self holds sway over awareness, the more I create a *place to allow the knife edge* and am *in death trapped.* The ironic consequence of *favoring life* is that this must be off-set by *in death trapped* (balance must be maintained!)

51.

This chapter really exposes, albeit subtly, the fiction that society fosters. Clearly, the world goes around NOT BECAUSE THIS IS DECREED BY AN AUTHORITY BUT BECAUSE IT IS NATURAL. This chapter essentially corresponds to HESITANT, HE DOES NOT UTTER WORDS LIGHTLY. WHEN HIS TASK IS ACCOMPLISHED AND HIS WORK DONE THE PEOPLE ALL SAY, 'IT HAPPENED TO US NATURALLY.'

I suppose I take it even further, for in my view, no one is responsible for what happens either good or bad. Reality is, rather, *of the way born, of virtue reared. Of long duration, of giving birth. Of well balanced, of malicious. Of support, of overturning.* Humans, being social hierarchical animals, take credit (or dish out blame) for what is actually quite NATURALLY so. The Bhagavad Gita puts it well: "All actions take place in time by the interweaving of the forces of Nature; but the man lost in selfish delusion thinks that he himself is the actor".

When, in the 60's, I'd hear people blaming leaders (generals, corporations, etc.) for the world's ills, I'd always respond with the view that there would be no leaders without willing followers. Followers are the 'horse' that draws the 'leaders' cart. That is the nature of a social species; we are simply driven to *rule* and be ruled. Because we are so innately tribal in nature, I suppose this will always remain something of a well-kept (yet open) secret.

This chapter served as a core model for raising my kids. That meant, my main service would be **to not get in the way**. Rather, allow *virtue, things and power* (or as D.C. Lao puts it, CIRCUMSTANCES) to play themselves out naturally. I wanted them to be able to SAY, 'IT HAPPENED TO US NATURALLY.' So far, it has proven to be a successful experiment. It has outdone my initial expectations in fact, as any true experiment should, I suppose. Still, they are only in their early 20's so the experiment is still on. To be honest, I was mature enough by the time I had kids (40+) that I was able to raise them in the 'taoist way'. This would have been impossible to do if I had been a parent in my youth.

52.

The first part, 'AFTER YOU HAVE KNOWN THE CHILD GO BACK TO
HOLDING FAST TO THE MOTHER' and the ending 'USE THE LIGHT BUT
GIVE UP THE DISCERNMENT' feel to me like two ways of saying the
same thing. The *mother* is the 'big bang' of consciousness, the
light that got the ball rolling, so to speak. From the pure simple
light of that beginning evolved the *children* (the *seeds* or MYRIAD
CREATURES, of which we are one). *Squeeze exchange, shut the gates,*
is the sole way to *use the light and again return to clarity.* Not
doing so allows consciousness to run around chasing all the *seeds*
of existence and leads to exhaustion (*no relief*). In fact, though,
most of us avoid reaching such extremes by clinging to BELIEF
and habit as a way of staying safely 'inside the box' of sanity.

The only disadvantage of staying 'inside the box' is the ignorance
that goes with confining perception there. On one hand, this is
protective, for it keeps us from using the *light* to discern every
nook and cranny of sensory experience. The obstacle is that it
blinds us to the MYSTERY UPON MYSTERY lying outside words and
belief. The only sane way to *use the light* of consciousness fully
is to *squeeze exchange* (i.e., to GIVE UP THE DISCERNMENT). You
can do this by *using the light* to *observe* the *profound sameness*
in what at first glance appears as difference. For this, it is
helpful to regard all differences you THINK YOU KNOW as simply
reflections of your own needs and fears, rather than reality
in their own right. When the small bits and pieces of life are
seen as THE ONE interconnected whole, *practice of the constant*
is as easy and natural as breathing moment to moment.

Squeeze exchange, shut the gates is the only way to KNOW
CONTENTMENT. *Opening the exchange, and helping affairs,*
on the other hand, allows the flames of desire to burn
endlessly, hopping from one issue to the next to the end of
your days. What are these *affairs*? Most everything you cling
to, or chase after, depending upon your personality, e.g.,
politics, food, sex, speech, work, sleep, etc. I can't think of
anything that doesn't apply (including doing this blog).

This is not saying to avoid desire, and the clinging and chasing of *affairs* that follow. It is simply helpful to KNOW WHEN TO STOP. This exemplifies the problem with 'NOT KNOWING YET THINKING THAT ONE KNOWS.' Knowing when to stop is not a rational intellectual knowing, it is a gut knowing. So, when the gut wants to keep going, thinking will rationalize that need. This corresponds to MY WORDS ARE VERY EASY TO UNDERSTAND AND VERY EASY TO PUT INTO PRACTICE, YET NO ONE IN THE WORLD CAN UNDERSTAND THEM OR PUT THEM INTO PRACTICE. It doesn't matter what the head understands, it is what the gut knows that counts. Alas, we have not the least bit of control over that. We must learn it the hard way, i.e., IF YOU WOULD HAVE A THING WEAKENED, YOU MUST FIRST STRENGTHEN IT. As futile as it seems, knowing this is exceptionally helpful. Go figure!

53.

'This does not conform to the way either,' or as D.C Lau puts it, 'FAR INDEED IS THIS FROM THE WAY' raises a question. In chapter 1 we read the 'Taoist disclaimer', 'THE WAY THAT CAN BE SPOKEN OF IS NOT THE CONSTANT WAY'. Saying what the way does *not conform to* something is just describing *the way* from the other side of the coin, so to speak. *'The fields very overgrown, the storehouses very empty'* helps reconcile this seeming contradiction when I bring it down to my personal experience... my ultimate test of 'reality'.

I don't worry about your *fields being overgrown* because I won't accept responsibility over that. I do worry about whether my garden *fields being overgrown* because I've taken gardening *'fields'* as a personal life *way*. A BY-PATH for me would be to neglect it. Balance between caring for the garden and enjoying the sensual pleasures of life, *drink and food, wealth and goods,* etc., is the key. The by-path is HAVING TOO MANY DESIRES and pleasures that bring me out of balance. In other words, it is where a path takes you that determines how much of a by-path it will be, not the desire or pleasure per se.

I feel the *way* is more about follow-through in doing what I know (in my heart of hearts) to be my life's path – my duty, my <u>Dharma</u>. This constancy is why THE NAME THAT CAN BE NAMED IS NOT THE CONSTANT NAME. The way is not a 'what' that can be named, it is an approach we innately know is 'right' for us personally, but which we are often distracted, for a host of reasons, from giving follow-through (...KNOWN AS FOLLOWING THE CONSTANT.) Without that follow-through, life feels a bit 'yucky'; with balanced follow-through, life feels just about right. It is possible to KNOW CONTENTMENT.

At the top of this chapter, D.C. Lau translates, 'I WOULD, WHEN WALKING ON THE GREAT WAY, FEAR ONLY PATHS THAT LEAD ASTRAY. THE GREAT WAY IS EASY, YET PEOPLE PREFER BY-PATHS'. Comparing this the more literal translation reveals something interesting: *Going in the great way, alone bestow this respect. The great way is very smooth, yet people are fond of paths.* People are fond of paths, not 'by-paths'! (Although, I've always liked using the term 'by-path'.) I'm reminded of how animals prefer following paths. That behavior is what gives predators a great advantage. I imagine animals, including us, *are fond of paths* because they can relax and not be as keenly aware (and thus responsible) of where they are going. It is not really by-paths that are problematic, it is ALL PATHS, at least all that can be 'spoken of' or 'named' that allow us to go-on-automatic. The Great Way, then, is more like an intuitive responding to each moment to moment with, as Buddha put it, <u>Right Attentiveness, Right Mindfulness, Right Concentration, Right Effort</u>. That's work; no wonder we all *fond of paths*.

It is also helpful to see all this from a symptoms point of view. The hunger-gather instinct drives us to jump ahead, seeking benefit – to hunt and gather. The safe and advantageous circumstances of a civilized life allow us to do this without restraint (i.e., follow-through on that drive). In the wild, natural circumstances keep instinct in check and help maintain balance. With less 'natural-push-back' we can 'gather benefit' relentlessly as we pile on more *colorful clothes, culture, belted swords, drink and food, wealth and goods.* (Note: if helps to think of *belted swords* as a metaphor for adult toys: 'hot' autos, 'cool' electronics, and most everything related to recreation or comfort. *Belted* being the key word... i.e., frivolous. Now, I'm not saying these toys are bad, I am saying we have difficulty KNOWING WHEN TO STOP)

Confident in our *knowledge,* we overlook our priorities and rationalize our push for 'gathering' more. Over-the-top examples of this, seen in the rich people, are simply a *path* that plagues us all. However, people often fail to see this universality, and instead focus on 'them'... the *government* and wealthy people. Here, the 'fairness' instinct (see UNFAIR TRADE) drives us to judge and criticize the *government* and rich people and corporation for what feels to us like robbery. It is easy to get trapped in the gut instincts that drive our lives. A major step to being *possessed of the least knowledge* may be just recognizing and accepting this simple fact of life (i.e., what WE THINK THAT WE KNOW is largely driven by what we feel).

Possessing things (even POSSESSED OF THE LEAST KNOWLEDGE) is the same as being possessed by those possessions. We think (i.e., feel) we own them, when in fact they own us. In holding on to these, they provide the anchor for our imagined self. What we hold on to makes the illusion of "I" feel real, as Buddha so nicely pointed out in his Second Noble Truth, "the illusion of self originates and manifests itself in a cleaving to things". To let go of those 'possessions' is tantamount to committing suicide, in that we would be letting go of "I".

54.
References to *ancestors* and *sacrifice* in this chapter
make it feel a bit culturally dated. No matter,
I'll fix this... or get a head ache trying!

The subject of this chapter, WHAT IS FIRMLY ROOTED, is based on two words: (1) Shan (善) means: *good; satisfactory; good; make a success of; perfect; kind; friendly; be good at; be expert in; be adept in; properly; be apt to,* (2) Jian (建) means: *build; construct; erect; establish; set up; found; propose; advocate.* What does this really boil down to? I see these two words pointing to something we all sense, yet for which we have no 'answer'.

The eternal mystery is, "where did all this (me, we, earth, stars) come from?" We see that Nature is *perfectly established* and have created stories to answer the why, where, when, what of it all: on one end, we have the biblical stories, which are part history, part myth. At the other end, we have science... but in the end, all are stories. The 'biblical' story of China has a lot to do with *descendants offering sacrifice to ancestors.* I prefer science as it is less susceptible to bias, i.e., there are rigorous methodologies to prevent the 'theory' from getting ahead of the 'observation' (evidence). That said, science's weakness lies in its bias toward the material, tangible, and measurable. Essentially, the eternal question can never be answered, at least in NAMES and WORDS!

WHAT IS FIRMLY ROOTED CANNOT BE PULLED OUT; nor can 'it' be defined and answered. To me this is another way of saying, WHEN YOUR DISCERNMENT PENETRATES THE FOUR QUARTERS, ARE YOU CAPABLE OF NOT KNOWING ANYTHING? Nevertheless, whatever this *firmly rooted* 'it-ness' is, we would be wise to *use it.* To keep returning to the primal mystery is the challenge. It is only from that raw experience, moment to moment, that we can *know* the question. This is what having a proper sense of awe is all about, in my view. The reason THE OFFERING OF SACRIFICE BY DESCENDANTS WILL NEVER COME TO AN END is that WHEN THE PEOPLE LACK A PROPER SENSE OF AWE, THEN SOME AWFUL VISITATION WILL DESCEND UPON THEM. In other words, we are always sobered by the awe-full mystery and pulled back into 'its' reality, (only to leave again, of course).

Making *'offering sacrifice to ancestors never ceases'* relevant to us may need a broader interpretation. For example, *ancestors* is all which came before us personally, or before our species. *Sacrifice* is that which we do, or don't do, as participants in the MYSTERIOUS 'now' of evolution / creation. We (all living things) are *offering sacrifice*, whether we think so or not. And we are all in the process of becoming *ancestors*. Being self-aware of all this is less self-centric and 'cool', as they say. ;-)

The series, *'of cultivating in'* and *'use the'*, reminds me of the old adage about 'walking a mile in another man's shoes'. The world we see 'out there' is merely a reflection of ourselves – the biological 'in here'. Yet, we are under the illusion (bio-hoodwink) that we experience an 'objective' reality. That illusion works well throughout nature. Only we (I suppose) have DIFFICULTY WITH THIS BECAUSE WE THINK. *Using all under heaven to observe heaven* helps demolish our self-centric point of view.

Finally, if you have read various translations of the Tao Te Ching, you may have noticed some translators endeavor to make the English sound beautiful and poetic. There is some downside to that (naturally, everything has a price). The wonderful thing about the original Chinese is its ultra terse nature. Overall, fewer words means more mystery, inviting the reader to read-between-the-lines even more. Writing a translation that more people enjoy reading requires more BEAUTIFUL AND PERSUASIVE WORDS. The unique thing about the Tao Te Ching for me is that it's like a technical book on a spiritual subject (and thus less fun reading). A nice little irony, I'd say.

55.

This chapter makes common sense when understood from the eyes of A NEW BORN BABE. A baby is not self-consciousness (conscious of 'I am'), and so from its point of view, *poison insects don't sting it, fierce beasts don't seize it, birds will not grab it.* To be sure, this is not objective fact—the young and the old are a major food source for predators. It is, rather, simple subjective truth; there is just no 'I' to be eaten. This is a case in point of *profound sameness*, or of the Vedic Tat Tvam Asi, 'you are that'. This is two sides of the same coin: the eaten and the eater, the stung and the stinger. (Of course this is easier to see/feel when you are not concurrently being *stung*. Oh well, we all have to start somewhere.)

Within a few years a baby learns language, which enables it to think it is somebody, i.e., "I am __(place name here)__". Now being 'Somebody', there is somebody to be eaten, stung, and eventually die. This is where the importance of being *clear* and *honest (*DISCERNMENT*)* comes into play. Only through careful self-*honesty* can I return to be CAPABLE OF NOT KNOWING ANYTHING.

Only through being *clear* and *honest* can I see how 'I am' is fiction, even though 'I' feels real (pinch me and it hurts type of real). Feeling, and the thinking it drives, is unreliable (e.g., puppy love, tasty equals healthy, earth feels flat, speeding saves time). Being tentative and hesitant (AS IF FORDING A RIVER IN WINTER) in every perception is extraordinarily helpful and extraordinarily difficult.

When I'm slipping off balance, I need *clarity* and *honesty* to notice quickly enough to counterbalance. The main obstacle to being *clear* and *honest* is self-deception inherent in my story. By that I mean the desires and worries (stemming from visceral need and fear) that 'guide' my thoughts and life. Seeing the down range consequences of my own desires and worries requires *clarity* and *honesty* (which essentially requires courage).

When balance is lost, we compensate by EGGING ON THE BREATH, AND INCREASING OUR VITALITY. We are driven to extremes in a vain attempt to find the constant, the harmony—the balance. This easily turns into a vicious circle, as the initial loss of balance is what drives us to extremes in the first place. Extremes, ironically, seem to promise our emotions a return to balance. Sure, extremes do bring balance eventually (i.e., IF YOU WOULD HAVE A THING LAID ASIDE, YOU MUST FIRST SET IT UP, and so on), but only after much suffering and wasted energy. Why wait? If possible, why not tilt life this way...

> IT IS EASY TO MAINTAIN A SITUATION WHILE IT IS STILL SECURE;
> IT IS EASY TO DEAL WITH A SITUATION BEFORE SYMPTOMS DEVELOP;
> IT IS EASY TO BREAK A THING WHEN IT IS YET BRITTLE;
> IT IS EASY TO DISSOLVE A THING WHILE IT IS YET MINUTE.
> DEAL WITH A THING WHILE IT IS STILL NOTHING;
> KEEP A THING IN ORDER BEFORE DISORDER SETS IN.

Doing this requires me to be as *clear* and *honest* as I can in order to see what is actually going on, as it is going on. Regarding everything as a symptom of deeper unseen underlying forces invites awareness to take a moment, peel back the covers, and peek beneath appearances. Only by seeing the invisible, does it become '*easy to deal with a thing while it is still nothing*.'

56.

I was long perplexed by the idea that 'ONE WHO SPEAKS DOES NOT KNOW'. That seemed to negate any opinion, observation or thought that I had. Now I finally get it, I think. At least it doesn't perplex me much anymore. As I see it, there are two sides to this.

One side is about truth. From a *profound sameness* point of view, thinking and speaking can never reach the depth of all-inclusive knowing. In order to discern or say anything, I must harden, not *soften its[1] brightness.* Instead of seeing *profound sameness*, I need to discern discrete differences. Language requires this *sharpness*, even for the most mundane statements of 'fact'. This results in a symbolic abstraction of experience, and not extemporaneous knowing. Thinking and speaking are after-the-fact reporting of past experience—in a word, gossip. Mind you, there is nothing wrong with that, which brings me to the other side of this issue.

Gossip is the natural glue that connects social animal. Non-thinking social animals, like dogs, commonly use scent as 'gossip'. Bees use a dance of sorts. Elephants, whales, and other big-brained social animals use sounds, as rudimentary forms of speech. Speaking for us is like chirping for crickets, or tweeting for birds. It connects individuals of a social species to the group. Language connects us to our fellow beings. Knowing <u>is not</u> the purpose, which brings me back to the point of this chapter.

This chapter's 'ONE WHO KNOWS DOES NOT SPEAK; ONE WHO SPEAKS DOES NOT KNOW' highlights the view that our species has gone a bit overboard, relying too heavily on thinking and speech to *know* reality. Too much of a 'good' thing results in imbalance. In our case, heavy reliance on WORDS and NAMES (language) has weakened our ability to experience nature with sufficient IMPARTIALITY. Our mind chatter enables us to haul around our dead and gone past, and an imagined although unlikely future.

---

1 You may wonder what the 'its' refers to in *soften its brightness*. I think of '*it*' as a broad description of anything and everything that DIVERGES IN NAME AS IT ISSUES FORTH. The actual word is *qi* (其) which translates as: *his, her, its, their, he, she, it, they, that, such.*

Nevertheless, we're stuck with thinking and speaking. The more we believe what we think, the more we keep chasing our tail in circular rationalizations to prove the 'reality' of our symbolic mental world. I find it is possible to avoid some of this futile run-around by merely acknowledging that, 'knower not speak; speaker not know,' (and by the same token, 'knower not THINK, thinker not know'.

Spiritual ideas (all the way from God down to the stuff I write) reflect an irresistible and ironic attempt to speak to that which is beyond thought. I regard it all as just beating-around-the-bush. I can never put my finger on that which IMAGES THE FOREFATHER OF GOD (which makes it all the more intriguing, eh). From a symptoms point of view, I see this quest as simply the hunter- gatherer drive prodding me to keep looking for the ultimate tasty morsel of truth THAT CAN BE SPOKEN OF. Everything is so much simpler than *it* appears in thought. That is why, TO KNOW YET TO THINK THAT ONE DOES NOT KNOW IS BEST.

57.

NOT BEING MEDDLESOME is another way to consider the notion of *using non responsibility*. Both meddling and taking responsibility come from a desire on the part of the "responsible" MEDDLING person to control the situation in order to have an outcome that agrees with their ideal objective. The DESIRE to have things go your way is the fly in the ointment of life.

But what about the desire for "good"? The problem with GOOD AND BAD is that one person's "good" (pleasure) is another's "bad" (poison). Being *without desire*, means being *without responsibility* for either good or bad. That may feel shocking at first, but consider Nature for a moment. Looking at the natural world, I see no good or bad - IMPARTIALITY rules the day. Good and bad are obviously projections of what personally brings us pleasure and pain. Simply said, if it's pleasurable and I like it, it's good. If it's painful and I dislike it, it's bad. If animals could talk, they'd formulate a similar set of words for their emotional experience of pleasure and pain.

Of what are *taboos, sharp tools,* and *laws* symptomatic? Our instinctive, boundless need for comfort and security. *Taboos* are restrictions that evolve in cultures to preserve the security of the status quo. This stability is useful to an extent, but eventually serves to undermine the people's ability to adapt to the changing conditions nature throws their way. *The poorer the people* is the end result. *Sharp tools* enable people to circumvent nature in order to maximize comfort and security. *Tools* allow us to get life done quicker; *confusion grows* as we get ahead of ourselves in our rush to "progress".

Finally, *laws multiply* as group cohesion and mutual trust wanes. Most members of prehistoric, hunter-gatherer groups lived their entire lives together from birth to death. That connection fostered intuitive trust and mutual obligation. As that sense of intimate connection wanes, it becomes easier for people to *rob,* cheat and lie. As we transitioned from hunter-gatherer tribal existence to civilization, everyone beyond one's family became a stranger to some degree. Indeed, today even member of nuclear families have become strangers somewhat as they share less and less common purpose in activities than previous generations did (work, music, food, etc.). (See Ethics, Do They Work Any More?) It is a "lonely brave new world" in ways we've yet to fully realize.

The world I experience is largely a reflection of how I feel. Thus, when I HOLD FIRMLY TO STILLNESS, the whole world feels more tranquil than otherwise. *"I love stillness",* is the heart and soul of what we call meditation and prayer. It is one sure way for *people to straighten themselves. Stillness* is more than meditation and prayer though: a sigh, a cigarette break, a tea break, a nap,... many are the ways of *stillness.*

On the other hand, rushing around taking *responsibility* and getting things done is symptomatic of what we feel deficient in life (i.e., Nature abhors a vacuum). The imperfection we see in the world is simply a reflection of what we feel missing, and so hunger for. Saying *I do nothing and the people transform themselves* can be very misleading if it comes across as implying that *doing nothing* results in their objective transformation. Although, that is the first impression many have.

It may be more accurate to see both as happening in concert together; one doesn't cause the other. Rather, when I feel a need to change something, I will act. When I feel contentment with how things are, *I do nothing* (much). When I feel CONTENTMENT, everything is perfect; I AM FREE FROM DESIRE AND THE PEOPLE OF THEMSELVES BECOME SIMPLE LIKE THE UNCARVED BLOCK. (I suppose a more accurate way to put this would be: *I am free from desire and thus my perception is transformed and I see the people simple like the uncarved block.* (Alas, what we gain in accuracy, we lose in the poetry).

58.

WHEN THE GOVERNMENT IS MUDDLED, THE PEOPLE ARE SIMPLE; WHEN THE GOVERNMENT IS ALERT, THE PEOPLE ARE CUNNING speaks not only to big government but also to small scale governance - from the governance of ourselves, to parenting, to employing, and on up the hierarchical chain.

For me, this addresses the wisdom of taking life step-by-step, like a JOURNEY OF A THOUSAND MILES, compared to forcing life to conform to my agenda (any ideal of what should be). The former allows me to respond to each step as it unfolds in a simple, *honest,* and *straightforward* way. The later, agenda driven approach *scrutinizes* the steps along the way, and CONTENDING WITH THEM, I focus on *imperfection* rather than ON THAT WHICH IS NATURALLY SO.

The difficulty of imposing our agenda (ideals) onto life is that we will find ourselves swinging more from one *extreme* to the other. The more acutely aware we are of the *good, mainstream, and straightforward,* the more acute can become the opposite. Simply put, our sorrows lie in that which we hold most dear. (THESE TWO ARE THE SAME, BUT DIVERGE IN NAME AS THEY ISSUE FORTH.)

We tend to believe that somehow we can have all the *good, mainstream, and straightforward,* and somehow escape the other side of the coin. I like to think of this as being just another biological HOODWINK to get us to act in the world. After all, nature has no need to enlighten us as to how it operates. For all other species, this works out well and balance is maintained. Because we approach life with such idealized versions of how life 'should' be, we react far out of proportion to what is actually so. Our ability to THINK enables us to make mountains out of molehills.

Viscerally knowing that this is how 'it' is, one can't help but be *upright, yet not cuttingly so;. Honest, yet not stabbingly so; Straightforward, yet not wantonly so; Honorable yet not gloriously so.* Seeing both sides of the coin makes it all VERY EASY TO PUT INTO PRACTICE (and downright impossible to do otherwise! , 'IT HAPPENS TO US NATURALLY.').

59.

First, I must ask, what prevents me from FOLLOWING THE WAY FROM THE START and causes me to be less *frugal*. One glaring factor is the tendency to put *limits* on myself[1]. From birth, I was "brain washed" into my culture's paradigm, beginning with being given a NAME. Being NAMED right off the bat is not a promising way to "follow the way from the start"[2] , yet what choice did I have back then? The same goes for the TABOOS, cultural myths, and RITES instilled in me from infancy.

I regard all this as symptomatic of society's need to keep large populations of virtual strangers living in the semi-harmonious illusion of belonging to the same tribe. When we all GO UP TO THE TERRACE IN SPRING, we feel a sense of communal connection. However, this is a far cry from the intimate birth-to-death intimacy experience by hunter-

---

1   How does being *frugality* help me *to be limitless?* On the face of it, *limitless* and *frugality* feel like opposites. Here clearly, STRAIGHTFORWARD WORDS SEEM PARADOXICAL. All I can say is, the more far reaching the view, the more useless words become at conveying it. Eventually, only PRACTICING THE TEACHING THAT USES NO WORDS remains.

2   This is why we did not name our children for a year after they were born. Assigning labels (names) removes some of the inherent mystery. There would be plenty of time for that in the future we rightly thought.

gatherer tribes. Sure, they would have had their issues. Like any animal, barnyard politics always plays some role[1].

Many facets of civilization aim at enhancing the illusion of communal connection. We lose more and more of the real thing as population increases (no wonder we say, REDUCE THE SIZE AND POPULATION OF THE STATE). One of the main features of civilization is the codification of '*limits*'. These limits (taboos, rites, rituals) maintain social stability as long as everyone is onboard and keeps to their "proper place". Just imagine if everyone was a freethinker, a non-thinker, or even CAPABLE OF NOT KNOWING ANYTHING. I imagine mega-civilization would collapse, and we'd all return to hunter gathering again. Now, would that be a step back, or a step forward? (Of course, this an unanswerable question, i.e., FORWARD AND BACKWARD PRODUCE EACH OTHER.)

The remarkable feature of the Tao Te Ching is how it shows me a way to leave taboos, rites, BENEVOLENCE AND RECTITUDE behind, or at least head in that direction. Merely letting go of who/what I think I am, looking inward and RETURNING TO MY ROOTS is a step in the right direction. When I no longer THINK THAT I KNOW my *limits*, who else can? Am I not my own worse enemy? OVERCOMING MYSELF is the greatest hurdle I face.

60.

This chapter reminds me of how easy it is to go to extremes. Balance is so hard to maintain, and perfect balance is impossible to realize[2]. Fortunately, I eventually came to realize this is natural, i.e., **balance is balanced by imbalance**. Ah yes, STRAIGHTFORWARD WORDS SEEM PARADOXICAL. For me, life is a process of getting

---

1   My experiences among the Akha hill tribe people in Laos and the Dayak people in Borneo showed me that politics thrives at every social level. It is just that the simpler the level, the greater the trust, and the more direct the resolutions of grievances. Simply said, there are no terrorists at that level.

2   Perfect balance is impossible to realize only in the sense that impossible expectations are impossible to realize. I see nature as being in a dynamic state of perfect balance. My desire to hold onto any moment creates an impossible expectation. I am my own worst enemy.

closer and closer to the happy medium between too much, and too little. In other words, CIRCUMSTANCES BRING ME TO MATURITY. Cooking an egg, like BOILING A SMALL FISH, takes less action (heat) than beginners imagine; as a result the inexperienced overcook it. Likewise, in life we tend to over do, over protect, over plan, over THINK, over DESIRE. In the natural wild, HEAVEN AND EARTH'S RUTHLESS edge would push back on us, slow us down, resulting in a happy medium of sorts. Freeing ourselves from nature's restraints, as we have, makes maintaining reasonable balance all the more challenging. Ironically, the more we are able to satiate our every desire, the less we are able to KNOW CONTENTMENT.

Boiling a small fish reminds me of the saying, "too little, too late". If we were not so preoccupied with doing what requires less doing, we would be aware of what truly needs "more, sooner". Eagerly jumping into actions is symptomatic of deep-seated personal fears and needs, projected outward in one's actions. When life is action-packed-full to the brim, there is no space to see. HOLD FIRMLY TO STILLNESS to watch our needs and fears, rather than jumping in, gives us space to see when action would be most timely[1]. Ironically, such delayed gratification results in CONSTANT 'gratification'. (i.e., short-term pain; long-term pleasure).

As I see it, words such as *spirits* and GOD symbolize for us what exists beyond what we think we know. We are much better at defining existence than the ancients were. Having less factual knowledge at their disposal, they relied on 'fuzzier' rationales to support their myths. For example, someone getting sick might be seen as the body being *hindered* by bad *spirits*. Now, we get out the microscope and see E. Coli by the millions... Ah ha! But really, isn't this simply an updated version of the "what we think we know".

The crux of the matter is not that different. The ancients thought they knew; we think we know; future generations (10,000 year

---

1   Watching our needs and fears, rather than jumping in may be a good example of chapter 70's MY WORDS ARE VERY EASY TO UNDERSTAND AND VERY EASY TO PUT INTO PRACTICE, YET NO ONE IN THE WORLD CAN UNDERSTAND THEM OR PUT THEM INTO PRACTICE, especially the "put them into practice" part! Still, it helps to know THE WAY.

from now perhaps) will look back on our quaint understanding from their future time, at which time they will think they truly know. Nothing will have changed. Only when we face the void, will we be truly BE CAPABLE OF NOT KNOWING ANYTHING. The older a person gets, the more that becomes possible, i.e., death is moving closer. Still, I wouldn't hold my breath!

So, why do we need to THINK WE KNOW? I'd say fear drives us to see the INDISTINCT AND SHADOWY... DISTINCTLY! Names and words help us nail that MYSTERY UPON MYSTERY firmly down. This utility of names and words makes language inevitable... and natural I might add. Nevertheless, these deceive us. Still, when conditions are fairly balance, *neither assists in hindering, therefore, each ascribes virtue to the other.*

61.

The virtue of the humble, *lower position* is universally acknowledged. Yet, I am also drawn to success and the 'higher' position—not surprising seeing how animals, and especially humans, want to have 'it' both ways (e.g., decrease taxes not benefits, eat rich food not get fat, and countless other double-dealings). Happily, I am able to notice this and take the *lower position* with increasing grace as each year passes. You might say the *female* (time) only reveals herself after much of the *male* (energy) has spent himself.[1]

A key issue for me is the wax and wane dynamic that complements ALL THE STREAMS OF THE WORLD UNITING. Chapter 36 puts it wonderfully: IF YOU WOULD HAVE A THING WEAKENED, YOU MUST FIRST STRENGTHEN IT; IF YOU WOULD HAVE A THING LAID ASIDE, YOU MUST FIRST SET IT UP. Interestingly, noticing one phase, or the other, but not both as inextricably connected is all too easy.

---

1 *Female* and *male* here have nothing to do with gender; women have just as much *male* as men have *female*. These just express themselves differently among us all. The surface only appears different; the deeper we look the more *profound sameness* we see.

Indeed, I think we are innately blind to Nature's omnificent cyclic nature. In an ironic way, we suffer the illusion of expecting that action (the waxing, strengthening, 'setting it up' phase) leads directly to resolution. It does, in a long-term way, just as *all the streams of the world unite... at the lower reaches.* The illusion is that one's CONTENTMENT is tied directly to successful action. The further irony is that the *lower position, the female* is felt as the *position* one must avoid at all costs[1]. We are innately driven to CONTEND long and hard to reach the top. Yet, reaching the top, all we can ever see is *the lower position.*

Personally speaking, it has taken years of living to fully appreciate and viscerally feel nature's 'game'. Now, that doesn't mean I get to quit playing the game prematurely (before death). However, it does permit me to UNDERSTAND more deeply the game's rules. While all in nature experience the game's dynamic, only humans think they know. The snag here is how the dynamic itself drives our thoughts to think that success brings peace. Sure, it does for about a minute before we find ourselves at the end-of-the-line once more. That subtly is lost on us. Only after years of being hoodwinked by our biology, do we begin to see a possible resolution: ONE DOES LESS AND LESS UNTIL ONE DOES NOTHING AT ALL, AND WHEN ONE DOES NOTHING AT ALL THERE IS NOTHING THAT IS UNDONE.[2]

Really, isn't this drive to succeed just Mother Nature's way of keeping us alive, resisting entropy until the full-on entropy of our last dying breath? Yes, it is nature's way. However, if we're going to circumvent nature's restraints as we are want to do, we would be wise to understand a little deeper

---

1   We begin each moment from a *lower position* drawn toward a 'higher position', *the male*, MERIT. The illusion that resolution and peace come with success drives us to strive on. The beautiful irony of this is that we begin each moment from resolution (*the lower position*) and essentially go in full circle (or perhaps a 'mysterious' spiral) only to arrive back at the beginning. It helps to know it's a game—not real—no matter how real it feels.

2   This has less to do with actual doing; it's more about our actual expectation of accomplishment. Without dreams of success bugging us to over-do, we naturally tend KEEPS TO THE DEED THAT CONSISTS IN TAKING NO ACTION, with an emphasis of **taking!** Simple necessity (need) drives action, more than imagined necessity (desire).

how she HOODWINKS us as well. Otherwise, we're bound to lose balance, stumble repeatedly and suffer needlessly.

Nevertheless, understanding that nature is hoodwinking me doesn't prevent me from 'enjoying' the illusion. Just as knowing a magician's tricks are just tricks doesn't hinder my sense of awe at his illusions. I find the true benefit of knowing I am being hoodwinked lies in helping me KNOW, YET THINK THAT I DON'T KNOW. This cuts down on the alternative: "Not to know yet to think that one knows will lead to difficulty".

62.

This chapter makes a bit more sense in the original Chinese than in D.C. Lao's translation. I doubt I'll do any better though. This is the curious side of attempting to convey knowing through words. There is also the peculiar effectiveness one language (here Chinese) can have over another (English here). Although, perhaps this isn't actually that unusual. Think of how the Eskimos have dozens of words to refer to the subtle characteristics of snow. In this case, the difference lies not in any unique Chinese words used in the original Tao Te Ching, but in its terseness. Maybe this reflects an ancient Chinese sense that more words obfuscates, i.e., TO USE WORDS BUT RARELY IS TO BE NATURAL. In Chinese, it is possible to say more with fewer words. (Correlations [1] takes that even farther... alas, a leap too far for most.)

Is this saying that using more words is somehow less natural? Not exactly. Rather, the less we expect words to mean what they say, the more room we make for intuitive understanding. In other words, our attempts to HAMMER IT TO A POINT are less enlightening than groping around for THE SHAPE THAT HAS NO SHAPE. Saying less has the potential to convey more of the ESSENCE, if one already knows—at some level. This goes back to my view that we only truly understand cognitively what we already know intuitively (i.e., sub-thought).

---

1 See centertao.org/essays/correlations

Especially endearing to me is the view: *Even though surrounded by jade and presented with horses, Not equal to receiving the way*, or as D.C. Lau translated it, HE WHO MAKES A PRESENT OF THE WAY WITHOUT STIRRING FROM HIS SEAT IS PREFERABLE TO ONE WHO OFFERS PRESENTS OF JADE DISKS FOLLOWED BY A TEAM OF FOUR HORSES. Here is where 'giving' and 'receiving' truly produce each other. I set this in motion through IMPARTIALITY. This means not passing judgment, but instead observing the myriad creatures (i.e., everything) in their own right. This is the only true *present of the way* I can offer, and in offering that I am *receiving the way*. Chapter 16 speaks beautifully to this experience...

THE MYRIAD CREATURES ALL RISE TOGETHER
AND I WATCH THEIR RETURN.
THE TEAMING CREATURES
ALL RETURN TO THEIR SEPARATE ROOTS.
RETURNING TO ONE'S ROOTS IS KNOWN AS STILLNESS.

On gifts, the Bhagavad Gita says this, "A gift is pure when it is given from the heart to the right person at the right time and at the right place, and when we expect nothing in return. But when it is given expecting something in return, or for the sake of a future reward, or when it is given unwillingly, the gift is of Rajas, impure".

It really is the thought (or rather feeling) that counts, and for me, the ultimate gift is non-judgment. As Christ puts it, "Judge not, that ye be not judged[1]. For with what judgment ye judge, ye shall be judged: and with what measure ye mete, it shall be measured to you again. And why beholdest thou the mote that is in thy brother's eye, but considerest not the beam that is in thine own eye? Or how wilt thou say to thy brother, Let me pull out the mote out of thine eye; and, behold, a beam is in thine own eye? Thou hypocrite, first cast out the beam out of thine own eye; and then shalt thou see clearly to cast out the mote out of thy brother's eye."

---

1   I imagine many Christians take this to mean God will judge us later in Heaven. I find it is immediate. Any judgments I make are only reflections of my own needs and fears. Being such, they are actually self-judgments. As needs and fears wane, I see and act more impartially. Seeing *judgment* for the two-way-street it is helps me be self honest: When I judge, I look inward to find what I am needing or fearing at the moment.

63.

I see various ways to consider the idea of Doing that which consists in taking no action; and Laying plans for the accomplishment of the difficult. At first glance they may even seem contradictory—apparently doing nothing on one hand and yet lay plans on the other. These virtues and do good to him who has done you an injury (*respond to resentment using kindness*) may also appear to be moral prescriptions. Are they?

I'd say they are, if that is what you want to see. There is more to this than meets the eye though. I find *do without doing* useful because life usually sorts itself out better when I don't jump in right away and meddle. This is another way of counseling patience. In action it is timeliness that matters also speaks to patient action that is timed to maximize efficiency (benefit/cost).

Respond to resentment using kindness sure sounds like a moral prescription. Christ echoes this view when he says, "But I say unto you, Love your enemies, bless them that curse you, do good to them that hate you, and pray for them which despitefully use you, and persecute you".

I find this impossible to pull off sincerely. Feeling *resentment* is a symptom of foiled expectations. On the other hand, if I know contentment (i.e., have zero expectations) I naturally feel *kindness* within, and so *respond* to others kindly. This parallels the Bhagavad Gita's, "A gift is pure when it is given from the heart to the right person at the right time and at the right place, and when we expect nothing in return."

We tend to ignore the deeper how's and why's, and instead tout moral ideals to fix societal ills. I suspect this is no more effective than the 'snake oil' remedies of old. We only wishfully think they work; history proves otherwise. Only through deeper understanding do we have any hope of fixing pretty much anything. Buddha hit the nail on the head—he fleshed out the basic how's and why's (Four Noble Truths) and then proposed Right Understanding as a first step to fixing things. These Truths are utterly clear, yet usually fall on deaf ears[1]. Doesn't this prove that we simply understand what we already know, and we simply know what we already need and fear (DESIRE)? It is all very humbling!

The habit of considering things *excessively easy* is probably a normal symptom of youthful naïveté. Certainly, youth lacks the experiences that prods the more mature to consider consequences down the road. Not surprisingly, youth can encounter *excessively difficult*[2]. As chapter 16 puts it, WOE TO HIM WHO WILLFULLY INNOVATES WHILE IGNORANT OF THE CONSTANT. Fortunately, as the years go by, wisdom deepens. On the other hand, there are plenty old-yet-foolish, and young-yet-wise. Nevertheless, every person grows wiser and more mature as they age, relative to where they started. After all CIRCUMSTANCES BRING [ALL OF] THEM TO MATURITY.

Ah, too bad that hard won wisdom has to go the grave with us. Yep, and the next generation gets to learn it all over again. Looking back on things I've read, like the Tao Te Ching, I recall how uplifting the spiritual ideals sounded, and I longed to incorporate them in my life. Decades later, rather than incorporating them in me, I am becoming them naturally—IT HAPPENS TO US NATURALLY. There is an important distinction. The spiritual ideas are universal and reflect maturity. The only way one becomes mature is through circumstances and time. The 'teachings' don't teach, they are merely comment on the experience. They are biographical universals, not models that we can shoehorn our lives into—THAT IS WHY I KNOW THE BENEFIT OF RESORTING TO NO ACTION. THE TEACHING THAT USES NO WORDS, THE BENEFIT OF RESORTING TO NO ACTION, THESE ARE BEYOND THE UNDERSTANDING OF ALL BUT A VERY FEW IN THE WORLD.

---

1 During my years in East Asia I noticed how unaware most Buddhists there were of Buddha's core view. Of course, the same is true in the West. People obviously PREFER THE BYPATH of form and overlook the foundation of function. Again, proving that our needs and fears (DESIRE) determine what we see (understand)? That's enough to make anyone who realizes this TENTATIVE, AS IF FORDING A RIVER IN WINTER!

2 Considering something *excessively easy or difficult* can often be a projection of one's own needs and fears, having nothing to do with age. Those emotions form our imagined sense of what lies down the road.

64.

Sure, IT IS EASY TO MAINTAIN, DEAL WITH, BREAK, OR DISSOLVE something while it is essentially nothing. A question worth asking is how does 'nothing' become something in the first place (besides the slightly mystifying SOMETHING AND NOTHING PRODUCE EACH OTHER)? One obvious cause is our old 'friend' desire.

I know, DESIRE gets such a bad rap. I think of desire as a composite of need + thought. Thought is uniquely human, while need is the universal driving force for all life. Honestly though, I see this breaking down even further; just as something and nothing produce each other, so also do need and fear. So desire is actually more like a blending of need, fear AND thought. Two of these are essential survival instincts. Thanks to human CLEVERNESS, only we are capable of taking these a step further, ending up with mountains of something out of molehills of nothing. So yes, *'Taking this, the wise person desires non desire'*, certainly makes sense.

Of course, the wisdom to *desire non desire, not value difficult to obtain goods, and learn non learning* is only evident to those who feel the no-brainer sense of this already. Our failure to UNDERSTAND this is the most straightforward reason for why the world is the way it is. I often feel mystified that people can be so irrational—not so much the nameless masses or the foolish and uncouth. I mean, we all know 'we' don't have a clue. What baffles me more are the leaders of society, the cognoscenti elite, that run things. As chapter 75 puts it, THOSE IN AUTHORITY ARE TOO FOND OF ACTION. Alas, they are no wiser than the poor and meek. If anything, just the opposite; they are even less likely to have LITTLE THOUGHT OF SELF AND AS FEW DESIRES AS POSSIBLE. Their drive to lead the pack and change the world makes them even less likely than others to 'DESIRE NOT TO DESIRE, NOT VALUE GOODS HARD TO COME BY, AND LEARN TO BE WITHOUT LEARNING'. (Who knows, perhaps Jesus had this partly in mind when he said, "Blessed are the meek: for they shall inherit the earth".)

Yet, something in me, even to this day, expects more of them... the leaders of society. Why? It's so irrational on my part! My

192

social ideals (driven by a fairness instinct'?) coming face to face with the real of 'what is' leaves me feeling continually awestruck. If I didn't realize the natural science behind this disconnect (ideal vs. real) I'd probably feel angry. Without a doubt, the more IMPARTIALITY I bring to what I observe, the more kindliness I feel. While it can be difficult seeing things as they are, it's even harder remaining IGNORANT[1].

Happily, this chapter ends with some useful peace-of-mind advice. It is stated awkwardly; perhaps seeing it from another angle will help: *Learn non learning* tells me to take much less seriously all that I've come to realize, (i.e., WHEN YOUR DISCERNMENT PENETRATES THE FOUR QUARTERS, ARE YOU CAPABLE OF NOT KNOWING ANYTHING?) Only then do I find myself able to *turn around people's excesses, in order to assists all things naturally and never boldly act.*

Don't take this to mean I actually do something 'out there' to MAKE GOOD THE MISTAKES OF THE MULTITUDE, OR HELP THE MYRIAD CREATURES TO BE NATURAL AND TO REFRAIN FROM DARING TO ACT. That would be flat out impossible… although, Lord knows countless "do gooders[2]" try. Just the opposite works, in fact; merely understanding what is happening helps me 'make good the mistakes of others', WITHOUT RESORTING TO ACTION. 'To be natural' is 'to be just so' (自然 ziran). Seen this way, it is easy to find beauty in how-it-is, and not push to remake the world to fit an ideal view of how-it-should-be.

In other words, when I can see GREAT PERFECTION SEEMS CHIPPED, it becomes easy to let it be—*easily manage, easily plan, easily melt, easily scatter.* The Taoist path is about changing our point

---

1   I can't imagine ignorance being bliss for anyone who THINKS. Neither can I imagine nature, animals, infants, trees, and such, being ignorant or having desire. It is thinking that makes both ignorance and desire what they are. When we THINK, we step into a whole other world – a virtual world of ideals for what should or shouldn't be – and we pay a price.
2   As they say, the road to hell is paved with good intentions. Of course, we can't help trying to do good; social instinct drives us. The GOOD we are pushing is only a projection of our own desires, which accounts for the unintended and unfortunate consequences that pile up in the wake of our activity.

of view rather than the world 'out there'. What we see out there is truly a reflection of who we are, what we fear, what we need—our desires, our agenda. As the agenda changes, the world we see changes. We are told, *'the sage desires not to desire, and does not value goods which are hard to come by'*! Desire is the true culprit that causes us to 'RUIN THINGS WHEN ON THE VERGE OF SUCCESS'[1].

65.

Nothing is more 'OF OLD AND EXCELS IN PURSUIT OF THE WAY' than nature. That nature HOODWINKS living creatures to bring about instinctive interaction has become utterly obvious to me now. I first realized nature was tricking me when I began examining my irrational, lustful, attraction to women. Or course, I knew about this intellectually ever since biology class in high school. However, this went deeper.

The difference here was the dawning of a visceral intuitive sense of these natural forces acting on me. It was quite liberating to see the puppeteer pulling the strings! Curiously, it took another few decades to truly appreciate how extensive nature's hoodwink really was. Truth be told, I am still in awe. Why did it take so long?

Wishful thinking blinded me for decades. I cherished the illusion that I could be the master of my fate. Civilization and education shielded me from the harsh wild side of Mother Nature, which further convinced me that I could outwit her. Simply put, my story was what I wanted to hear.

We've all heard our species' centric talking point: "Animals merely respond through blind instinct; we can *intelligently* rise above instinct". Alas, we are intoxicated by our own CLEVERNESS, believing we can get away with "murder"

---

1   Or as I translated it, *People in their affairs always accomplish some, yet fail*. I first became keenly aware of some of this while working with wood. When sawing by hand, for example, I'd always tend to rush it. This invariably lead to ruin, if not materially, then spiritually (i.e., lack of CONTENTMENT). I eventually realized that the only way forward was through TURNING BACK. Finish the task at hand, deal with it completely before jumping on to the next 'bauble' of desire always leaves me with a better taste in my mouth.

without consequences. Our excessive intelligence makes us a difficult species for nature *to govern*. We are like spoiled children, and like them, are not any the happier for it.

Also, like children, CIRCUMSTANCES BRING US TO MATURITY. Maturity affords us enough self-honesty to begin to see underlying *patterns*. The issues of life: battles, arguments, attraction and aversion, gain and loss, worries, etc., all have their individual 'color'. KNOWING THE MODEL that underpins these seemingly disparate events offers us a way to DEAL WITH A THING WHILE IT IS STILL NOTHING. By dialing down the 'color' of distinction, we can avoid being swamped by the details.

Noticing underlying patterns—the common denominator—is another way of describing *profound sameness*. *Knowing and investigate the pattern*, the constant, that connects life's disparate issues is called *profound moral character* given that it becomes less possible to deceive one's self through self-rationalization / justification. How do we know *profound sameness* when we see it? That's simple: IMPARTIALITY increases and HYPOCRISY drops off.

Alas, nature hoodwinks us into seeing sameness as boring and differences as interesting and exciting. It is easier and more fun to know one side of the coin (or the other). *Knowing these both and investigate their patterns* as a whole is not. Indeed, history is replete with folks passionately aligning themselves to one side or another. Nothing ever changes; it just goes round-and-round. On the other hand, the more one sees the whole, the more COMPLETE CONFORMITY happens to us naturally.

Reaching great conformity is also another way of saying to FOLLOW THE WAY AND THE WAY ONLY. *Conformity* to each moment as it happens is difficult for we tend to project (THINK) our fears and needs ahead to the next moment. We struggle to control and lead life, rather than follow life. Imagined fear drives us to over protect ourselves from that which will not happen, and ironically, distract us from dangers ever present.

66.

D.C. Lau's translation of this chapter left me with mixed feelings today. For example, Therefore, desiring to rule over the people, one must in one's words humble oneself before them. I do see this playing out in real life, yet I also notice how people are drawn to those who are less than humble. Similarly, desiring to lead the people, One must, in one's person, follow behind them does not address the traditional practice of a commander leading his troops in battle. Finally, the real world of ruling over people is based on contending and overcoming your opponent whether as a 'alpha male' in a gorilla tribe, or as president running for office.

Reading the literal Chinese may shed a more realistic light on this. It says, *Yes, accordingly, a wise person, Desiring to be above the people, must using speech be below; Desiring to be ahead of the people, must using life be behind.* This refers to *a wise person,* not just anyone, tyrant or otherwise. For me this speaks more of attitude than of practice. *Desiring to be above the people* versus Desiring to rule over the people. Rising *above* in the sense of virtue, integrity, self-honesty, compassion, and not ruling over as D.C. Lau translated it. Certainly, these qualities help one who is actually 'rule over the people' or 'lead the people', but this is secondary.

I find a closer fit lies in a sense of governing or stewardship, not ruling over. The best stewardship is possible only when one's personal character is '*above*', which is closer to the point of this chapter. This chapter's guidance helped support my "be patient and let it unfold" approach to raising my children. It worked wonderfully well. Rather than 'ruling over' my kids, I was more of a shadowy presence. I provided a pathway for them to follow, yet did not pressure them to walk it. As chapter 72 puts it, It is because you do not press down on them that they will not weary of the burden. It was to be their choice alone. Granted, I was approaching fifty years of age when I took on fatherhood. I could never have pulled off such a 'taoist approach to parenting' had I been twenty years younger!

Perhaps all this applies more to small, family-tribe CIRCUMSTANCES. Clearly this is one downside of leaving the hunter-gatherer lifestyle for civilization. We've lost the readily available guidance of elders common in an ancestral tribal family structure. Interestingly, this chapter also speaks to the role a 'God' would play in people's lives... *Dwells above, yet the people are not weighed down, Dwells ahead, yet the people are not impaired.* There you go: God equals mature parental figure; mature parent figure equals God. The idea of God is simply a natural outcome of what people long ago imagined to be an ideal parent (or perhaps an ideal 'alpha-male' tribal leader).

67.

If THE WHOLE WORLD SAYS THAT MY WAY IS VAST AND RESEMBLES NOTHING, why are we driven to say what 'it' resembles? Some examples of 'resemblances' that come to mind are God, Allah, Nature, Peace, Love, Tao, etc (Tao is the only one that comes with a disclaimer, i.e., "*The way possible to think, runs counter to the constant way*".) Curiously, the view that "IF IT RESEMBLED ANYTHING IT WOULD, LONG BEFORE NOW, HAVE BECOME SMALL" is one shared by few. I suppose giving name and definition to INDISTINCT AND SHADOWY experience is our way of placing 'it' upon a pedestal[1]. Clearly, such pedestal-placing behavior is at least partly an emergent property of our social, hierarchical nature. However, there's another side to this too.

This chapter also parallels chapter 2's, IT IS BECAUSE IT LAYS CLAIM TO NO MERIT, THAT ITS MERIT NEVER DESERTS IT. Although, written in this order puts the cart before the horse, in my view. More accurate would be, 'it is because we don't feel merit that we feel

---

1   My long felt reluctance to elevating things to 'pedestal' status must be genetic. I seem to instinctively level, if not knock down, anything that sticks up. I expect this is the key reason a Taoist point of view feels so comfortable and natural to me. IMPARTIALITY seems only natural; it is my own agenda that skews my view. Whenever I scratch the surface of my perceptions, *profound sameness* appears. That we are by-and-large a hierarchical species (i.e., set things on pedestals) is what accounts for so few people drawn to a Taoist point of view. In other words, the philosophy that an individual adopts is most likely the one that says what they innately want to hear. What could be more natural!

compelled to lay claim to merit'. Likewise, from a symptom's point-of-view, we define, praise and put 'it' upon a pedestal BECAUSE we fail to feel ONE with 'it'[1]. The 'resemblances' we name simply indicate our yearning for what we feel missing. Put another way, the resemblances we name reveal our inner weakness--WEAKNESS IS THE MEANS THE WAY EMPLOYS. Our weakness drives us to define 'it'. Ironically, in defining 'it', it becomes small returning us back to square one. This drives some to become fervent bomb throwing fundamentalist of one neurotic stripe or another.

I find that *loving* and compassion requires some *bravery* on my part. Pigeon-holing-judgments are easy to make and cowardly compared to the courage I must draw upon to withhold judgment (i.e., FEARLESS IN BEING TIMID). *Loving* also entails restraint. Passionate *loving* (or hating) emotion, focusing narrowly as it does, is plainly elitist pedestal-placing behavior. Focusing the mind's light in one direction leaves the rest of the 'big picture' in darkness. *Thrift* preserves some of that light for the other side of the coin.

If *kindness, thrift* and *not daring to act* are more beneficial, why is the opposite often more easy? Clearly, *daring, spreading out,* and getting out *in front* feel like sure paths to success and survival. Concerns that they may end in *death* are out of sight, out of mind. We also tend to think we are the exception to the rule. Deeper still, this *daring, spreading out,* and leading *in front* serves social dynamics; it stirs the tribal pot! It is hard to stir up support for war, for example, without the passionate "we're the best, we're right, we'll win".

However, the deepest reason may be in how the urge to do the opposite of what is prudent influences the course of evolution, albeit in a round-a-bout way. It is another of Mother Nature's HOODWINKS I dare say. Here-in I see an ingenious side to nature's game: Any individual that becomes aware of the hoodwink can

---

1   Why do we fail to feel one with 'it'? As I see it, words and names (and the language they enable) cut both ways. Cognitive thinking allows our DISCERNMENT [TO] PENETRATES THE FOUR QUARTERS. The unintended consequence of that strength is the flip side. Our ability to be CAPABLE OF NOT KNOWING ANYTHING is crippled.

better avoid the hook and improve their chance at survival. Wisdom, in the final analysis, may just lie in becoming keenly aware of the hoodwink. Certainly, knowledge, I.Q., talent, etc., don't seem to confer much if anything to wisdom. Indeed, for all I know, it could be just the opposite. Even age is only relatively helpful. It is no accident that chapter 3 says, HE ALWAYS KEEPS THEM INNOCENT OF KNOWLEDGE AND FREE FROM DESIRE, AND ENSURES THAT THE CLEVER NEVER DARE TO ACT. Alas, we are masters at WILLFULLY INNOVATING WHILE IGNORANT OF THE CONSTANT. Nature's hoodwinks are evolutionary 'tests'. Species that pass the test persist; those that don't perish.

68.

My *enemy*, in a broadest sense of the word, is anyone or anything that is 'wrong'. Wrong being whatever stands in the way of what I DESIRE. This makes DESIRING NOT TO DESIRE an ironic notion, doesn't it. This chapter also gives practical insight on dealing with this *enemy*, whether it is desire itself, or that which thwarts winning my heart's desire. It turns out that *contending* with what is 'wrong' only intensifies the 'wrong' I feel. I only end up in a vicious circle as this *enemy* grows even larger.

I first noticed this while walking to work in winter in Japan. I noticed how, along with others, I was grimacing and complaining about the cold. The Bhagavad Gita with its message of surrender[1] offered me the sound path I needed at the time. As I began to cease *battling* the cold, the less cold I felt. The cold wasn't wrong, bad, or the *enemy* any longer; life mellowed. The idea of surrender in a spiritual sense is not the outright capitulation it usually suggests; yet it is just that—capitulation. This is a good example of STRAIGHTFORWARD

---

1   These are two example of the Bhagavad Gita's message of surrender:

For concentration is better than mere practice, and meditation is better than concentration; but higher than meditation is surrender in love of the fruit of one's actions, for on surrender follows peace. (12:12)

The renunciation of selfish works is called renunciation; but the surrender of the reward of all work is called surrender. (18:2)

WORDS SEEM PARADOXICAL and perhaps of FEARLESS IN BEING TIMID. Fear accounts for surrender of the ordinary kind; just the opposite with surrender of the spiritual kind.

Wanting life to be other than it is makes life a more sorrowful and stressful journey. It is just such impatient, chomping at the bit DESIRES that stress me most. This happens when I dwell on the ideal of where I-desire-to-be juxtaposed with where I-THINK-I-am now. I avoid much of this by retaining only enough ideal to PERSEVERE WITH PURPOSE, and let go of (forget!) the rest of the ideal. In other words, ideals are potent, and more than a little turns them poisonous.

The last line of this chapter, *This is called matching Nature's ancient utmost,* is closer to the literal Chinese than D.C. Lau's THIS IS KNOWN AS MATCHING THE SUBLIMITY OF HEAVEN. However, both mean truly the same thing, don't they? This meaning is also expressed elsewhere in the Tao Te Ching as EMPTINESS AND STILLNESS, as VAST AND RESEMBLES NOTHING, as THE THREAD RUNNING THROUGH THE WAY, and of course as the VIRTUE OF NOTHING. This is to say, it is not the words that truly matter. Meaning really lies in depth and breadth of one's interpretation.

It is this 'force of nature', the *utmost ancient of nature,* that evokes in me A PROPER SENSE OF AWE. How can such *sublime* nothing-ness drive the universe, from accelerating galaxies to stirring the hunger that drives my ducks to seek out bugs hither and thither. This same process operates at all levels of existence. The more I sense this throughout my day, the smoother the day turns out. Indeed, always keeping watch on this "forest" of NOTHING helps avoid becoming blind-sided by the "trees" of something.

For as long as I can remember, my core *enemy* has been ignorance along with a commensurate lack of watchfulness. However, I now realize ignorance and watch-less-ness are just other aspects of 'nothing-ness'. Throughout the day I experience my own ignorance and lack of watchfulness, yet, by accepting these as core aspects OF THE WAY, I can persevere without *contending* or meddling with myself, or with others.

We are bio-hoodwinked into seeing the internal and the external as poles apart—like black and white, material and spiritual, mind and body, and so on. Through Taoist eyes, I truly see no such difference. I see the *battles* I wage within myself directly expressed in my dealings with others. Being aware of this direct connection is key to *employing the ability of other. Others? Others* is only the reflection of myself; myself is only the reflection of *others*. Whew!

69.

A valuable lesson I learned from years of global hitch hiking was the benefit of DARING NOT TO PLAY THE HOST BUT PLAY THE GUEST, (i.e., not taking the initiative). Granted the wisdom of *dare not act as host* came gradually. Circumstances gave me no choice but to *act as visitor*. Although, I fought this at first for I was a 110% *rash*, impatient and action oriented American lad. Several times *rashly opposing nearly lost me treasure* (i.e., life, body parts). Fortunately, these CIRCUMSTANCES wore me down enough for wisdom to slowly seep in.

The *act as host* approach to life shows up in various ways, most noticeably as impulsive buying, eating, driving, working, etc. In every case, there is an object ahead, either literally or in the mind's eye, to be gained, conquered, solved, or just dealt with. In our pre-civilized wild state, this innate 'just do it' drive would be counter-balanced by the natural lack of opportunity to go hog-wild (i.e., buy, eat, drive, work, etc., as much as we desired). When hungry we'd simply have to hunt or gather up something to eat. Such RUTHLESS wild simplicity fosters sanity in all living things. WILLFULLY INNOVATING WHILE IGNORANT OF THIS CONSTANT interferes with this natural balance. Given all this, it is not surprising how progress often LEADS TO DIFFICULTY.

Another way of thinking of the *going without going, grabbing without an arm*, and such, is to imagine dealing with 'things behind', rather than 'things ahead'. Our thinking mind allows us to jump forward out of this moment into the imagined one just ahead. Balance lies behind us, and so, TURNING BACK is how we arrive. The special nature of *daring not to advance an inch* is also addressed as: HE WHO IS FEARLESS IN BEING BOLD WILL MEET WITH HIS DEATH; HE WHO IS FEARLESS IN BEING TIMID WILL STAY ALIVE. OF THE TWO, ONE LEADS TO GOOD, THE OTHER TO HARM.

To me, this parallels Buddha's last words before he died, "all things created pass away; strive on". Whatever is, eventually isn't, and so *without an arm* corresponds to "all things pass away". Nevertheless, "strive on"; keep on *grabbing*. Thinking allows us to approach life excessively goal oriented rather than process oriented. We look to the future objectives rather than watch the moment to moment where the actual "strive on" and *grabbing* take place. On balance, life is on the side of "striving" and *grabbing* at the most basic level—breathing, heart beating, with senses aware and *grabbing* the world around us. *Daring not to advance an inch, but withdraw a foot* pulls the mind back into the moment. This approach is also called: RETURNING TO ONE'S ROOTS IS KNOWN AS STILLNESS, and BLOCK THE OPENINGS, SHUT THE DOORS.

THIS IS KNOWN AS MARCHING FORWARD WHEN THERE IS NO ROAD, as D.C. Lau puts it, describes the essence of Hatha Yoga. In many postures, for example, you reach up as though you are touching the sky, even though touching the sky is impossible. You march forward when there is no road, you strive on even though all things pass away. This emphasizes the integrity of your approach to life, rather than on any particular accomplishment (which in the case of touching the sky is impossible from the outset). I suppose you could call this 'thinking <u>and</u> acting outside the box'.

The Bhagavad Gita expresses this *marching forward when there is no road* approach to life a little more earthly:

> 2:47   Set thy heart upon thy work, but never on its reward. Work not for a reward: but never cease to do thy work.

> 5:12   This man of harmony surrenders the reward of his work and thus attains final peace: the man of disharmony, urged by desire, is attached to his reward and remains in bondage.

18:12   When work is done for a reward, the work brings pleasure, or pain, or both, in its time; but when a man does work in Eternity, then Eternity is his reward.

70.

Every so often, the tonal nature of Chinese gives a curious twist, especially in something like the Tao Te Ching. I've been using the rising tone meaning of *wei* (唯): *only, alone*, for this character. Although sometimes it doesn't makes a lot of sense. The dipping tone of this character means *'yea'* which I've avoided using. This time I'm going to go with the third tone meaning which gives us this: *Man, yea, is without knowing...* etc. . Alone or only would also work, but this puts more pizazz into the statement... *yea!*

[Update: No, I went with my tried and true rising tone meaning, only, alone. This conforms to how it is generally used. Another point I'd add here is how 夫 fu (man, husband) perhaps took on a more 'sage like' meaning in the old days. However, now this makes the line say something closer to, *The sage alone doesn't know, and so I don't know.* Boy, you can say that again!]

Speech has its faction alludes to how *speech* is symptomatic of some deeper *faction* (tribal agenda, motive, aim). It helps to not take words at face value, but instead peek under the hood of motivation to ponder from what emotion the words spring. A similar process applies to *involvement* in living.

Underlying emotional needs and fears influence all action[1] whether *speech* or *involvement*. Seeing those underlying influences, in one's self and in others, can be helpful if not enlightening. Fear and need drive action, making us do what we actually do, in spite of what we may otherwise imagine

---

1   All action (or inaction) can be traced back to fear. Fear, as I define it, is our intuitive dread of entropy (loss, failure, death). This underlies the survival instinct in all living things. It is the subtle underbelly (cause) of the fear-based reactions (effects) with which we usually picture fear. See Fear Is The Bottom Line, Reward, Fear & Need, Fear Rules, and perhaps the glossary in One who speaks does not know?

doing. Our mind's 'ideal world' is boundless. We think we (and especially others) can "just do it", in the vein of FREE WILL. Truth be told, we are at the mercy of the fears and needs felt in our reptilian brain. The only possible influence I have comes through knowing -- moment to moment -- how little free will I actually have. Accepting this prods me to see and UNDERSTAND what is going on behind the scenes: ONLY THEN IS COMPLETE CONFORMITY REALIZED. Such *knowing self, following self* is the only way I've found TO ACCOMPLISH [MY] PRIVATE ENDS.

With a slightly different choice of word meaning, *'Speech has its faction'* becomes *'Words have an ancestor.'* This points to what underpins word meaning. In learning other languages, I've found that emotion holds the key. Feeling the emotion source-spring of a word make it 'native' (intuitive, fluent). Without that emotional connection to the sound of a word, the word is merely noise. Any meaning it conveys actually resides in how it translates to my native English. I stop translating only when I feel the meaning emotionally[1].

Seen in this light, the idea that *our words are very easy to know, very easy to do. Under heaven none can know, none can do* may make more sense. The emotion that gives a word meaning for me can often not be (or never be?) the same emotion you feel when hearing me say that word. Being in agreement only means we each trust we are, not that we actually are. It is somewhat surreal. A parallel of this occurs with color, what we each sense when we hear that something is blue can be quite different, especially if I am somewhat color blind in the blue end of the spectrum. Obviously the less concrete the words, the more NO ONE IN THE WORLD CAN UNDERSTAND THEM. Instead, we read into the words what we need (or fear) to hear.

---

1   This also applies to understanding and/or translating the Tao Te Ching. The reader can only understand what they already know within intuitively. That intuitive feeling you bring to the words is what gives it meaning. That is why understanding deepens over time as CIRCUMSTANCE BRING US TO MATURITY. In other words, the Tao Te Ching's point-of-view is deeper and broader than any words used to convey it. Words can never do it justice. This is what separates timeless words (usually scripture) from the rest.

Self knowing leads naturally to simplicity (*wearing coarse cloth*). Of course, in order to do any of this, you need to KNOW, YET THINK THAT YOU DON'T KNOW, to avoid being hoodwinked by your preconceptions. Admittedly, that is a tall order, and explains why *following self is noble.* By the way, it is interesting to note how D.C. Lau translates my subjective, *knowing self is rare, following self is noble,* as a more objective, THOSE WHO UNDERSTAND ME ARE FEW; THOSE WHO IMITATE ME ARE HONORED.

71.

Realizing I don't know puts the unknown (questions) ahead of the known (answers). The void, NOTHING, empty and silent all correlate to the unknown, the question... reality! *Not knowing this realization is a defect* because it becomes all too easy to think I know THE answer. Conversely, 'TO KNOW YET TO THINK ONE DOES NOT KNOW' values the question far beyond any answer.

Ever since my sobering wake-up call through CORRELATIONS, I've regarded questions and problems as being akin to invariable reality, and any resulting answer or solution as merely transitions to yet deeper questions or problems. Whether or not this is true makes little difference, practically speaking, as long as it makes my life a saner experience. I need all the help I can get. ;-)

Animals, including us, generally fear the unknown. This fear makes us impatient to know 'the answer' now. Answers allow us to THINK THAT WE KNOW, and that promises us peace of mind. Some of this may also result from an urgent need to fill our big-brain's imagination space. Like they say, nature abhors a vacuum. We have to fill it with something; filling mind space with questions (as a child does), more than answers (as adults do) helps us avoid thinking our way into a corner. This is not saying to avoid answers; just know what is at stake. In other words, well placed questions bare useful fruit. Only such fruit will holds the seeds for even better placed questions... a virtuous circle, as they say.

BEING ALIVE TO DIFFICULTY is accepting that life is difficulty. As Buddha said, <u>birth is suffering; growth, decay, and death are</u>

suffering. <u>Sad it is to be joined with that which we dislike. Sadder still is the separation from that which we love, and painful is the craving for that which cannot be obtained.</u> The more I try to avoid or escape difficulty, the more difficult life ends up feeling. The courage to bite the bullet, *taking his defect as a defect,* and get on with living, especially as Buddha puts forward in the other three truths, is actually the easiest to live. Yet, our pleasure seeking nature is always dragging its feet. It wants comfort and safety above all else. And so we struggle, torn between what we ideally desire from life, and what we are really faced with in life.

72.

D.C. Lau has translated 自知不自见 (literally, *self know no self see)* as, HENCE THE SAGE KNOWS HIMSELF BUT DOES NOT DISPLAY HIMSELF. This works fine. I've found that the deeper I know myself, the less I *display myself.* Displaying oneself can be one symptom of not knowing oneself. That said, I see another way to interpret this *'self know no self see'.* For starters, what does *self know* mean really? Personally, I suppose it means being as self-honesty as possible. The difficulty here lies in the thinking, i.e., TO KNOW YET TO THINK THAT ONE DOES NOT KNOW. No wonder it takes a lifetime!

I've found that the deeper I know myself, the more INDISTINCT AND SHADOWY I've become. There is less and less of me for me to see. Increasingly, I can't see myself - *no self see!* When we see ourselves, we are more likely seeing the story of ourselves we've come to believe true. To paraphrase chapter 1, THE [SELF] THAT CAN BE SPOKEN OF, IS NOT THE CONSTANT [SELF]; THE NAME THAT CAN BE NAMED, IS NOT THE CONSTANT NAME. In addition to this, there is the Hindu, <u>That Thou Art</u>. Ha! No wonder it takes many lifetimes!

'Without meddling with their dwelling place, without detesting their existence' may come closer to capturing the spirit of this than D.C. Lau's interpretation. *Without detesting their existence* is another way to put Christ's dictum, 'let ye without sin cast the first stone.' When your ideal of being dominates your mind's thought, you end up *detesting* every *existence* that doesn't conform to that story. It follows that you would cast stones or worse.

D.C. Lau's, IT IS BECAUSE YOU DO NOT PRESS DOWN ON THEM THAT THEY WILL NOT WEARY OF THE BURDEN was a guiding principles in raising my sons. Children will only rebel against 'Something'. The less you give them to rebel against, the smoother life usually flows. Helpful too was insuring that they felt a PROPER SENSE OF AWE. The adult quality that instills the utmost sense of awe in children is patience! Children understand the usual human emotions: desire, fear, anger, kindness. They don't understand patience because in its pure form, it is not an emotion. To me patience is a function of perspective; it's the essence of wisdom. (Note: Patience, being akin to the MYSTERIOUS FEMALE, STILLNESS and SILENCE, seems less of an awesome force than it is. Mysterious is right.)

'Loves himself without valuing himself' makes more sense seen as a symptom. In other words, when we truly love ourselves, we feel no need to value self. Conversely, when we feel inadequate, we need ego affirmation. How we are determines how we act, or more accurately, react. Although, I find we often tend to see it the other way around, i.e., how we act determines how we are. This could stem from our need for control in that it is easier to identify actions and repress them than to deal with who we are intrinsically. We let free will take care of that angle..

73.

As fear increases, I will *hesitate* to act boldly. Just the opposite happens when fearless. So, what does it mean to be FEARLESS IN BEING TIMID? Another way to phrase this might be, 'can you be fearless and yet timid'? This corresponds to KNOW THE MALE, YET KEEP TO THE ROLE OF THE FEMALE. I am only 'fearless in being timid' when my DISCERNMENT PENETRATES THE FOUR QUARTER. When I see beyond the current exigencies of the moment, and see the rapids which lie ahead on the river of life, I can HOLD FIRMLY TO STILLNESS and take no action that would exacerbate the flow. When to be *bravely certain* or *bravely hesitant*, more than anything else, determines life's outcome. Seeing as how *these both either benefit or harm*, it pays to be adept at each. However, *brave certainty* comes all too naturally, while *brave hesitation* is the essence of patience and wisdom. Therefore, just as I can't

DESIRE NOT TO DESIRE too much, neither can I over-do *brave hesitation*. Personally, this comes as close to <u>free will</u> as I can get.

Nature's ruthlessness, who know its cause brings to mind the <u>Judeo Christian question</u>, why does God cause innocents (like infants) to suffer? I remember how, in the wake of my ski accident's torn ligament, I naively thought "Why me?" Alas, HEAVEN HATES WHAT IT HATES, WHO KNOWS THE REASON WHY? Of course, looking at this more broadly, I see how one thing's gain MUST be another thing's loss (i.e., two sides of the same coin). In the flow of nature, gain and loss, GOOD FORTUNE AND DISASTER follow each other; desiring life to go just one way is so utterly irrational, and yet so common. It is a testament (and a warning) to the power of emotion!

Nature's approach[1] is often opposite to what our initial inclinations are; that's not surprising, for Nature isn't particularly concerned with survival. Life, on the other hand, is. Therefore we contend with our sights firmly held on *victory*. However, *victory* is always short lived, and by contending, we set in motion unintended consequences that defeat ACCOMPLISHING OUR PRIVATE ENDS. Allowing events to play out requires patience (*brave hesitation*), and usually works to our long-term advantage. On the other end we have, IN ACTION IT IS TIMELINESS THAT MATTERS which also plays a role. Hitler and WWII come to mind. A stitch in time saves nine million or so (DEAL WITH A THING WHILE IT IS STILL NOTHING). The art of living comes down to maintaining a balance of the two.

No words—silence—are often the 'loudest' *answering* with which one can reply. I found this marvelously so in raising my two sons. A few days of shunning, with not a word spoken, brought home my *answer* to certain behavior (like lying) more effectively than could all the nagging in the world.

Simple certainly under-pins *adeptness in victory*, yet ironically the *simplest* approaches are the most difficult. 'Easy' approaches with their unforeseen complications are our first choice; haste

---

1   What do I mean by Nature's approach? Not perhaps what is usually thought of as nature or natural in these days. The Chinese word offers a more all inclusive view that describes it better for me... *daziran_* (大自然) *the great self so.*

makes waste is no empty saying. Only *brave hesitation* gives enough time to reflect until a simple, optimum approach takes shape. A good example of this is the time I wanted to put a bridge across a small pond. The simplest would be a plank, but I desired a gentle arch in the bridge. I easily envisioned various plans, but they all required problematic method of joining wood (e.g., screws, nails with the inevitable shrinkage and rust that would follow). I *bravely hesitated* building anything until a simple, elegant solution 'bubbled up'. A year later, voila! I simply bent two 3/4" pipes into gentle arcs, drilled holes in 3x4 lumber and threaded the lumber onto the pipe.

Decades of gardening also offers an example of *comes simple, yet adept in planning*. For the first 10 years I overdid everything. 'Complex, and second-rate in planning' would be a fair description of my gardening then. Over the years complexity gradually dropped away. Now, 30+ years later, *simple, yet adept in planning* is a fair description of my gardening. I do just enough to get the results I want, when I want. Nothing is wasted. My gardening comes closest to modeling nature, and it only took a couple of decades of that all essential 'set it up' (i.e., IF YOU WOULD HAVE A THING SHRINK, YOU MUST FIRST STRETCH IT). This is another way of saying there are no short-cuts in life! Alas, we all have to learn the hard way. THEREFORE EVEN THE SAGE TREATS SOME THINGS AS DIFFICULT.[1]

74.

First note the curious grammar in the last line, *rarely never hurts his own hands* (希 有 不 = rare exist not). This double negative is the round about way of saying *he usually hurts his hand.*

This chapter reminds me of how I used to want to 'help' others avoid making mistakes. Undoubtedly this is caused by 'fairness &

---

1   This line is in D.C.Lau's translation of this chapter, but it's not in the original Chinese. I run across this from time to time; why does he do that? Often I imagine he uses poetic license to make it more readable. Conversely, I take as little poetic license as possible, which often makes my translation much less readable. This is a win-win actually, as reading both versions can help fill out the big picture.

friendly minded' mirror neurons which play a large role in many social mammal's DNA[1]. This instinct is ALWAYS helpful in social animals other than humans, and even for human in our earliest time. Civilization has made many of our natural instincts more problematic, however. For example, the instinct to eat as much high-energy food (fat, carbs, protein) when we came across it in the wild was a boon. We even store some of that away in fat cells for times of famine. Nowadays, that instinct leads to obesity and associated health problems. The drive to help others avoid making mistakes often turns out to be CHOPPING WOOD ON BEHALF OF THE MASTER CARPENTER (Nature being the *master carpenter* here). After all, stumbling is how we learn to walk and talk. Mistakes are the path to learning and successful life long accomplishment.

All my life, I've noticed how other people would warn me of the dire consequences of doing this or that, or of going here or there. None of it ever turned out to be so. Their warnings were actually a projection of their own fears. Thankfully, by the time I had children I had seen enough of this 'projected' fear to allow my kids to make the most of their stumbling. Not standing in the way of their stumbling and growth benefited them and, indirectly, the whole family. Allowing nature to take its course, letting mistakes happen is the path to GREAT PERFECTION. This avoids CONTENTION and favors CONTENTMENT more than anything else I've known (and I need all the help I can get).

75.

The closest parallel to *taxes* I see in nature is the parasite. Parasites that give as much as they take are symbiotic relationships beneficial to both organisms. Nitrogen-fixing bacteria are an example. The larger an 'organism' of the governed and governing, the more difficult it is to maintain such a symbiotic balance. Too many self-interested parties take more than they give, and like leaches suck away the juices for their own

---

1   I'm playing it safe by limiting it to "many social mammals", although I suspect that some form of this 'fairness & friendly' instinct exists at the core of every animals' DNA, right down to ants and bees.

benefit - not for the greater good of the 'organism'. At heart, the pragmatic conservative realizes this DIFFICULTY, while the liberal puts their eggs in the basket of an 'if only' idealism[1].

TOO FOND OF ACTION reminds me of trying to remove a bug from my tea cup. The more I stir up the water (fondest of action) the more chaotic the situation, the more difficult it is to fetch the bug. The most efficient way to deal with a problem is to be let the conditions settle down enough to perceive the *profound sameness*, and then take action with minimal *expectations*[2].

I would include the word personal when talking about how people *take death lightly*. They treat their own death lightly for they are preoccupied with *seeking life's flavor*, the promises of what life has to offer going forward. The problem: we really only have this moment; the next is only a promise. Even when fate fulfills the promise, we aren't fully present to appreciate it because we're still (or soon) off *seeking life's flavor* tomorrow.

Only the man without use for life means having no use for the 'objective' aspect of life. In other words, *use for life* comes down to the *flavor* one is *seeking* to get out of life. Here the eye is always looking out for the promise of some ideal future reward.

---

1   I'm not referring to particular political parties here. A pragmatic conservative in the Taoist sense would be more RUTHLESS. As D.C. Lau puts it, IT IS JUST BECAUSE ONE HAS NO USE FOR LIFE THAT ONE IS WISER THAN THE MAN WHO VALUES LIFE. Political parties, left or right, push their brand of 'if only' ideals in a tug-of-war that wages on and on. Perhaps a more impartial way to consider liberal vs. conservative is by way of correlations. For example:

    LIBERAL ≈ complex, struggle, evolves, definite, anxious, modern
    ———— ———— ———— ———— ———— ———— ————
    CONSERVATIVE ≈ simple, surrender, revolves, ambiguous, patient, ancient

2   D.C. Lau translated these lines as, IT IS BECAUSE THOSE IN AUTHORITY ARE TOO FOND OF ACTION, THAT THE PEOPLE ARE DIFFICULT TO GOVERN. While true, that seems to go beyond what the Chinese says. Two characters, have+do (有为) translates as youwei which means promising or young and promising. Thus for me, these lines really speak more to people's expectations, the promise of the future. Our expectations, and the DESIRE that drives them, are our greatest liability when it comes to FOLLOWING THE WAY.

This is at odds with making the most of one's moment. Like the old saying goes, a bird in the hand is worth two in the bush.

76.

This chapter can appear a little inconsistent with most other chapters. In this chapter we see, THE SUPPLE AND WEAK TAKES THE HIGHER POSITION. However, in chapter 61 we see, THE FEMALE ALWAYS GETS THE BETTER OF THE MALE BY STILLNESS. BEING STILL, SHE TAKES THE LOWER POSITION. The former makes it sound like the 'higher position' is the way to go; the later sounds like the 'lower position' is. This is where correlations help. Placing a few core active (yang) and passive (yin) words in the correlation line-up give us another way to consider this (see next page):

Of course, correlations accentuate the view from the "differences side of the coin", not from the *profound sameness* side. However, that is always the results when using of names and words (language), and why chapter 56 begins with, ONE WHO KNOWS DOES NOT SPEAK; ONE WHO SPEAKS DOES NOT KNOW. Even so, correlations[1] can help you set it up in order to lay it aside, as chapter 36 points out so well.

Consider the two side of these **Active/Passive** 'coins' below. The differences are stark; the sameness, mysterious just as it ought to be.

Active	Passive	Active	Passive
male	female	full	empty
strong	weak	order	entropy
higher	lower	difference	sameness

---

1   The Corrleations process can help you see *profound sameness* by 'tunneling' through the edge of difference, so to speak. The struggle to maintain consistency is essential to breaking through. By the way, here are some other general words that correlate with Yin and Yang:

Yin = below, slow, soft, yielding, diffuse, cold, wet, tranquil.
Yin is associated with water, earth, the moon, femininity, nighttime

Yang = above, fast, hard, solid, focused, hot, dry, aggressive.
Yang is associated with fire, sky, the sun, masculinity and daytime.

life	death	contention	cooperation
stir	still	sound	silence
yang	**yin**	**yang**	**yin**

The Tao Te Ching is no different in this way. It uses language to point to the *profound sameness* beyond language. Inconsistency, however, doesn't help get you there. The stark contradiction, for me anyway, lies in the yin and yang of it all. That is to say, in the placement of *lower, below* and *higher, above.* Why is there this inconsistency? Did some scribe simply get the character *below* and *above* switched around, and it has been passed on that way ever since? Living things do all they can to be strong, hard and unyielding. This is essential to counter the natural entropy that influences all matter, living or not. Of course, too much of a "good" thing can work against long-term survival. Balance is the way of long life and successful evolution. Contention must be balanced by cooperation, stirring by stillness, and so on. Still, a walk in nature soon reveals life's 'survival-of-the-fittest' bottom line. In the final analysis, life's bias is toward hanging tough and avoid death is biased towards holding on; death is giving up.

There is a distinct bias favoring the passive side of this process in all scriptures. I attribute this to the fact that THE PEOPLE SET TOO MUCH STORE BY LIFE [AND] ARE TOO FOND OF ACTION. We need all the encouragement we can get to HAVE LITTLE THOUGHT OF SELF AND AS FEW DESIRES AS POSSIBLE. Truth be told, we ALLOW OURSELVES TO HAVE DESIRES IN ORDER TO OBSERVE ITS MANIFESTATIONS, so much more than the ridding ourselves of desires side of the process.

Here is another instance of inconsistency. In other words, there would be no other way to put it: HIGHEST GOOD IS LIKE WATER. BECAUSE WATER EXCELS IN BENEFITING THE MYRIAD CREATURES WITHOUT CONTENDING WITH THEM AND SETTLES WHERE NONE WOULD LIKE TO BE, IT COMES CLOSE TO THE WAY. Water settles in the lower position, yet we say "highest good". To say "lowest good" would simply not make sense, and yet, might be more accurate from a purely Taoist point of view. All of this goes to shows why Taoism regards words and names problematic. For example, chapter 23 says, TO USE WORDS BUT RARELY IS

TO BE NATURAL, and chapter 32 notes that, AS SOON AS THERE ARE NAMES, ONE OUGHT TO KNOW THAT IT IS TIME TO STOP.

77.

Once in awhile the Tao Te Ching falls into what I'd call a 'humanist' trap. This lends support to the view than the Tao Te Ching is really the product of more than one thinker / author. Perhaps too, the 'taoist' point of view was passed down via aural tradition over generations before being finally written down. It's so long ago; I forgot. ☺

The view here that 'IT IS THE WAY OF HEAVEN TO TAKE FROM WHAT HAS IN EXCESS IN ORDER TO MAKE GOOD WHAT IS DEFICIENT. THE WAY OF MAN IS OTHERWISE' runs contrary to the broader view expressed in chapter 34... THE WAY IS BROAD, REACHING LEFT AS WELL AS RIGHT.

Even more at odds with this chapter is chapter 25, which in my view, expresses a simple rendering of the emergent properties principle. Chapter 25 ends with:

> MAN MODELS HIMSELF ON EARTH,
> EARTH ON HEAVEN,
> HEAVEN ON THE WAY,
> AND THE WAY ON THAT WHICH IS NATURALLY SO.

I can only guess that our species' fairness instinct (see OUR FAIRNESS INSTINCT) drives the egalitarian bias obvious in chapter 77. This sense of equality and fairness underlies so much (perhaps most) of our behavior, I suspect. I have now come to regard this to be a major influence in every facet of human life[1].

Indeed, this chapter expresses a sense of what I call implied free will. It is subtly expressed here, for instance, by: *The way of*

---

1   So, how do I know I'm not just projecting some need to see "the fairness instinct" as one of nature's master puppeteers? I don't really. On the other hand, I don't really care if I'm right or wrong. Ironically, this may make it more likely that I'm seeing 'it' as 'it' is. In any case, people have no trouble seeing instinct as the driving force in animal life. It's just in human life where people balk at the idea. Somehow we desire to see ourselves "superior" to other animals and blessed with free will, free choice.

nature decreases surplus yet benefits the insufficient. The way of man, as a rule however, decreases the insufficient so as to give to the surplus. The implication is that humankind somehow has a choice in the matter. It seems to imply that humankind could act more "naturally" than it does if it chose to. This view puts the cart before the horse (or rather the man before the biology).

The way I see it, an animal (including us) does what it does out of innate need and fear. What is the real reason that *the way of man, as a rule however, decreases the insufficient so as to give to the surplus?* Chapter 22 sheds light on this indirectly:

> HE DOES NOT SHOW HIMSELF, AND SO IS CONSPICUOUS;
> HE DOES NOT CONSIDER HIMSELF RIGHT, AND SO IS ILLUSTRIOUS;
> HE DOES NOT BRAG, AND SO HAS MERIT;
> HE DOES NOT BOAST, AND SO ENDURES.

Here, the view is that by not bragging he has merit; by no boasting he endures; by not considering himself right, he is illustrious. Again, the cart is before the horse[1]. My experience is just the other way around. The more I feel inner merit, the less I tend to brag; the more illustrious I feel, the less I need to consider myself right, and so on.

Similarly, the more CONTENTMENT I feel, the less I desire to *decrease the insufficient so as to give to the surplus.* It is out of need (visceral hunger) that greedy action arises. Greed is a symptom of not being content; greed is a natural consequence of NOT BEING CONTENT. Not being content drives animals, including us, to do what they do - period. The trick to balanced living is not shooting oneself in the foot. This entails doing that which has the best chance to make us feel more content; with contentment we naturally KEEP TO THE DEED THAT CONSISTS IN TAKING NO ACTION AND PRACTICE THE TEACHING THAT USES NO WORDS. Ah yes, all this is so VERY EASY TO UNDERSTAND AND VERY EASY TO PUT INTO PRACTICE, YET...

---

1   The way this is stated, i.e., "He does not brag, and so has merit", is accurate in the sense that this is how we tend to perceive it. Meaning, when someone doesn't brag we regard them in a more meritorious light. This 'judging a book by its cover' is a key bio-hoodwink that often trips us up.

78.

Yep, STRAIGHTFORWARD WORDS SEEM PARADOXICAL. The chief biological hoodwink all life experiences is lacking the perception that THE WEAK OVERCOMES THE STRONG, or as Jesus put it, "The meek shall inherit the earth". Accepting the HUMILIATION OF THE STATE is the only approach possible when I see the state as it actually is rather that how I would like it to be. Biological processes determine how people interact-- sometimes getting along, sometimes battling.

I can certainly imagine a world of peace and bliss, equity and justice for all. Yet, this is simply not how Nature works. Such ideals are simply dreams that reflect innate needs and fears—what we want, not what is. That's okay mind you; it's just very helpful to know **it is a dream**. Believing a dream is real is fine for a movie, but for living daily life?

Only a person capable of seeing things as they are, and not as desired, would be A KING WORTHY OF DOMINION OVER THE ENTIRE EMPIRE. LORDS AND PRINCES (and even politicians) such as this are rare I suspect. Instead, I see the *hard and strong* standing their ground, CONTENDING self-righteously with their ENEMIES. We hear much talk of bipartisanship on one hand, and see actions that are just the opposite on the other.

Only when opposing forces wear each other out, can the *yielding and weak* conclude matters. Loss is the foundation of compromise. People can't compromise as long as their sense of compromise is more about what their opponent needs to give up. You would think this self evident, which goes to show the blinding power of desire; indeed, desire is the fuel that powers the BLIND SPOT AND ITS MANIFESTATIONS.

Of weakness and loss through death, victorious and powerful.
Under heaven there's no one who does not know - no one can do.

In other words, entropy is always the victor in the end! Saying that *under heaven there's no one who does not know* may be a bit of an overstatement. However, that *no one can do* is certainly dead right.

Naturally, *no one can do* because life's core drive is to resist entropy at every turn, right up to our final breath. While I can't actually, through free will, PUT THIS KNOWLEDGE INTO PRACTICE, this knowledge does give me peace of mind when I feel *yielding and weak*. Heck, it may even help my ACTION LEAD TO IMPARTIALITY.

79.

I've always had an issue with the way D.C. Lau's translated the end of this chapter: IT IS THE WAY OF HEAVEN TO SHOW NO FAVORITISM. IT IS FOREVER ON THE SIDE OF THE GOOD MAN. How can nature on one hand "show no favoritism" and on the other hand "be on the side of the good man"?

One of the Chinese characters involved here helps me resolve this. This character, *shan* (善) means: *satisfactory; good; make a success of; perfect; kind; friendly; be adept in; properly*. This word, *shan*, is the "good" at the end of this chapter. It is also the "perfect" at the beginning of the chapter (i.e. How can this be considered perfect?).

My difficulty comes from having this translated as "good" or "perfect". As I see it, there is no "bad" or "imperfect" in nature. We are SO PARTAKING OF THE 'TAI LAO' OFFERING in our notions of 'GOOD and BAD'. Good and bad are human values, which simply mirror what we generally like and dislike, and our preferences for comfort and security, e.g., we dislike death, it's "bad"; we like life, it's "good".

This inconsistency clears right up when I use some of the other meanings of *shan*, i.e., satisfactory, be adept in, make a success of... are all preferable to perfect and good. Nature is adept in all she does. Nature makes a success of all she does. Nature is always satisfactory. Nature is always on the side of adeptness; after all, that is evolution, plain and simple.

As to nature showing no favoritism, favoritism has nothing to do with being adept. Favoritism is giving your son the job even though he is not adept. Ulterior motives drive favoritism. Nature has no ulterior motives, that I can see anyway.

The wise person is the one not driven by their agenda (DESIRES, needs, fears), so it takes a lot more to trigger their fairness instinct. It is much easier to be impartial, and not punish people or exact 'fairness' when you HAVE LITTLE THOUGHT OF SELF AND AS FEW DESIRES AS POSSIBLE.

80.

BRING IT ABOUT THAT THE PEOPLE WILL RETURN TO THE USE OF THE KNOTTED ROPE sure puts a free will slant on this chapter. So, how in the heck is one supposed to ENSURE THEY WILL NOT USE TOOLS OF WAR? The Chinese word for "bring it about" and "ensure" as used here is *shi* (使) which translates as: *send; tell somebody to do something; use; employ; apply; make; cause; enable; envoy; messenger; if; supposing.* That is quite a string of meanings, with some conveying a stronger sense of FREE WILL than others, although none as strongly as "ensure" does, I suppose.

Making or causing someone to feel *content* is a tall order. Societies have struggled to do that for ages. That is one of the goals of religion, although without great success, as I see it. Truth be told, isn't religion merely a symptom of feeling disconnected and the unhappiness that causes. This endemic sense of disconnection is a byproduct of civilization and THINKING, and religion is the palliative civilization and thinking creates to treats that symptom. My, what a clear example of how Nature balances herself in straightforward ways.

Chapter 33 says, HE WHO KNOWS CONTENTMENT IS RICH. I dare say it would be far, far easier to make or cause a person to become rich money-wise than contentment-wise. At best, a better phrasing here might be *'help the people'.* To be fair, religion does supply some helpful tools (prayer, meditation, devotional rites, etc.), but it is up to the individual 'craftsman' (us individually) to use them religiously. Hah! That sounds like a catch-22 (a no-win, double bind situation).

This chapter makes more sense to me if seen as a comment on what makes life run smooth. These tips are really symptoms of personal contentment. The more *content* I feel, the more *peaceful in my life, and happy in my customs*. *Travel* is always a symptom of some degree of discontent. Even a trip to the toilet arises out of physical discontent. Thirst and hunger are similar symptoms of elemental discontent, and evoke the need to travel somewhere for food and water. In ancient, hunger-gatherer times, that would amount to scrounging around until the need was satiated and contentment returned. Now a days for many that amounts to just a short trip to the kitchen.

As a result, what happens with all the extra free time and energy civilized living affords me? Various desires, stemming from elemental need, arise to fill the void[1]. The only way I can *enable the existence of various tools, yet never need them* is by acknowledging the need I feel, yet forgoing the impulse to satiate it impulsively (if at all). Feel it, but cease to act upon it. This is an aspect of action-less action, (为无为 act without act) spoken of in chapter 3. D.C. Lau translated this as: Do THAT WHICH CONSISTS IN TAKING NO ACTION, AND ORDER WILL PREVAIL.

81.

I have to wonder what kind of words could qualify as "TRUTHFUL WORDS"? *True speech* would be that which presents the whole picture, both sides of the coin, the pros and cons. Words that only voice what we want to hear, and avoid voicing what we fear or dislike would be less *true*.

Hearing words we want to hear easily persuades us. Skilled politicians and salesmen know and use this hoodwink deftly. This also is what makes truth so illusive. Not that it is rare or hidden; truth is omnipresent. It just isn't what we want to perceive - it's not *beautiful* enough. *True* truth lacks contrast. Perhaps that is

---

1 IT IS EMPTY WITHOUT BEING EXHAUSTED brings to my mind an interesting thought: When one reaches a point approaching full contentment, biological dynamics stir and spawn elemental need. That restlessness gets us off our butts and on to the next 'project'. Naturally, it is not only us; this must be true for all life! Within us, however, need whips up imagination and voilà... a fresh batch of desires are born (need + thinking = desire).

an odd thing to say; let's take a closer look: Chapter 2 pries into this when it says, THE WHOLE WORLD RECOGNIZES THE BEAUTIFUL AS THE BEAUTIFUL, YET THIS IS ONLY THE UGLY; THE WHOLE WORLD RECOGNIZES THE GOOD AS THE GOOD, YET THIS IS ONLY THE BAD.

Beautiful and good are only cognitively perceptible in contrast to an awareness of ugliness and bad. Such perceptions are simply reflections of what we like and dislike; of what we want and don't want; of what we are attracted towards and from which we are repelled. It is simple neurology, a biological hoodwink—a BIO-HOODWINK, as I like to call it. The same applies to truth vs. false doesn't it? *True* truth must transcend the contrast of opposites. (Herein lies THE BENEFIT OF THE TEACHING THAT USES NO WORDS.)

So now, ask yourself, is there **good** or **bad** in nature? Does nature play favorites; does nature love some things more than other things? In nature's book, are some things more *beautiful* than other things? In my view, the answer is a resounding no. Thus, if *speech* is to reflect THAT WHICH IS NATURALLY SO, it can't be both *beautiful* and *true*. I hate to resort to the word transcendent, but here I must… One requirement of *true* truth, in the transcendent sense of the word, is IMPARTIALITY. How can any perception that pulls you in (beauty) or push you away (ugly) be transcendently *true*?

"The sage does not hoard"
In thinking over "THE SAGE DOES NOT HOARD", I reflect back upon times I've hoarded. Really though, *accumulate* is a better description; it is less pejorative. Also correlated to *accumulate* is holding on, clinging, seeking, grasping. While never really hoarding stuff, I sure sought after and clung to what I felt precious at the time. I don't do this much any more. Besides, I now recognize the obvious—seeking after or clinging to things (or ideas) are simply symptoms of that for which I feel or felt deficient. What has changed? I simply feel an approaching ENOUGH now. Indeed, why would anyone seek that for which he or she felt enough? They would not. So, what did I feel lacking?

In general, perhaps I lacked a deep ENOUGH sense of life-meaning. Looking back, I can see how powerfully that drove what I did. I clung to what promised me life meaning at the time. For example, while living in Singapore, I had an English girlfriend who worked at the Changi Air Base. We'd ride the bus from Singapore to the base on Sunday night. I clung to the last moments we'd share before taking the bus back alone to Singapore. I really was dependent on that relationship for life-meaning, and so I clung to it.

Over time, I realized the poverty of this approach... poverty because I felt incomplete. That is why we say, "HE WHO KNOWS CONTENTMENT IS RICH", and similarly, *wealth doesn't know* contentment. In fact, wealth can be very problematic as Jesus alluded to when he said, "It is easier for a camel to go through the eye of a needle, than for a rich man to enter into the kingdom of God".

We put many of our happiness eggs in the money basket despite it being VERY EASY TO UNDERSTAND that money does not buy happiness. Not only does money not buy happiness, it easily detracts from happiness. On the other hand, money does buy us comfort and security! Then the bio-hoodwink lures us in by equating happiness with more comfort and security. Naturally, this linkage would be largely *true* in wilderness circumstances.

The human ability to circumvent natural boundaries allows technological innovations to increase comfort and security exponentially. Evolution didn't 'plan' on that. Without natural limits, increasing comfort and security leads to physiological and psychological imbalance, and overall happiness actually decreases. We become neurotic and fall into a vicious cycle: decreasing contentment drives us to pursue comfort and security, which creates more imbalances, which makes us even less happy. THE BIO-HOODWINK WORKS IN MYSTERIOUS WAYS.

Well, perhaps not so mysterious once you are willing to see life STRAIGHTFORWARDLY. In my view, an ongoing awareness of these dynamics can actually help moderate them... if you so DESIRE, and that, as we know, is the hitch!

When is enough, enough?
One of the main errors we make in society is thinking we
can change life from the outside in. Meaning for example,
we think that we can chose to be less selfish—more giving.
A *true* sense of giving is the natural result of feeling enough.
Without that root, any ostensible giving correlates more to
RITES, RECTITUDE AND BENEVOLENCE. Yes, this can help glue
the fabric of society, but unintended consequences always
ensue. It is messy, but then that's life. I suppose this all ties in
with the 'wandering mind is unhappy mind'. *Accumulating,*
or simply holding on, focuses the mind (emotions actually)
and supplies us with a sense of self-meaning. Of course,
Buddha pointed that out in his second truth, "the illusion of
self originates and manifests itself in a cleaving to things".

Healing the Imbalance
*Nature's way benefits, and yet doesn't harm. The holy person's
way acts, and yet doesn't contends.* Normally, benefit accrued for
one comes at a loss for another. Likewise, life's actions normally
involve contending with opposing forces. TO HAVE STOPPED IN
TIME, before harm or contending occurs is a very fine line. Nature
has no difficulty maintaining the IMPARTIALITY this requires.

Unlike non-thinking animals, we haul around a personal agenda
(TOO MANY DESIRES) and often end up crossing that balance line.
We seek *healing* from the difficulties caused by this imbalance.
When you begin to feel that this is our common cause, *considers
people's personal healing his own* begins to happen naturally.
This is why THE WAY has none of the prescribed morality
found in all other religions. Morality is an ideal easily touted,
impossible to practice; THE HIGHEST VIRTUE is a reality hard to
describe, easy to practice—unavoidable even—once you see
that of which you would rather otherwise remain IGNORANT.

HAVING BESTOWED ALL HE HAS ON OTHERS, HE HAS YET MORE;
HAVING GIVEN ALL HE HAS TO OTHERS, HE IS RICHER STILL clearly
deviates somewhat from the original, in my view, in order
to promote a pseudo virtuous moral ideal. Again, much of
civilization relies on such ideals to hold together large populations.

The fear is that otherwise society would break apart into a barbaric every-man-for-himself chaos. It just may be that we are far more barbaric (nukes, pollution, famine and war) in our ostentatious morality than if we lived more in tune with our selves as we *truly* are rather than as we wish we were—honesty is the best policy.

Other Offerings

Blowing Zen guides you step-by-step from producing sound to playing Zen Buddhist Meditation music. Also included are detailed build-your-own shakuhachi instructions. Instructional recordings are available on CD and online.

For centuries, Zen monks have been using the Shakuhachi to train mind and breath through the practice of Sui Zen (blowing Zen). Preview this book at Centertao.org/zen-book and listen to samples at Centertao.org/hear-zen.

Hatha Yoga: The Essential Dynamics guides you step by step from beginning through advanced Yoga using vectorial information for 138 postures as taught by B.K.S. Iyengar.

The full page, large print format enables you to learn (or remember) at a glance, what you need to be doing while your are doing it. You can preview this book at, Centertao.org/yoga-book

Family Tradition: ToneWay Music Method and Song Reference demystifies music by teaching a more intuitive, play by ear, approach to learning string instruments and singing. Includes 350 traditional songs.

This is traditional 'people music', especially doable by anyone, of any age, with a yearning to sing and play. Preview this book at, Centertao.org/tone-book

Shamisen of Japan teaches you how to professionally play and make the Tsugaru Shamisen, simply and enjoyably! It's really two books in one!

Includes instructions for building your own shamisen, a learning guide for playing shamisen, and 16 traditional shamisen pieces. Watch the free shamisen crash course, and join the growing shamisen community at Bachido.com!

Made in the USA
San Bernardino, CA
20 December 2013